TAKING CONTROL
Autonomy in Language Learning

TAKING CONTROL

Autonomy in Language Learning

Edited by
Richard Pemberton, Edward S.L. Li,
Winnie W.F. Or and Herbert D. Pierson

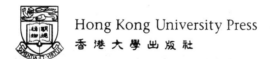

Hong Kong University Press
香港大學出版社

Hong Kong University Press
139 Pokfulam Road, Hong Kong

© Hong Kong University Press 1996

ISBN 962 209 407 4

Printed in Hong Kong by Caritas Printing Training Centre

Contents

Contributors

Phil Benson is a Lecturer in the English Centre at the University of Hong Kong, where he coordinates self-access language learning.

Rocío Blasco García is a professional translator and part-time teacher in the Language Centre at the University of Hong Kong.

Elsie Christopher is an Instructor in the Language Centre at the Hong Kong University of Science and Technology.

Leni Dam is an educational adviser and in-service teacher trainer at the Royal Danish School of Further Education in Copenhagen, Denmark. She also teaches at a comprehensive school in Copenhagen.

Edith Esch is Director of the Language Centre at the University of Cambridge, UK.

David Gardner is a Senior Language Instructor in the English Centre at the University of Hong Kong.

Susanna Ho is an Instructor in the Language Centre at the Hong Kong University of Science and Technology.

Rena Kelly, formerly Manager of the Language and Communication Division at Temasek Polytechnic, Singapore, is now Lecturer in Business Communication in the Faculty of Management at Deakin University, Melbourne, Australia.

Winnie Lee, formerly an Instructor at Hong Kong Polytechnic University, is now an Instructor in the English Language Teaching Unit at The Chinese University of Hong Kong.

Lienhard Legenhausen is Professor of Second Language Acquisition/ Foreign Language Pedagogy at the University of Münster, Germany.

David Little is Director of the Centre for Language and Communication Studies and Associate Professor of Applied Linguistics at Trinity College, Dublin, Ireland.

Lindsay Miller is an Assistant Professor in the English Department at City University of Hong Hong.

John Milton is a Senior Instructor and CALL coordinator in the Language Centre at the Hong Kong University of Science and Technology.

Raymond Ng, formerly a Lecturer in the English Department at City University of Hong Kong, is now teaching and studying in Brisbane, Australia.

David Nunan is Director of the English Centre and Professor of Applied Linguistics at the University of Hong Kong.

Valerie Pickard is a Language Instructor in the English Centre at the University of Hong Kong.

Herbert D. Pierson, formerly Director of the Independent Learning Centre at the Chinese University of Hong Kong, is now an Assistant Professor in the Institute of ESL at St. John's University, New York, USA.

James Purchase is a Research Assistant in the Language Centre at the Hong Kong University of Science and Technology.

Philip Riley is Professor of Linguistics and a member of the Centre de Recherches et d'Applications Pédagogiques en Langues (CRAPEL) at the University of Nancy 2, France.

Diana Simmons, formerly a Lecturer in the National Centre for English Language Teaching and Research at Macquarie University, Sydney, Australia, is now a Lecturer in the School of English Linguistics and Media at the same university.

Barbara Sinclair is a Lecturer in TESOL in the School of Education at the University of Nottingham, UK.

Ian Smallwood is a Senior Instructor in the Language Centre at the Hong Kong University of Science and Technology.

Vance Stevens, formerly coordinator for CALL and Self-Access Learning at Sultan Qaboos University, Oman, is now Director of ESL Software Design at Courseware Publishing International, Cupertino, California, USA.

Chihiro Kinoshita Thomson is Director of Language Studies in the School of Asian Business and Language Studies at the University of New South Wales, Sydney, Australia.

Peter Voller is a Language Instructor in the English Centre at the University of Hong Kong.

Preface

The papers that make up this book originated at an international conference on 'Autonomy in Language Learning', held in Hong Kong from 23-25 June 1994, and jointly organized and sponsored by the Language Centre, Hong Kong University of Science and Technology and the Independent Learning Centre, The Chinese University of Hong Kong.

We would like to thank our keynote speakers at the conference (Edith Esch, David Little, David Nunan, Philip Riley, Barbara Sinclair and Ken Willing), the presenters and all the participants for helping to make the conference such a success. Richard and Herbert would also like to thank the organizing committee members, and in particular, their co-organizer Austin Conway, without whom the conference would not have been possible. And we would like to express our gratitude to our two universities and the British Council for their sponsorship of the event.

Many people have contributed to the making of this book. We would particularly like to thank David Little for his insightful and constructive comments in the early stages. Many thanks are also due to: all the contributors (we hope the wait has been worth it!); the editors of *Die Neueren Sprachen* for giving us permission to publish the chapter by Leni Dam and Lienhard Legenhausen; Ada Fan Shui-fun and Carra Kee Suk-mun for their extremely efficient word processing; John Law for all his help with troublesome graphics; Norma Pemberton for her transcription and checking of the bibliography; Barbara Clarke of Hong Kong University Press for starting the project and providing the impetus in its early days; Dennis Cheung for overseeing the project once it was underway; and Clara Ho for her patience and technical skill in bringing the book to publication.

Finally, to everyone who is involved in helping their students develop autonomy, or considering doing so — we hope this book gives you food for both thought and action.

Richard Pemberton, Edward Li, Winnie Or and Herbert Pierson

Introduction

Richard Pemberton

The chapters that follow provide insights into a field of language learning that has been attracting an increasing amount of attention over the last 20 years. Numerous books for language teachers have appeared during this period on the subjects of learner autonomy, self-directed learning, self-access systems and individualized/independent learning (e.g. Harding-Esch 1976; Altman and James 1980; Holec 1981; Geddes and Sturtridge 1982a; Mason 1984; Riley 1985; Dickinson 1987; Wenden and Rubin 1987; Brookes and Grundy 1988; Holec 1988; Ellis and Sinclair 1989; Little 1989; Sheerin 1989; Willing 1989; Gathercole 1990; Little 1991; Wenden 1991; Dickinson 1992; Page 1992; Esch 1994; Gardner and Miller 1994; Dam 1995); special issues of the journals *Die Neueren Sprachen* and *System* were devoted to learner autonomy in 1994 and 1995, respectively; and the aim of developing autonomy in language learning has been incorporated, to greater or lesser degrees, into many countries' national curricula.

The reasons for this trend are varied, and have to do with factors as diverse as: educational philosophy; language-learning theory; political beliefs (from widely differing perspectives); the need to adapt to rapid changes in technology, communications and employment and the increasing recognition that the ability to learn is more important in today's environment than a set of knowledge; the opportunities provided by technological developments and increased communication links around the world; and attempts to expand educational provision at the same time as cutting costs. However, with people from a wide variety of backgrounds using terms like 'autonomy' and 'independence' for a variety of purposes, there is a massive potential for misunderstanding, and so we turn first to the question of terminology.

Terminology

The word *autonomy* appears in nine of the titles listed above, and a glance in recent language teaching and applied linguistics journals is likely to confirm the impression that it is taking over the buzzword status that *communicative* and *authentic* held in the 1980s. There are a number of problems associated with this growing popularity (see, e.g., Little 1994c), two of which concern us here. The first is that, as can be seen from the range of terms used in the book titles mentioned above, different terms are often used to refer to the same thing. The second, related, problem is that the same term is often used to mean different things. Before we go any further, then, we need to clarify what concepts we are addressing in this book, and what words we are using to express them.

The goal of the contributors to this book is to help learners develop the potential to take control of every stage of their own learning, from the setting of goals through to evaluation. In this, they share some common ground with proponents of learning systems which allow (or can allow) learners varying degrees of choice over the learning process, such as 'distance learning', 'flexible learning', 'individualized instruction', 'open learning', 'self-access learning' and 'self-instruction'. Where they differ, however, is that the systems just mentioned are ways of organizing learning and not approaches which have as their central aim the development of a particular capacity in the learner.

Self-instruction, for example, is taken either to refer to learning without a teacher (e.g. Little 1991: 3) or learning "without the direct control of a teacher" (Dickinson 1987: 5). *Distance learning* is a way of organizing learners which usually only allows learners control over access (the time, place and pace of their study). *Open learning* (of which distance learning is a subset) allows choices within the curriculum as well as in access; it does have taking responsibility for learning as a goal, but it appears fundamentally to be an institutional response to the need to take on board more students while at the same time cutting costs (Lewis 1995). *Individualized instruction* involves the use of activities designed to meet the needs of individual learners, but it is the teacher who prepares or adapts materials, sets objectives and evaluates the learner's ability to perform required skills (Logan 1980). *Flexible learning* is a similar approach to language learning at secondary level in the UK in which the teacher or department provides materials and activities; the learner has some choice over what to do when, but there is usually little opportunity to negotiate about learning goals or method of evaluation (Page 1992: 83; Evans 1993). *Self-access learning* refers to learning from materials/facilities that are organized in order to facilitate learning;

much reference is made to this type of learning in the book, but again, the learning may range from self-directed to teacher-directed.

The labels that remain to us in order to put our aims into words are, of course, 'learner autonomy' and 'self-directed learning'. *Self-directed learning* is a concept which has been widely promoted and researched in the adult education field, particularly in the USA. In the literature, the term has been used in two senses: to mean both the process of/the techniques used in directing one's own learning, and the change of consciousness that is the result of such learning (Brookfield 1985). Candy (1991: 23) further distinguishes between four aspects of the term:

1. a personal attribute (personal autonomy);
2. the willingness and capacity to conduct one's own education (self-management);
3. a mode of organizing instruction in formal settings (learner-control); and
4. the individual, noninstitutional pursuit of learning opportunities in the "natural societal setting" (autodidaxy).

Similar distinctions (and therefore the possibility for misunderstanding) exist in the definitions of 'learner autonomy' and 'self-direction' in language learning. Here the classic definition, referring to *autonomy* as "the ability to take charge of one's own learning" is that of Holec (1981: 3), and you will find several definitions of this type in the early pages of each of the first four chapters of the book. Central to this definition of autonomy is the concept of knowing how to learn. Holec sees autonomy as an *ability* or *capacity* that needs to be acquired (i.e. learning how to learn) and as separate from the learning that may take place when autonomy is being or has been acquired; this learning Holec labels *self-directed learning*, which clearly, in the context of this book, has similarities with Candy's third meaning 'learner-control'. In this view, then, 'autonomy' is a capacity and 'self-directed learning' is a way in which learning is carried out.

This distinction is accepted by most writers in the field, apart from Dickinson (1987: 11) who calls the potential to accept responsibility for one's learning "self-direction", and complete responsibility for one's learning, carried out without the involvement of a teacher or pedagogic materials, "autonomy". Autonomy is seen generally as a capacity that is rarely, if ever, realized in its 'ideal' state: as Little (1991: 5; see also Chapter 13) emphasizes, because of the essential human need to interact with others, "the freedoms conferred by autonomy are never absolute, always conditional and constrained". Nor is autonomy seen as being a steady state: as many have pointed out, an autonomous learner may well choose teacher-direction at certain stages in his or her learning, and is likely to be autonomous in one situation, but not in another.

Having made some attempt to clarify the profusion of terms and meanings that cloud the whole issue of autonomy, it is as well to point out that the term 'autonomous language learning' (eschewed by Holec on the grounds that 'autonomous' should not be used of a process) is now found quite frequently, and indeed occurs in this book. This can cause some confusion, as the term may refer to self-directed learning or to learning (usually self-directed) that is carried out by autonomous learners; but the sense will usually be clear.

The focus and aim of the book

The title of the book thus embraces both the means and the end of learner autonomy. Some, like Candy, may argue that 'taking control' over the learning situation is not a sufficient condition for the development of autonomy, and that in formal educational situations the 'ghost' of the instructor lingers on, making it less likely that autonomy will be developed. We would agree with the first point, but we believe that experience is a necessary condition, a vital factor in the development of autonomy. Moreover, as Holec (1981) points out, it is unrealistic to expect learners to want or be able to learn how to learn without being in a position to direct their own language learning at the same time. As for the second point, we do not believe that educational institutions make the acquisition of autonomy impossible, and we discuss this point further below. The focus of the book is on *fostering learner autonomy within educational institutions*, and while several chapters reveal difficulties that may be faced, all are predicated on the belief that — given appropriate support — learner autonomy in these environments is an achievable goal.

The aim of the book is threefold: to examine key aspects of current theory and practice in the field; to exemplify the range of learning and research projects that are under way; and to highlight some of the problems and possibilities that lie ahead. The book combines a wealth of theoretical perspective with a wide range of practical examples, drawn from both classroom and self-access learning in a variety of cultural contexts. The division of the book into sections on Introductory perspectives, Learners and the learning process, Materials, Technology, and Evaluation provides a framework for readers to examine their own thinking on major issues and to consider how their thinking might most effectively translate into reality. We believe that the book makes an important contribution to the debate about learner autonomy, and we hope that it will be of value both to those already involved in helping language learners develop autonomy, and to those who are thinking about doing so.

Current issues of debate

A number of issues concerning autonomy in language learning have come to the fore in recent years. It may help to discuss some of those of particular relevance to this book by considering the following questions:

1. In what situations is learner autonomy an appropriate goal?
2. What type of autonomy should we aim at?

In response to the first question, it might be argued that learner autonomy is inappropriate in certain educational or cultural settings. We have already mentioned Candy's doubts about the likelihood of self-directed learning that is carried out in formal institutions leading to learner autonomy. There is a perception among certain adult educators, perhaps inspired by the example of Allen Tough (1971) and his Learning Projects (all of which were carried out by learners without any contact or input from educational institutions — i.e., in Candy's terms, autodidacts), that self-directed learning equates with adult learning outside of formal education. Leni Dam and Lienhard Legenhausen's chapter in this book (Chapter 17), along with Leni Dam's other publications (e.g. Dam and Gabrielsen 1988; Dam 1994, 1995), answers the query about whether self-directed learning can be carried out and autonomy developed with children. All the work emanating over the years from the Centre de Recherches et d'Applications Pédagogiques en Langues (CRAPEL) and other institutions, all the work represented in the titles listed at the beginning of this introduction, and indeed the chapters in this book, attest to the possibility of developing learner autonomy in formal institutions. As Little (1991) says, autonomy involves a psychological relation between the learner and what is to be learned, and can therefore occur anywhere; and the freedoms that exist despite restrictive educational environments mean that the "counsel of despair" (ibid.: 40) can be rejected. (See also Gremmo and Riley 1995: 154-6.)

The doubts about cultural appropriateness are more serious. Evidence from adult education has been unclear, often consisting of anecdotal reports (see, e.g., Brookfield 1985: 11; Nolan 1990; Brockett and Hiemstra 1991). Riley's (1988) admittedly impressionistic account of the differing responses of four national groups to self-directed learning has rightly set alarm bells ringing around the world. This is particularly true in South-east Asia, where a large number of self-access centres and self-directed learning projects have sprung up in recent years. Questions have been raised, for example, about the appropriateness of the goal of autonomy for Asian learners (e.g. Jones 1994) and of asking culturally diverse groups of learners to assess their own progress (Thomson, Chapter 6). At the same time, others do not see cultural obstacles as being insurmountable (e.g. Nunan, citing Willing 1988, Chapter 1; Esch, Chapter 3; Little, Chapter 13) or provide evidence that traditional learning practice and cultural traits may actually contribute to the development of learner autonomy (Ho and Crookall 1995; Pierson, Chapter 4). The debate continues.

In response to the second question ('What type of autonomy should we aim at?'), two oppositions might be suggested: individual vs. social; and psychological vs. political. Many of the contributors to this book have stressed the vital importance of interaction and negotiation to the development of autonomy (see especially Chapters 2, 3 and 13). Those working in self-access centres are called upon to find ways of helping learners to participate in social interaction (Benson 1995). Holec's definition has been altered to add a social dimension to the existing individual one:

> Learner autonomy is characterized by a readiness to take charge of one's own learning in the service of one's needs and purposes. This entails a capacity and willingness to act independently and in co-operation with others, as a socially responsible person. (Dam 1995: 1)

All this reflects a growing commitment to the importance of interaction and collaborative learning, and an insistence that learning does not take place in a vacuum and that self-direction does not mean learning on your own. Alongside this emphasis on the social nature of learning, a re-emphasis on the political nature of autonomy has started to emerge. Not surprisingly, the more a concept is discussed, the more likely it is to appear 'normal' and at the same time to be 'normalized' by mainstream culture. This is the argument made by Phil Benson (Chapter 2) as he outlines the gradual trend to overlook the political foundation for Holec's (1981) definition, and to concentrate on an individual, psychological version of autonomy. Benson's call for a return to a more political view of learner autonomy is echoed in a recent article by Little (1996), in which he contends that learner autonomy is essentially a political concept, and makes the point that to argue for the removal of psychological barriers between school knowledge and the learner's knowledge is in fact a political act that challenges existing power structures. This is an aspect of learner autonomy that has received relatively little attention from language teachers until now; assuming that teachers do not continue to avoid problematic issues (Benson, in press), that situation is likely to change.

The organization of the book

As with any collection, it would have been possible to organize the book in a variety of different ways. For example, a section on Culture was at first envisaged (this is central to the chapters by Pierson and Thomson, and is touched on in many others, such as those by Nunan, Esch and Little). The chapter by Little could easily have fitted into the Introductory section, as could the chapters by Nunan and Sinclair into the section on Learners and the learning process, the chapters by Dam/Legenhausen and Nunan into the section on Materials, and the chapter by Stevens into the section on Technology. You may like to follow up these connections or prefer to make connections of your own.

The book is organized into five sections. The first section, 'Introductory perspectives', sets the foundation for the book, and discusses important theoretical and practical issues that are followed up later on: the relationship between learner-centred teaching and the development of learner autonomy (David Nunan, Chapter 1); the mainstreaming and depoliticization of the once radical version of autonomy (Phil Benson, Chapter 2); criteria for learning environments that are likely to promote learner autonomy (Edith Esch, Chapter 3); and the question of whether cultural factors predispose certain groups of learners against autonomy (Herbert Pierson, Chapter 4).

The next section then tackles the element that is central to the success or failure of learner autonomy: 'The learner and the learning process'. In the section, a variety of projects are reported on in which teachers interact with learners or organize a learning experience with the aim of helping learners direct their own learning and develop their autonomy. The interactions/opportunities described are: strategy training (Diana Simmons, Chapter 5); self-assessment (Chihiro Thomson, Chapter 6); counselling (Rena Kelly, Chapter 7); conversation exchange (Peter Voller and Valerie Pickard, Chapter 8); and peer assessment (Lindsay Miller and Raymond Ng, Chapter 9).

Section 3 focuses on a factor that is fundamental to the way learning is organized: 'Materials'. In Chapter 10, Barbara Sinclair considers how much explicitness is appropriate in learner-training materials. In Chapter 11, Winnie Lee analyzes learner perceptions of authentic and textbook materials, and in Chapter 12, Elsie Christopher and Susanna Ho report on a group film discussion project carried out in self-access mode.

Section 4 examines a related area: 'Technology'. First, David Little considers how far learner autonomy can be fostered by various computer-based technologies (Chapter 13). Two of the technologies that Little discusses are exemplified in the chapters that follow: David Gardner and

Rocío Blasco García report on learner use of an interactive video program (Chapter 14) and John Milton, Ian Smallwood and James Purchase describe the features of a prototype computer program designed to aid language use (Chapter 15).

In the final section, the attention turns to 'The evaluation of learner autonomy'. In this section, the papers are concerned with the evaluation of learning that takes place in autonomous or self-access settings. In Chapter 16, Philip Riley explores methodologies appropriate for research into self-directed and self-access learning. Then Leni Dam and Lienhard Legenhausen report on a project comparing the vocabulary acquisition of an autonomous secondary school class with that of traditional classes (Chapter 17). Finally, Vance Stevens analyzes data from a project investigating the use of help features in a self-access CALL program (Chapter 18).

You will find more detailed introductions to each chapter at the beginning of each section.

Future directions

In terms of content, the issues of debate mentioned earlier, along with others discussed by the contributors to this book, will continue to engage those involved with promoting autonomy in language learning for some time to come. Other avenues for future research have been suggested by, among others, Skehan (1989: 134, 140), Candy (1991: 438ff.) and Gremmo and Riley (1995). There is certainly no shortage of areas worthy of investigation. However, there is obviously still a long way to go if we are to convince educational decision-makers of the need to match lip-service to the goal of learner autonomy with appropriate changes in educational practice.

What sort of research approaches and methods should we employ in trying to achieve this aim? Candy (op. cit.: 426ff.) argues that the positivistic approach is inappropriate for the study of self-directed learning, and that instead we should use "interpretive" methods that focus on the personal meanings and perceptions of individual learners. Riley (Chapter 16) clarifies the debates over positivist/antipositivist and quantitative/qualitative research approaches. Some of his suggestions are similar to those of Candy, but he argues for a "mixed" approach that "rejects the either/or terms of the qualitative vs. quantitative debate and the absolute distinction between objectivity and subjectivity". The guidelines and suggestions in his chapter should prove useful to those starting to carry out research in the area.

I

Introductory perspectives

One of the main purposes of this book is to provide an account of the concept of autonomy as it relates to second language learning and to discuss how this goal can be translated into practice. In this introductory section, which sets a theoretical foundation for the book, the concept of learner autonomy is discussed from the varying perspectives of teachers, learners and self-access centre managers. David Nunan (Chapter 1) presents examples of how learner- and learning-centred classrooms can help develop learner autonomy, while Phil Benson (Chapter 2) argues for a critical approach to autonomy that addresses issues of social control. Edith Esch (Chapter 3) proposes criteria for learning environments that are likely to promote learner autonomy, and Herbert Pierson (Chapter 4) uses evidence from ancient writings and recent research to argue that autonomy may not be as antithetical to cultures outside the European democratic tradition as might be supposed. Each chapter raises important theoretical and practical issues relating to learner autonomy that are followed up, directly or indirectly, later in the book.

In the first chapter, David Nunan explores the concepts of learner-centredness, learning-centredness and learner autonomy. Nunan argues that autonomy is a relative concept, and that curricula and classrooms which help the learner to develop learning strategies or skills (e.g. the ability to plan, reflect on and evaluate their own learning) can lead to a degree of learner autonomy. Nunan supports his argument by reference to research studies of learner-centred approaches to teaching which led to improvements in language skills and in the ability to take responsibility for learning. Finally, he provides practical illustrations of how "learning skills" (and hence, learner autonomy) might be developed in an "autonomy-focused" classroom through syllabus and materials design. (This is taken up in more detail by Barbara Sinclair in Chapter 10). Nunan's chapter usefully reminds us that, as educators, we do not need to regard autonomy as something achievable only by those learning entirely outside institutions and under their own steam; we can — and should — make a start in our own classrooms.

In Chapter 2, Phil Benson takes a somewhat contrary position to that of David Nunan. While not denying that the concept of autonomy has important psychological dimensions, Benson maintains that in the years since Holec's definition in 1979, there has come to be an emphasis on psychological autonomy, individual choice and learner-training techniques, while the political aspect of autonomy has largely been overlooked. This has occurred as the once radical concept of autonomy has been absorbed into the mainstream of educational thinking. From the viewpoint of critical language pedagogy, Benson argues for a more radical, critical version of autonomy that sees it not as an ability or the handing over of responsibility within the learning situation, but rather as a right, as a concept involving control of the learning process, of resources, and of language.

Benson's analysis addresses broad issues of control and power more overtly than any other chapter in the book. Some of us may find these issues uncomfortable, particularly in the current educational climate, and dealing with them can be problematic, as Benson demonstrates. But a consideration of where exactly we stand in terms of the issues Benson raises (e.g. collective decision-making, social change and the extent of control available to learners) is overdue and will also surely give our work (both collectively and individually) a sharper focus.

Benson's emphasis on the social and collaborative nature of learner autonomy is echoed in Chapter 3, in which Edith Esch proposes criteria for language-learning environments which are likely to promote learner autonomy. The criteria that she puts forward are: the provision of choice and flexibility within the system; the capacity of the system to be adapted, and of materials to be modified, according to the learning plans or paradigms of the user; the existence of support sytems which encourage reflection through social interaction; and the provision of collaborative learning activities and networks. In her discussion, Esch stresses the importance of three factors that she sees as essential for the development of learner autonomy: learning by doing, reflection and conceptualization, and interaction and negotiation.

At a time of rapid changes in technology and communication, Esch considers ways in which the latest advances may be used to promote or counter learner autonomy, a topic discussed further by David Little in Chapter 13. She concludes that the main obstacle to learner autonomy is likely to be, not cultural differences (as some have suggested), but the onset of standardized language skills-training packages "where no engagement of the learners' cognitive abilities and social responsibilities is required".

The relationship between learner autonomy and culture is explored in more detail in Chapter 4.

In this chapter, Herbert Pierson responds to objections that cultural impediments prevent autonomous language learning from establishing itself as a goal of education in older, less dynamic traditional learning cultures rooted outside mainstream Eurocentric cultures. Using Hong Kong Chinese learners as his basis for discussion, Pierson contends that contemporary structural factors in Hong Kong, rather than deep-rooted cultural factors, might make learners less amenable to autonomy as a goal and make them less confident in following a language course based on the principles of autonomous learning. To support this view he draws on the authority of ancient Chinese writers as well as contemporary Chinese intellectuals and institutions to demonstrate that there exists in a culture as old as China's a clear tradition and support for learner autonomy. He thus concludes that experiments in autonomous language learning cannot be dismissed out of hand on the basis of purely cultural arguments. Pierson ends by outlining some of the ways in which one institution has set out to promote learner autonomy, conscious of the fact that all learners, whatever their cultural background, are individuals.

1

Towards autonomous learning: some theoretical, empirical and practical issues

David Nunan

Introduction

In this chapter I shall look at some of the theoretical, empirical and practical issues associated with the concept of learner autonomy. In the first part of the chapter, I shall provide my interpretation of some of the key terms associated with learner autonomy, as well as providing a rationale for autonomous learning. The second part of the chapter contains a selective review of some research which illuminates issues of relevance to autonomous learning. Finally, I shall look at some of the practical implications of fostering autonomy in language learning. This final section will be illustrated with materials for developing autonomous learning in both ESL and EFL contexts.

The central point I would like to make in the chapter is that autonomy is not an absolute concept. There are degrees of autonomy, and the extent to which it is feasible or desirable for learners to embrace autonomy will depend on a range of factors to do with the personality of the learner, their goals in undertaking the study of another language, the philosophy of the institution (if any) providing the instruction, and the cultural context within which the learning takes place. Each of these factors will, of course, interact, so that a learner whose personality and preferred learning style is positively oriented towards autonomy might, in an institutional or cultural context in sympathy with autonomy, become largely autonomous, and, in a context antithetical to autonomy, develop little in the way of autonomy.

A second, related point, is that some degree of autonomy can be fostered in learners regardless of the extent to which they are naturally predisposed to the notion, by systematically incorporating strategy training into the learning process.

Defining terms

In this first part of the chapter, I should like to explore some key terms that have been variously interpreted by different practitioners and comment-ators at different times. These terms are 'learner-centredness', 'learning-centredness' and 'autonomy'. To begin with *learner-centredness*: the basic idea behind the concept is simple, although not, I trust, simplistic. A learner-centred curriculum will contain similar components to those contained in traditional curricula. However, the key difference is that in a learner-centred curriculum key decisions about what will be taught, how it will be taught, when it will be taught, and how it will be assessed will be made with reference to the learner.

Information about learners, and, where feasible, from learners, will be used to answer the key questions of what, how, when, and how well. Other themes to emerge in writings on learner-centredness include an emphasis on the active involvement by learners in communicating in the classroom (Scarcella and Oxford 1992), a focus on the use of authentic materials (Cathcart and Vaughn 1993), and incorporating into the curriculum learning-how-to-learn goals alongside language goals (Ellis and Sinclair 1989).

My own interest in seeing things from the learner's point of view developed when I realized that I could not do the learning for my learners — that in the final analysis, they would have to do their own learning, and that the best thing I could do was to help them find ways of doing their own learning. Supporting this notion is the realization of the complex and indirect relationship between instruction and learning. When I began as a language teacher, I thought, perhaps with the arrogance of the young, that my learners ought to learn what I taught. It was a shock to discover how naive was the idea that learners learn what teachers teach. It is a fact of life that learners do not learn what teachers teach in the simplistic one-to-one way implied by many curricular specifications and assessment tools.

However, it is a serious error to leap from an acceptance of the notion that learners must ultimately do their own learning to embrace the doctrine of learner autonomy. While I believe that learner autonomy is an end towards which all teachers and learners ought to work, it is a mistake to assume that learners come into our classrooms with some kind of natural endowment to choose both wisely and well. In fact there is substantial evidence to suggest that many learners are not so naturally endowed. This is where the notion of *learning-centredness* makes its appearance. A learning-centred classroom is constituted with dual complementary aims. While one set of aims is focused on language content, the other is focused on the learning process. Learners are therefore systematically educated in the skills and knowledge they will need in order to make informed choices about what they want to learn and how they want to learn. Rather than assuming that the learner comes to the learning arrangement cashed up, as it were, with critical learning skills, the sensitive teacher accepts that many learners will only begin to develop such skills in the course of instruction.

Learner-centredness, then, is not an all-or-nothing concept. It is simply not the case that classrooms are either teacher-centred or learner-centred. It is a relative matter. As I have already implied, it is also not the case that a learner-centred classroom is one in which the teacher hands over power, responsibility and control to the students from day one. I have found that it is usually well into a course before learners are in a position to make informed choices about what they want to learn and how they want to learn, and it is not uncommon that learners are in such a position only at the end of the course.

So far, I have dealt with learner-centredness and learning-centredness, suggesting that the latter can provide a basis for the former. They may also lead towards learner autonomy. The concept of *autonomy* has been characterized in various ways, as has its relationship to the concepts of self-direction, learner-centredness and individualization. Holec (1981: 3) defines autonomy as "the ability to take charge of one's own learning". This is elaborated as follows:

"*To take charge of one's learning* is to have, and to hold, the responsibility for all the decisions concerning all aspects of this learning,
i.e.: — determining the objectives;
— defining the contents and progressions;
— selecting methods and techniques to be used;
— monitoring the procedure of acquisition properly speaking (rhythm, time, place, etc.);
— evaluating what has been acquired." (ibid.)

Towards learner autonomy: the research background

In the preceding section, I tried to sort out some of the terminological issues associated with the terms 'learner-centredness', 'learning-centredness', and 'autonomy'. In this section, I turn to the question: Is there any evidence that learner- and learning-centred teaching actually leads in the direction of learner autonomy? Is there any evidence that the active engagement of the learner in the learning process has any effect on learning outcomes? Do learners have views on what they want to learn and how they want to learn it, and what happens within the learning process when their views are actively solicited?

Quite a few years ago now, I carried out a comparative study into the learning preferences of teachers and learners in the Australian Adult Migrant Education Program (Nunan 1987). When I compared the preferences of learners and teachers in relation to selected learning tasks and activities, I found some stark contrasts and dramatic mismatches. They disagreed on issues to do with error correction, teacher explanations, the use of games and video, the use of cassettes, and pair work. About the only thing that they did agree on was the importance of conversation practice. Now I am not suggesting that student views should be acceded to in all cases. However, I would argue that at the very least, teachers should find out what their students think and feel about what they want to learn and how they want to learn.

In 1988, Ken Willing reported the findings from a large-scale study into the learning styles and learning strategy preferences of adult immigrant learners of English as a second language in Australia. With 517 learners, Willing had a substantial data base. Using a questionnaire and interviews, Willing investigated possible learning-style differences which could be attributed to a range of learner biographical variables such as ethnic background, age, level of education, time in the target country, and speaking proficiency level. The study came up with certain surprising findings. In the first instance, learners did have views on the learning process, and were capable of articulating these. Perhaps the most surprising finding was that none of the biographical variables correlated significantly with any of the learning preferences:

> ... none of the learning differences as related to personal variables were of a magnitude to permit a blanket generalization about the learning preferences of a particular biographical sub-group. Thus, any statement to the effect that 'Chinese are X' or 'South Americans prefer Y', or 'Younger learners like Z', or 'High-school graduates prefer Q' is certain to be inaccurate. The most important single finding of the study was that for any given learning issue, the typical spectrum of opinions on that issue were represented, in virtually the same ratios, within any biographical subgroup. (Willing 1988)

In Europe, Dam and Gabrielsen (1988) investigated the extent to which young learners were capable of making decisions about the content and processes of their own learning. Beginning in the early 1980s, and continuing for a six-year period, they investigated whether eleven-year-old learners of English as a foreign language in Denmark were capable of being involved in planning, organizing, managing and evaluating their own learning. They also wanted to know how such a collaborative process could be maintained over a six-year period, and what effect such a collaborative approach would have on the development of communicative competence in their learners. They found that learners, regardless of their aptitude or ability, were capable of a positive and productive involvement in selecting their own content and learning procedures. Furthermore, learners were also positive in accepting responsibility for their own learning. Interestingly, the researchers found that difficulties reported by teachers had less to do with learner resistance than with the problems of redefining teacher roles.

In a very different context, one of my own graduate students in Australia, Assinder (1991), came up with a similar result when her students were given an opportunity to determine what content was to be learned and how the content was to be dealt with in class. Assinder developed a peer-teaching, peer-learning model, in which students prepared video materials to present to one another. Her own observations, as well as student evaluations, confirmed the success of this experiment in student-initiated teaching and learning. Assinder reported increased participation and responsibility, increased accuracy, and sustained motivation. The learner-oriented nature of the experiment is evident in Assinder's conclusion:

> I believe that the goal of 'teaching each other' was a factor of paramount importance. Being asked to present something to another group gave a clear reason for the work, called for greater responsibility to one's own group, and led to increased motivation and greatly improved accuracy. The success of each group's presentation was measured by the response and feedback of the other group; thus there was a measure of in-built evaluation and a test of how much had been learned. Being an 'expert' on a topic noticeably increased self-esteem, and getting more confident week by week gave [the learners] a feeling of genuine progress. (Assinder 1991: 228)

Widdows and Voller (1991) sought the views of university students in Japan. They report that, contrary to popular wisdom, these learners have definite views on what they want to learn and how they want to learn. These views conflict with the 'official' curriculum of the university. In their report, they state that:

> The most important result of this survey is the dichotomy between what students want to learn and experience in university English classes, and what they are actually taught there. ... Students do not like classes in which they sit passively, reading or translating. They do not like classes where the teacher controls everything. They do not like reading English literature much, even when they are literature majors. Thus it is clear that the great majority of university English classes are failing to satisfy learner needs in any way. Radical changes in the content of courses, and especially in the

types of courses that are offered, and the systematic retraining of EFL teachers in learner-centred classroom procedures are steps that must be taken, if teachers and administrators are seriously interested in addressing their students' needs.

A study by Kumaravadivelu (1991) focuses on the multiple perspectives on reality in the classroom. His research demonstrates the mismatch between teacher intention and learner interpretation, and underscores the naivety of assuming that learners will learn what teachers intend for them to learn. His study identifies ten potential sources of mismatch between teacher intention and learner interpretation, and shows how, if we are aware of these, differing interpretations need not be negative, but — if identified and properly handled — can give learners an opportunity to negotiate further in order to tease out a problem in their own way (Kumaravadivelu 1991: 106).

Heath (1992) investigated what happens when ESL learners in the United States are collaboratively involved in selecting content, reflecting on learning tasks, and involved in their own self-evaluation. She used a simple but nonetheless ingenious device for collecting her data. She wrote to the high school students of an associate asking them to collect data on their uses of oral and written language. These students were all in Basic English classes. They had major deficiencies in their written language skills and some of them were considered to be 'mentally deficient'. Heath asked these students:

> ... to work together as a community of ethnographers, collecting, interpreting, and building a data bank of information about language in their worlds. They had access to knowledge I wanted, and the only way I could get that knowledge was for them to write to me. They collected field notes, wrote interpretations of patterns they discovered as they discussed their field notes, and they answered the questions I raised about their data collection and their interpretations. (Heath 1992: 42)

As a result of their involvement in this process, the students learned that communication is negotiation, and they got to reflect on the important relationships between socialization, language and thought. In substantive terms, all students moved out of the Basic English in 'regular' English classes, and two moved into 'honors' English. As Heath reports, "Accomplishments were real and meaningful for these students."

In addition, Heath was able to conclude that:

> If the students learned that communication is negotiation ... what did the teacher and researcher learn? [We] gradually recognized that the best way to assess students' progress was to ask them to analyze their own written work. They had recorded, described, and interpreted patterns of oral and

written language in their homes and the work settings of their parents, as well as their own classrooms. Why couldn't they look at their earlier letters and compare them with later letters. ... The evaluative process, usually imposed by the teacher, became one in which students helped determine how one letter might be 'better' than another, and how far they had come between September and May in their writing. (ibid.: 43)

Another study employing a deceptively simple methodology, but from which some fascinating results emerged, is Slimani (1992). Slimani sought to determine what learners actually learn from classroom interaction. Her question was as follows: What is it that individual learners claim to have learned from interactive classroom events (this claimed learning she terms "uptake")? She further asks what is it that happens in the lesson that can account for this uptake? Her learners were a group of Algerian learners of English as a foreign language who were preparing to undertake engineering studies in English. Slimani found that topics initiated in the classroom by the learners were much more likely to be nominated as having been learned than those nominated by the teacher. In other words, when learners had an opportunity to contribute to the content of the lesson, that was the content which learners would claim to have learned.

In a major study in Singapore, Lim (1992) sought evidence for a correlation between classroom processes and learning outcomes. In this study involving 1,600 junior college students, she found that the frequency or quantity of learner participation related significantly to qualitative aspects of learner participation such as the range of speech acts and the control of conversational management techniques (e.g. turn maintenance and topic initiation). Learner participation in class also related significantly to improvements in language proficiency as measured by proficiency tests. Finally, there was a high correlation between activation of language outside the classroom and participation in class.

Lim's results are mirrored in an investigation by Hall (1991). Hall wanted to know how two-way information gap tasks, in which students have to share different kinds of information in order to reach a teacher-planned outcome, contribute to the acquisition of mathematical vocabulary. Subjects for the study were eleven- to thirteen-year-old students of mixed proficiency. There were three matched groups of eight students in the experiment. The experimental group used split information tasks in a pairwork learning arrangement. The first control group used the same content, but completed the tasks as an individual worksheet without the benefit of interaction. The second control group received teacher-fronted instruction. All students were pre-tested, underwent a four-week instructional period, and were then retested on four different measures: multiple choice comprehension, sentence anomaly detection, free recall writing, and an oral interview.

While the post-test scores showed that all groups in Hall's study benefited from the task-based learning, the group which worked interactively on the information gap tasks did so to a significantly greater extent than the two control groups. Hall detected a strong correlation between the generative use of vocabulary items and the students' success in manipulating the items during attainment tasks. He concluded that:

> It would thus appear that spoken output in the context of split information tasks is an important factor in aiding the acquisition of target vocabulary items. (Hall 1991: vi)

Recent research has also focused on the effect of encouraging learners to self-monitor, and to self-evaluate. Over the course of a semester, Nunan (1994) investigated what happened when a group of thirty undergraduates undertaking EAP courses were given opportunities to reflect on their learning through the use of guided journals. It was found that opportunities to reflect on the learning process led to greater sensitivity to the learning process over time. Learners were also able to make more effective use of the English they were learning in the EAP courses by making connections between EAP and their content courses. The degree to which the process fostered autonomy varied dramatically from learner to learner, and seemed to be basically a personality rather than cultural variable. Finally, all learners developed skills for articulating what they wanted to learn and how they wanted to learn.

What implications can we derive from this research? I believe that there are at least six of them, which are listed as follows:

1. There are identifiable differences in the ways in which different learners approach the task of learning another language and these will be reflected in the extent to which they either desire autonomy, or are capable of developing it.

2. Autonomy is enhanced when learners are actively involved in pro-ductive use of the target language, rather than merely reproducing language models provided by the teacher or the textbook.

3. Autonomy is enhanced when learners are given opportunities to select content and learning tasks and also when they are provided with opportunities to evaluate their own progress.

4. Autonomy is enhanced when learners are given opportunities to activate their language outside the classroom.

5. Autonomy is enhanced when learners are encouraged to find their own language data and create their own learning tasks.

6. Autonomy is enhanced when learners are encouraged to self-monitor and self-assess.

Comparing 'institution-centred' and 'autonomy-focused' classrooms

In this section, I should like to contrast what, for want of a better term, I shall call *institution-centred* classrooms with ones attempting to operationalize the principles set out above. I shall do this by looking briefly at the different stages in planning, implementing and evaluating a language course, and compare what might happen in an *autonomy-focused* classroom, which is designed to develop autonomy in the student, with what one might expect in an institution-centred classroom.

At the syllabus-planning stage, in the institution-centred classroom, it is the institution or the teacher who makes all the decisions about what will be taught and when it will be taught. These decisions will be made with little or no reference to the actual or potential communicative needs of the learner. In an autonomy-focused classroom, on the other hand, the selection and sequencing of content will be made with reference to the sorts of uses to which the learner will want to put the language outside of the classroom, and learners themselves will be involved in the selection, modification and adaptation on both content and process. This involvement on the part of the learner can be encouraged by the use of subjective needs assessment instruments such as the needs assessment questionnaire shown in Figure 1 below.

In selecting learning experiences, in an autonomy-focused classroom, the teacher will introduce a range of learning activities and tasks. There will also be an attempt to identify the learning style preferences of the learner, and use these as the starting point in making methodological selections. There is a further element which distinguishes an autonomy-focused from an institution-centred classroom. In the former, the learners will be encouraged to reflect on their learning experiences, and to evaluate the opportunities made available to them in class. In this way, they learn not only about the target language, but about the learning process itself. This need not be an elaborate, time-consuming or difficult process, as the example below demonstrates.

We would like you to tell us which of the following uses of English are important for you. Please put an 'X' in the box beside each if you think it is ' Very Useful', 'Useful', 'Not Useful'.

	Very Useful	Useful	Not Useful
Do you want to improve your English so that you can:			
1 Tell people about yourself	☐	☐	☐
2 Tell people about your family	☐	☐	☐
3 Tell people about your job	☐	☐	☐
4 Tell people about your education	☐	☐	☐
5 Tell people about your interests	☐	☐	☐
6 Use public transportation	☐	☐	☐
7 Find new places in the city	☐	☐	☐
8 Speak to tradespeople	☐	☐	☐
9 Speak to your landlord/real estate agent	☐	☐	☐
10 Buy furniture/appliances for your home	☐	☐	☐
11 Deal with door-to-door salespeople	☐	☐	☐
12 Communicate with your friends	☐	☐	☐
13 Receive telephone calls	☐	☐	☐
14 Make telephone calls	☐	☐	☐
15 Do further study	☐	☐	☐
16 Get information about courses/schools etc.	☐	☐	☐
17 Enrol in courses	☐	☐	☐
18 Get information about the education system	☐	☐	☐

19 Help children with schoolwork ☐ ☐ ☐

20 Apply for a job ☐ ☐ ☐

21 Get information about a job ☐ ☐ ☐

22 Attend interviews ☐ ☐ ☐

23 Join sporting or social clubs ☐ ☐ ☐

24 Join hobby or interest groups ☐ ☐ ☐

25 Watch TV ☐ ☐ ☐

26 Listen to the radio ☐ ☐ ☐

27 Read newspapers, books, magazines ☐ ☐ ☐

28 Give, accept, refuse invitations ☐ ☐ ☐

29 Make travel arrangements ☐ ☐ ☐

30 Talk to your boss ☐ ☐ ☐

31 Talk to doctors/hospital staff ☐ ☐ ☐

32 Talk to neighbours ☐ ☐ ☐

33 Talk to your children's teachers ☐ ☐ ☐

34 Talk to government officials ☐ ☐ ☐

35 Talk to English-speaking friends ☐ ☐ ☐

36 Get information about goods and services ☐ ☐ ☐

37 Complain about, or return goods ☐ ☐ ☐

From this list, choose five you want to learn first.

1 ....   2 ....

3 ....   4 ....

5 ....

Figure 1: A needs assessment questionnaire (adapted from Nunan 1988)

At the beginning of a unit of work, learners are told:

In this unit you will:

Report what someone says

"The police said that I was lucky to get out of the accident alive."

Say what people have been doing

"They've been working on the project for months."

(Nunan 1995a: 33)

At the end of the unit, learners are told that these are the language skills they have practised in this unit. They are then asked to evaluate how well they are able to:

Report what someone says?   ☐ yes   ☐ a little   ☐ not yet

    Find or give an example: ....

Say what people have been doing?   ☐ yes   ☐ a little   ☐ not yet

    Find or give an example: ....

(Nunan 1995a: 40)

Ultimately, of course, the autonomous learner is one who is able to create his/her own learning objectives.

In terms of assessment and evaluation, classrooms which have the development of autonomy as a goal will place great store on training learners in techniques of self-assessment, ongoing monitoring, self-evaluation and reflection. Once again, the teacher should not assume that learners have these skills at the beginning of the learning process, nor that all learners will appreciate the potential value of self-monitoring and reflection. However, during the course of instruction, they will be provided with opportunities for engaging in self-monitoring activities and using these as a way of developing their language skills as well as their sensitivity to the learning process. The following probe, adapted from a reflective task in Nunan 1995b, illustrates one way in which this can be done.

PLEASE COMPLETE THIS FORM BETWEEN NOW AND NEXT WEEK

NAME: _____

UNIVERSITY NUMBER: _____   DATE: _____

This week I studied: _____

This week I learned: _____

This week I used my English in these places: _____

This week I spoke English with these people: _____

This week I made these mistakes: _____

My difficulties are: _____

I would like to know: _____

I would like help with: _____

My learning and practising plans for next week are: _____

_____

Brindley (1989) provides an excellent introduction to learner assessment and self-assessment. His book contains many practical ideas for involving learners in their own monitoring and assessment for those readers interested in implementing the ideas set out in the preceding section.

Conclusion

In this paper, I have explored the concept of autonomy in relation to language teaching and learning. In characterizing and exemplifying the concept, I made the point that it is not absolute, but rather a relative concept. The feasibility of fostering autonomy will vary from learner to learner, from classroom to classroom, and from institution to institution. In the second part of the paper, I provided a selective review of research which, in my view, has implications for learner autonomy, and in the final part of the paper, I illustrated ways in which autonomy might be reflected in pedagogy by contrasting an autonomy-focused with an institution-centred classroom. While this contrast is, to some extent, an oversimplification, I hope that it serves to illustrate ways in which teachers can modify their current practice to encourage a greater degree of self-reflection and autonomy.

2

Concepts of autonomy in language learning

Phil Benson

Introduction

It is often taken for granted that we know what learner autonomy for language learning is although the concept is, in fact, commonly represented in at least three different ways. For some, learner autonomy is an ideal state, seldom actually achieved, where learners are fully responsible for decisions about their own learning. For others, it represents a set of skills that can be learned. And for others still, autonomy is an inborn capacity that is suppressed as we go through the processes of institutional education. These appear to be significant differences, but their implications have seldom been discussed. Indeed a casual observer of the literature on the topic might easily gain the impression that the concept of learner autonomy for language learning is entirely unproblematic. As the starting point for any discussion of the concept, however, three points need to be acknowledged:

1. For every paper published on autonomy in language learning there are at least twenty on autonomy and self-direction in other fields of learning. In North American adult education in particular, self-direction is a tried and tested concept. Evaluations of it, even those made by some of its advocates, are by no means universally positive.

2. Autonomy is a multifaceted concept with political, psychological and philosophical ramifications. Its application in the field of language learning is highly problematic, and we cannot expect to find an off-the-shelf concept of autonomy neatly packed and ready for use.

3. Nobody has yet succeeded in developing a version of autonomy that specifically takes account of the nature of language and language learning. Little (1991) has taken us a long way in this respect, but we

must nevertheless recognize that, so far, we have no theory of autonomous *language* learning.

As concepts currently on the radical edge of language learning methodology, learner autonomy and self-direction are open to critique from more traditional positions. In the field of adult education, more trenchant critiques have come from the direction of critical pedagogy. In this chapter, I want to explore the relevance of these critiques to the field of language learning and discuss what a more critical approach to learner autonomy for language learning might involve.

Autonomy and critical pedagogy

In a paper published in *Adult Education Quarterly*, Stephen Brookfield (1993), a leading North American authority in the field of adult education, reports on what amounts to an ideological crisis in the field of self-directed learning. He argues that self-directed learning, having become "comfortably ensconced in the citadel, firmly part of the conceptual and practical mainstream" (p. 227), is increasingly open to attack from the direction of critical theory. From the perspective of critical pedagogy, he says of self-directed learning that an "alternative form of practice that began as a challenge to institutional adult educational provision has become technocratic and accommodative" (p. 228). Self-direction is further open to criticism for its promotion of individualism and its failure to confront issues of power and control in learning. It is in response to this critique that a number of educators, including Brookfield himself (also Hammond and Collins 1991; Garrison 1992), have launched attempts to rescue the radicalism of self-directed learning by framing the concept in more critical terms.

In the field of language learning there is apparently no crisis of the kind Brookfield reports for adult education, but the signs are there. Wenden (1991: 11), for example, observes that encouraging learners to become more autonomous is a goal with which few language teachers would disagree. This suggests that the concept of autonomy is indeed beginning to enter the mainstream of language learning methodology. As it does so, there is a risk that the concept will become, as Little (1991: 1) puts it, "fossilized". An attempt to rescue the radicalism of autonomy in language learning, by outlining what a more critical version of the concept might look like in concrete terms, may not, therefore, be premature.

Concepts of autonomy in language learning

The concept of autonomy as it has developed in the field of language learning is complex and multifaceted. To illustrate what I see as a series of shifts in the concept over a period of years (which now appear synchronically as a range of perspectives), I want to focus on three important contributions to the literature: Holec (1981), Allwright (1988) and Wenden (1991). Little (1991: 6) describes Holec's (1981) report to the Council of Europe as a "foundation document" in the field. Holec's starting point is explicitly political as he places learner autonomy among educational innovations that "insist on the need to develop the individual's freedom by developing those abilities which will enable him to act more responsibly in running the affairs of the society in which he lives" (p. 1). Defining autonomy as "the ability to take charge of one's own learning" (p. 3), Holec stresses three key components in this and other work:

1. a dual emphasis on the *ability* to carry out autonomous learning and on the learning structures that allow the *possibility* of developing and exercising that ability (1981: 6; 1985: 187; 1988);
2. an insistence that autonomy can only be developed through the practice of self-directed learning (1980; 1985: 180);
3. a principle of full control by learners over decisions relating to their own learning and a concept of teaching or counselling as support (1985: 184; 1987).

Holec's approach is theoretically rigorous (some might say extreme), but it has also proved its practicality in guiding self-directed learning at CRAPEL, Nancy for a number of years.

The second contribution to the literature that I want to discuss (Allwright 1988) is selected not because it is a major theoretical statement (which it does not claim to be), but because it articulates much of the doubt that has arisen about how far the kind of approach advocated by Holec can be generalized. Allwright begins his paper by suggesting that autonomy is a term "associated with a radical restructuring of our whole conception of language pedagogy, a restructuring that involves the rejection of the traditional classroom and the introduction of wholly new ways of working" (p. 35). From this somewhat alarmist premise, he goes on to suggest that there might be ways to promote autonomy within the context of whole-class instruction. His proposal is that teachers can, if they look, identify and encourage the autonomous classroom behaviour of their students. Allwright does not attempt to redefine autonomy on this basis, but his paper nevertheless represents an important stage in shifting the focus of autonomy away from the structural conditions of learning and towards the capacities and behaviour of the learner.

In Wenden (1991), Allwright's tentative suggestions are placed within a broader theoretical framework. In this work Wenden attempts to situate the methodology of learner training (learner *strategy* training in particular) within the wider theoretical context of learner autonomy. In so doing she further reduces the structural element in the definition of autonomy. In one passage, she defines autonomy in the following terms:

> In effect, 'successful' or 'expert' or 'intelligent' learners have learned how to learn. They have acquired the learning strategies, the knowledge about learning, and the attitudes that enable them to use these skills and knowledge confidently, flexibly, appropriately and independently of a teacher. Therefore, they are autonomous. (p. 15)

In this formulation, the learner's behaviour is in itself a sufficient condition for autonomy. This emphasis on learner behaviour is also apparent in an exercise in which readers are invited to divide the learners that they are presently teaching into those who are already autonomous, those who would be open to training and those who might be resistant to it (p. 11).

This shift in emphasis away from the structural conditions for autonomy perhaps makes learner autonomy a more accessible and palatable concept to a larger number of practising teachers. But before applauding such a development unconditionally, we need to look closely at its wider implications. I want, therefore, to comment on three shifts associated with this development: from situational to psychological, from social to individual and from meaning-orientation to task-orientation.

1. The search for ways of promoting autonomy without radical re-structuring of the learning process has led to a shift from a concern with situational or external aspects of autonomy to a focus on psychological or internal capacities. This shift could be interpreted as a depoliticization of the concept of learner autonomy which would be welcomed by many. However, an element of political ambiguity may be introduced if the influence of external social constraints on the development of learning skills is minimized. A psychological version of autonomy that emphasizes learners' responsibility for their own successes and failures in learning could easily be used to support political doctrines of non-intervention and self-reliance.

2. The shift from situational to psychological is also a shift from social to individual. Individual learning styles and preferences are stressed and individual choice tends to be emphasized over collaborative processes of decision-making. Again, a shift which appears at first sight as

'depoliticization' could lend support to doctrines of individualism that lead to social atomization and disempowerment.

3. The shift from situational/social autonomy to psychological/individual autonomy also involves a shift in emphasis from questions about the purposes and content of language learning (*why* learners are learning languages and *what* they want to learn) to questions about methods (*how* they should go about learning). This corresponds to a shift from constructivist meaning-oriented views of language and learning towards more task-oriented approaches. In constructivist views of learning (Candy 1989), the acquisition of knowledge is seen as the construction of meaning, a process in which the construal of experience through language is central (Mezirow 1991: 19). By contrast, in task-oriented approaches to learning both knowledge and language tend to be taken as given. Learning a language is seen as a task that must be carried out before learning through that language can occur. The 'learner training' approach to autonomy, in particular, shows a tendency to focus on the 'best' processing techniques for a given set of linguistic skills or body of knowledge. This is accompanied by a corresponding tendency to de-emphasize fundamental questions about the purposes and content of language learning. Politically, this could be interpreted as a tendency to encourage passive acceptance of dominant ideologies of language learning.

A critical approach to autonomy in language learning

This interpretation of shifts in the concept of autonomy in language learning is made from the perspective of critical language pedagogy (Pierce 1989; Pennycook 1989; Benesch 1993) which argues that language learning and language teaching are intimately bound up with issues of power and that to deny their political character is to take up an ideological position in favour of the status quo. But critical language pedagogy itself stands in need of some mechanism through which to engage both learners and teachers in critical work. In this sense, the concept of autonomy may fit well with critical approaches to language learning. In the remainder of this paper, I want to explore what a more critical version of learner autonomy for language learning might look like in concrete terms.

The issue of control lies at the centre of a critical approach to autonomy, operating at three inter-related levels: control of the learning process, control of resources and control of language. I use the word *control* in preference to *responsibility* because it places an emphasis on the *right* to autonomy.

1. Control of the management of the learning process is also at the centre of much of the current discussion on autonomy. This discussion is often framed in terms of an artificially constructed power relationship between teachers and learners in which autonomy is seen as a question of teachers handing over control to learners. From a critical perspective, however, the control that teachers exercise in the learning process is underwritten and constrained by broader structures of power. Assessment in particular is rarely under the full control of teachers, since criteria for assessment are inscribed both in social conceptions of language use specific to the social context of learning and within the norms of the language itself. Teachers have a certain amount of power to hand over to learners. They can also work to gain greater power for themselves and their students. It may be equally important, however, to help to raise learners' critical awareness of the social constraints under which language learning takes place. This could involve a process that I call collective analysis of the social context of learning. This process has some parallels with Hammond and Collins's (1991: 58) "situation analysis", which they describe as "critical questioning of, reflection on, and consciousness-raising about the normally taken-for-granted aspects of the situation within which learners and educators function". The social context of language learning involves both the functions of the language in the educational system and the wider society, *and* the learners' attitudes towards those functions. The aim of analysis is for learners to establish "subject positions" (Pierce 1989: 405) in relation to the functions of the language and the constraints that they imply so that they can make decisions about *what* and *how* they learn in the context of decisions about *why* they are learning the language.

2. Control of resources is an issue raised by Brookfield (1993: 238), who argues that an "inauthentic, limited form of self-direction is evident when our efforts to develop ourselves as learners remain at the level of philosophical preferences because the resources needed for action are unavailable or denied to us". In the context of language learning, control of resources could cover a diverse range of issues from native speaker vs. non-native speaker teachers to the content of textbooks and learning materials to issues of time and workload. Control of resources may constitute an argument for some form of self-access *and* the need for greater student control of what it makes available. As in the case of control over management of learning, control of resources may involve both direct control and a degree of critical awareness of resource constraints.

3. Control of language comes close to what Candy (1988) calls "subject matter autonomy" or the knowledge-based component of autonomy. Subject matter autonomy is seen as a correlate of constructivist approaches which emphasize the creative element in learning and posit the ability to call into question the judgements of experts as a fundamental aim of autonomous learning. In the language-learning context, native speakers might be considered as the experts in question, and subject matter autonomy as the learner's right to question native-speaker judgement of normative appropriateness. Control over the norms and content of the target language has been identified as a key issue in situations where, as in the case of English in South Africa, it has become an object of political contention (cf. Pierce 1989). More generally, it can be said to define the goal of autonomous language learning as the negation of the teaching-learning distinction, or the transformation of the *learner* into a *user* or *producer* of language.

The social and transformative character of learner autonomy

In conclusion, I want to suggest that by fronting issues of control in learner autonomy, two fundamental issues are raised: the social character of autonomous learning and autonomy as a philosophy of transformation.

Learner autonomy and self-directed learning have been strongly associated with individualization and even isolation in learning, but the implications of a more critical version of autonomy are social. Greater learner control over the learning process, resources and language cannot be achieved by each individual acting alone according to his or her own preferences. Control is a question of collective decision-making rather than individual choice. Yet collective decisions are also arrived at by individuals achieving consensus and acting in concert. From the perspective of Habermas's Critical Theory, Garrison (1992) argues that learning is necessarily social because of a need to validate meaning in dialogue with others which necessitates shared control of the learning process. He argues, however, that there is a distinction between external and internal processes and activities in that external control may be shared while internal self-directedness in constructing meaning is absolute (p. 141). In view of an overwhelmingly individualistic trend in current approaches to learner autonomy in language learning, I have chosen here to place an emphasis on the social. But it is clear that the relationship between psychological and social aspects of both learner autonomy and language learning is something that we currently know too little about.

Current thinking on learner autonomy also seems to have veered away from any connection with social change. But again, it seems clear that attempts to raise issues of control will necessarily bring both learners and teachers into conflict with entrenched relations and structures of power. To take a simple example, it is often the case that when a teacher asks a group of learners in an institutional setting for their input on the learning process, they request a reduction in the assessed workload. Such requests can often be justified on the grounds that lower workloads tend to promote deep, meaning-oriented approaches to learning, yet they are also likely to problematize the teacher's role as mediator between students and institution. Even a request as simple as this, if it is taken seriously, introduces an agenda of change. Because steps towards autonomy invariably problematize roles and power-relations, autonomization is necessarily a transformation of the learner as a social individual. In other words, autonomy not only transforms individuals, it also transforms the social situations and structures in which they are participants.

This point perhaps sums up what has been the major thrust of my argument in this chapter. As concepts of autonomy in language learning have multiplied and become more complex, there has emerged a growing tendency to avoid issues of power and social change. Approaches have become prominent which attempt simply to train learners in skills that prepare them for an abstract autonomy deferred to an indefinite future. In contrast to this trend, I have argued for a version of learner autonomy that stresses issues of control and the social and transformative character of learning. I have also argued for a version of autonomy that takes account of the specific nature of language and language learning. This view of autonomy also has important implications, I believe, for research, which needs to focus much more on the social character of independent learning and on relationships between language autonomy and social autonomy. In the course of this work, we have a great deal to learn from critical theory and its applications beyond the field of language learning.

3

Promoting learner autonomy: criteria for the selection of appropriate methods

Edith Esch

Introduction

The concept of autonomy has shaped views on education for thirty years in Europe, mainly through the influence of the work of the Modern Languages Project of the Council of Europe. It is a concept which arises from a fundamentally optimistic view of man according to which learners are able to be in charge of their own learning.

However, technological advances have changed the context within which language education takes place almost out of recognition. Satellite communications and high-speed networks transform the way we think about communicating with students. With two-way video links for conferencing, it is a matter of time before research students have supervisions with tutors who are hundreds of miles away. For research, fast and accurate information retrieval systems and huge digitally stored databases can do in minutes what used to take weeks or months. In our domain, access to foreign language input for learning is now normally available outside teaching institutions and we are slowly moving towards wall-to-wall multimedia, multilingual environments. This new culture sets the stage for new ways of thinking about the transmission of linguistic knowledge which is reflected in the emergence of a new discursive world, with new functions such as advising, new roles such as helper, new activities such as collaborative learning, and new tools such as "learning technology" — all taking place in virtual environments.

The question arises whether there is a fundamental conflict between, on the one hand, autonomy (the notion that language learners should be encouraged to be in control of their own learning path) and on the other, the slavery or control exercised over learners by technological means. Two views currently prevail:

1. One view is that the concept of learner autonomy may be a bit romantic but is very useful. It is good to encourage self-reliance because of ever-increasing numbers of students and ever-increasing costs of teachers. But fundamentally, of course, learners cannot, by definition, take charge of their own learning. How could they since they do not know the language they are learning? To direct students is the function of teachers and technology can help them effectively. Indeed, teachers are increasingly familiar with technology and the younger generation can design new imaginative and motivating programmes. According to this view, once enough self-instructional interactive programmes and multimedia packages can be transported and distributed over networks, there will not be any problems any more and the foreign language problem will be solved. We will be able to celebrate the dawn of universal communication.

2. The other view is that whatever method or technology is being used for language learning and teaching, it is essential that it should be placed within the framework of educational values and the educational aims pursued by teachers should be made explicit. The pursuit of learner autonomy is such an aim. Naturally, if technology — whether pencil and paper or computer does not matter — can be used effectively and cost-effectively in disseminating arrangements which appear to support the development of autonomous learners, it should be used and exploited to the full. This is the view that I will put forward in this chapter.

I will first clarify what I mean by 'promoting learner autonomy'. Given the nature of autonomy, it is absurd to talk about 'appropriate methods'. The methodological domain I will be dealing with is consequently restricted to that of the environment, conditions and resources provided for language learners. This environment is more — or less — likely to support autonomous learners. Five criteria will then be proposed for language-learning environments likely to provide this support and illustrated with examples of ways in which we have tried to support and/or promote learner autonomy in my institution — the Language Centre, Cambridge University, UK. In the third part of the chapter, I will come back to the concept of autonomy as a culturally-bound concept. I will argue that in language education, intercultural variations may be less important than politically motivated semantic shifts in discourse.

What is meant by 'promoting learner autonomy'

To start with, I wish to argue for the validity of my enterprise given the nature of autonomy. Following David Little (1991: 3), the easiest is to state what autonomy is not, thus listing the usual misconceptions associated with the concept. First, it is not self-instruction or learning without a teacher. Secondly, it does not mean that intervention or initiative on the part of a teacher is to be banned. Thirdly, it is not something teachers do to learners, i.e. a new methodology. Fourthly, it is not a single easily identifiable behaviour. Finally, it is not a steady state achieved by learners once and for all.

To state what it is, I will refer to three classic definitions only.

1. Autonomy is defined by Henri Holec (1981) as a capacity or fund-amentally critical ability to reflect on one's experience and to "take charge of one's own learning", after Bertrand Schwartz's (1977) "ability to assume responsibility for one's own affairs".

2. David Little (1991) labels this capacity a set of "conditional" freedoms, which, in a given learning context, make it possible for individuals to determine their objectives, define the content and process of their own learning, select their methods and techniques, and monitor and evaluate their progress and achievements.

3. Finally, John Trim (1976) talks about autonomy as an adaptive ability, allowing learners to develop supportive structures within themselves rather than to have them erected around them. 'Vertebrates rather than crustaceans' would be both more appropriate to societies with democratic structures and to the demands of constantly changing situations in adult life.

Thus by definition, in talking about 'promoting learner autonomy' I am only arguing for the provision of circumstances and contexts for language learners which will make it more likely that they take charge — at least temporarily — of the whole or part of their language-learning programme and which are more likely to help rather than prevent learners from exercising their autonomy. In doing so, I am pursuing a fundamentally Darwinian view of humans as adaptive organisms able to develop and to design their own structures. Humans are not only able to adapt to different languages and different learning conditions, but also to progress in their ability to learn, by becoming aware of the processes through which they learn, by conceptualizing their learning experience, by being actively engaged in steering the process and by taking responsibility for organizing their learning experience. Such a view (Schank and Birnbaum 1994) is reassuring for educators whose morale has been suffering badly in the past twenty years from the consequences of Chomsky's declarations about the irrelevance of linguistics and psychology to language teaching.

To sum up, while autonomy is a property of learners, or teachers for that matter, we are dealing with the *characteristics of systems* which can be described not only as 'not incompatible with autonomy' but 'supportive of autonomous learners'.

Creating a supportive environment for learner autonomy: five evaluation criteria

The problem is now clarified: the task is to identify criteria whereby we can evaluate whether a practice is more likely to support rather than suppress learners' ability to make their own decisions. To give one example, availability of choice for language learners seems a good candidate. Obviously, the same criteria can be used to identify practices/methods/ systems which are likely to prevent learner autonomy from surfacing. For example, programmed instruction is very unlikely to support learner autonomy.

Naturally, if a practice or method scores very high on one of these criteria, it is in no way a guarantee that language learners will be autonomous. On the contrary, the more choice people have, the more they may need support. In fact, it is people who have autonomy "thrust upon them" who are difficult to deal with (Trim 1976). Conversely, if a practice scores very low on one of the criteria, it does not mean at all that it is impossible to act autonomously (although it might make it more arduous). For example, Trotsky explains in his memoirs that at the very beginning of his political career, when he had been put in prison for subversive activities, he thought it would be very useful to learn foreign languages to be able to publish outside Russia when out of prison. He chose the comparative method: he asked for copies of the Gospel in several European languages and used them to learn the languages. This was autonomy at its best.

The following five criteria are proposed for the evaluation of arrangements and the management of support systems, whether human resources or materials provision. The first two criteria, Choice and Flexibility, essentially concern the management of the overall system for maximum learner access. The third criterion, Adaptability/Modifiability, concerns the management of language-learning materials by learners. The last two criteria, Reflectivity and Shareability, concern the ways in which learners can interact with other humans for support in the domain of language learning *per se*, in the domain of the management of the learning task, or simply for social communication.

Choice, or the provision of genuine alternatives

The relevant question is: are alternatives provided to learners whenever possible? It must be clear that the meaning of choice is substantive. It must be a genuine choice for the learner, not a gimmick the aim of which is to make the learner fit into predetermined categories. A self-access resource centre is a good start to help provide choice. At Cambridge, the resource centre provides traditional multimedia materials in over 100 languages, with a reference section, computer-assisted language learning, eleven languages available all day direct by satellite, and one four-hour video tape in each language received by satellite every night available for use the following day. Learning how to use the centre is done by means of introductory sessions, a users' guide and videotapes. Students can choose:

1. whether they work on their own or with help (or attend classes in a number of languages);
2. when and how often to come;
3. whether they come on their own or with a friend;
4. which language to study;
5. which medium to use;
6. which types of materials to start from (authentic or didactic);
7. what activities to carry out; and
8. what kind of evaluation they wish to undergo (formal, informal, summative or formative).

Apart from genuine choices, the advantages of a self-access resource centre are manifold because they provide for rich and varied input for acquisition in a non-normative environment. For example, in a major language, there would not only be a choice between pedagogical materials and 'raw' authentic data but within each category there would also be plenty to choose from. For example, there would be courses with a communicative approach and a notional-functional syllabus, but also others with situational material or even audio-lingual materials. In the same way, there is a wide range of 'raw data' whether they are magazines or audio recordings or TV programmes direct by satellite. TV is a favourite with students, but it is good because it is a constant reminder not that foreign languages are there simply to be learned but that there are whole communities of people out there who are sending out messages for interpretation. On the learning side, TV provides what Bruner (1983) would call "contextualized" and/or "situated" speech in a wide range of registers and, of course, it is the students' own interests and personal motivation which guides their viewing.

Another aspect which contributes to a rich linguistic environment in our centre is the fact that there are many languages available, the very existence of which are unknown to the average student. Again, this serves as a constant reminder that there are hundreds of other linguistic communities in the world and by itself, this acts positively against ethnocentrism.

Thirdly, and this is perhaps the most important, the very range of materials implies a non-norm-oriented view of linguistic knowledge and language-learning methods. This non-normative approach relaxes rather than builds learners' anxieties concerning what they should do. At the same time, it is a statement that, to quote Sharwood-Smith (1993) "there are no rules floating about to be grabbed and swallowed up". What is swallowed in is data, not rules.

Flexibility

This criterion refers to the flexibility or rigidity of structures. Once a particular choice has been made, how easy is it to self-repair and to change options? Of course, this depends on the student's type of difficulty. Let me here briefly mention the low-level trouble-shooting system we have. It is a 'Square One Kit' in which all the information students need to have to use the resource centre is available. In particular, it includes a user's guide and all the factual information students need to use the system, so that at any point they can 'come back to Square One'. But the kit also gives information about the advisory service, which I will describe in a moment.

Adaptability/Modifiability

This criterion addresses the capacity of the system to modify or change to suit the learning plans or strategies of different learners. A typical test of *adaptability* will be in the arrangement and classification of language-learning resources, and in particular the extent to which categories for the description of materials are imposed on the learner. An example is the classification scheme to be adopted for self-access raw data materials. The problem is two-fold; on the one hand, one needs to find descriptive categories which make sense from the point of view of the librarian such as nature, location and description of a document, and on the other, learner-relevant criteria must be created to support the retrieval operation by different categories of learners who may have very different needs or learning priorities. The problem, of course, is that whatever the range of choice you can offer, you need to be in the paradigm which is relevant to the learner to make it possible for the learner to negotiate it. The following anecdote will illustrate the point.

I live in England but every year I go to France for the holidays and I speak French with my children. One summer when my son Philip was about three I drove to France with him and he was very excited about the whole business of being on holiday in France. We stopped in a village shop to buy food and I told Philip to choose some biscuits. The lady of the shop asked him what kind of biscuits he wanted and to her absolute amazement, Philip replied "*French* biscuits".

Thesaurus construction within a self-access system addresses this problem of learner-relevant paradigm very precisely. The librarian of the Cambridge Language Centre is building up such a thesaurus. Briefly, it is a set of search terms meant to facilitate the process of browsing and to support the retrieval of materials. The process involves specifying the usage of terms, so that searching is itself a language-learning process. For example, the word 'occupation' would be followed by 'World War 2' as well as by 'employment'. Thesaurus terms can be combined so that the scope of the search can be constrained, e.g. to one language only. Thus, in the example above, a search for 'Occupation: World War 2' would guide a learner to all the materials concerning this topic across all the languages but could easily be constrained to only the French or German material. A thesaurus is an open-ended and dynamic tool — which can eventually integrate the learners' own terms — and it makes materials catalogued in the TINlib audio-visual database more easily and widely accessible.

Modifiability is slightly different. I am referring, in particular, to the possibility for learners of transforming documents and playing around with them. For example, one of the collaborative activities we encourage students to carry out is doing puzzles. These are entertaining at an advanced level mainly because they elicit talk that reveals which linguistic categories and strategies students are using when carrying out a task. For example, a whole short story is 'dismantled' into paragraphs which are then shuffled at random and distributed to two teams whose role is to reconstruct the short story. This requires learners to read their 'cards' very quickly, to make hypotheses about the structure of the story and support them with linguistic evidence, and then to negotiate with the other team. A psychological advantage here is that there is a 'correct answer' available but most often it is not needed. Modifiability, unfortunately, is seriously limited at present because of copyright issues.

Reflectivity/Negotiability

This criterion refers to the ability of the system to provide means for learners to reflect and look back on their learning experience in a negotiated way through language. At Cambridge, we have a system aiming at *individual learner support* through the learning advisory service and another system for *collective learner support* through learner-training courses.

The *learning advisory service* was set up as an intelligent human interface available to users for face-to-face interaction. Its specific brief is to improve students' 'learning to learn' ability. It is a system of intervention which aims at supporting students' methodology of language learning by means of 'conversations', i.e. by using language in the framework of social interaction to help students reflect on their learning experience, identify inconsistencies or changes and steer their own path. An important aspect is that initial contact, which may be before or after using the self-access system, is normally on the initiative of the student. The adviser interacts with learners by means of interviews, orally (face to face or by telephone) or in writing (by letter or e-mail). The service is also a way of stating that 'learning by doing' is not enough. Learners require help in making explicit their methodology and their representations of the learning process. The adviser provides for second language acquisition what Bruner called a "Language Assistance Support System" (LASS).

Learner-training courses have a comparable function but they aim at groups of learners who have common learning needs. They amount to group advising with a collective focus. The idea is that students work together and reflect together on their language-learning experience with the help of an adviser. Courses have so far been experimental and can take various forms. They are not advertised but offered to students who have come to see the adviser because they have difficulties in a particular area. This process of self-selection is considered by us to be crucial. Students are written to and asked to commit themselves to come to the course, the aim of which, explicitly, is to help them learn to learn, not to learn a particular language. At the same time, whenever possible, the course is conducted via the medium of the target language. At the first meeting, the students learn to know each other and work out what their respective needs and priorities are. For example, one group decided to split into two, one to concentrate on the lexicon and vocabulary development and the other on grammar. Students make all the decisions themselves. Intervention occurs only if requested. The tutor's role is to record what's going on, to help make sure that there is an agreed statement of what the plan is for the following session at the end, i.e. what activities are to be carried out with what intentions, and to distribute these 'minutes' at the beginning of the following session.

These courses have been remarkable for two reasons: first, although they are totally voluntary, participants tend to get hooked. Secondly, there is evidence that sharing the hands-on, task-based approach as a basis for reflection has increased students' understanding of categories for language-learning activities such as 'listening' or language categories such as 'vocabulary'. As a result, their use of the resources and in particular of the catalogue is improved.

These courses provide a 'learning by doing' experience for students as well as an occasion for reflecting on the way they learn. This is very valuable for learning and again I refer to Bruner's concept of "situated" speech in discourse. The value of learners' engagement in a task as a way to deeper understanding also appears to be increasingly supported by research in the cognitive sciences. Finally, such courses demonstrate to students that they are able to organize their own course and to control all the aspects of the management of learning.

'On the spot' negotiated learner support provided by a help desk is to be contrasted to that of advising in the examples above. Whereas the concept of advising is essentially methodological and associated with the development of a coherent metalanguage, this is a system which permits intervention into the language-learning process at a very different level, much more akin to the kind of intervention available in class, where an individual learner can ask either the teacher or the student sitting next to him/her for help.

The concept of 'help desk' will be tested in the framework of a research and development project called HIPERNET funded by the European Commission under the RACE (Research in Advanced Communications for Europe) programme. This will test a high performance multimedia network for distributed language training. The help desk will be a point where individual learners working at workstations on the network will be able to call somebody else (either an adviser or another learner) if they have a problem they wish to solve. Not only will they see each other but they will also share a screen with their interlocutor so that they can easily refer to or locate a difficulty by marking it. The HIPERNET help desk facility is also intended to facilitate collaborative planning between students to negotiate offers of cooperation with other students who are working on the network in order to plan and carry out simulated tasks. A students' plan will be recorded so that they can refer to it later on, revise it if necessary but also gain very valuable information for self-assessment. They will see for themselves any discrepancy between what they thought they would be doing and what they have actually done.

Shareability

This criterion refers to the ability of the system to provide means for learners to share activities and/or problems and difficulties with others. It is different from negotiability. The latter is fundamentally about negotiating meanings and change brought about by the learning experience. Shareability is both more 'convivial' and more linguistic. It has to do with doing things together, whether it is problem solving in relation to a complex task, planning a communicative task, or working out the correct pronunciation of a word and checking one's production.

At Cambridge, where over 60 languages are spoken by students at postgraduate level, there is a special arrangement supported by the advisory service to create supportive social conditions and networks by means of exchange pairs and pairing up of students. The concept is twofold: there is a pedagogical aspect that students learning a second language, and particularly if they work in a technologically advanced environment, should have the possibility of anchoring their language learning in social relations. It can be with a native speaker of the target language, or it can be with another student who is learning the same language. It is both a kind of dating system which helps individuals find friends and a way of creating a network of learners who can share the experience of language learning. The other aspect is that it is one of the means which can help the acculturation of non-native speakers of English who are in the university community so it is a case where a shared experience is used explicitly and positively as a socially cohesive device. This kind of exchange can be done in other ways. Nowadays, there are high-tech versions of what we called 'pen friends' when I was a child. Right now, The Chinese University of Hong Kong students are the 'electronic pen friends' of the students of the Chinese Department in Cambridge.

Where is the evidence that these are appropriate methods to promote autonomy? As I was very careful to explain earlier, there is no evidence that Cambridge students are more or less autonomous **because** of the way the Language Centre is organized, as it would be meaningless to seek such evidence. What I can say is that in the context of Cambridge University where independent thinking and the ability to take responsibility for one's decisions in the management of learning is highly valued, the system works for language learning. Use of the Private Study Laboratory has increased by over 70% in the past five years, and the number of users of the advisory service increased by 57% last year and keeps increasing. It is worth noting that for 75% of these students it is entirely 'free', hence self-motivated. Thus I am only ready to claim that these are methods which work with learners who believe autonomy is a good thing.

Let me summarize what I have said so far using the image of a college bridge over the River Cam (see Figure 1).

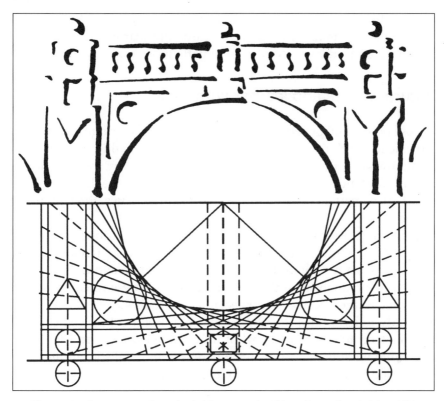

Figure 1: Representation of a bridge over the River Cam, Cambridge, UK

A language is comparable to a bridge between individuals or between groups. You can learn to build a bridge in several ways:

1. You may find out how to build a bridge entirely on your own, working on the design, the materials etc. as you go along until you step on the other side of the river. The risks of falling in the water are many but at the end of the process you will have learned a lot about yourself and about learning as well as being able to cross the river.

2. You may go through the same process with a team of friends, which requires negotiating over the method and design. This is likely to be more fun and if you fall in the water, you may get help.

3. You may agree with one or more people to start from the two banks of

the river at the same time until you meet in the middle, which requires careful joint negotiations.

4. Finally, and this is particularly important in the context of higher education, you can reflect on the experience of bridge building and, with the assistance of an engineer, turn your learning experience into conceptualized knowledge representations as you are learning.

Cultural values and learner autonomy

Because of its familiar setting to me, the image of the bridge over the Cam leads me to my third part. This concerns the way in which the concept of autonomy is culture-bound and why this affects the way we select and use methods for language learning and teaching. Coming back to the issue of values raised earlier, but in particular to cultural values, three points can be made.

First, there are cultural orientations reflected in attitudes, values and types of behaviour which have implications for the way students approach the task of learning. For example, a recent study of Jin and Cortazzi (1993) is based on an analysis of the expectations of Chinese research students who come to the UK and the expectations of their supervisors or tutors. The study reflects how, in cultures which are of a collectivist character, students tend to expect relations of mutual dependence, and to want to conform to what the group wants whereas individualistic cultures stress the development of independence, creativity and critical thinking from an opposite perspective. The way the transmission of knowledge is carried out in a society deeply affects expectations towards language norms and conventions about language use.

Secondly, and although I do not wish to underestimate the importance of this issue, cultural differences may not be the main barrier to the promotion of the concept of autonomy in countries with a group-oriented tradition such as China. To start with, there exists a Chinese tradition of transmission of knowledge which does not in any way contradict that of the gradual uncovering of higher knowledge through hard work, and in which the concept of obedience is not an impoverished concept referring to 'obeying orders' behaviour but on the contrary, is associated with self-knowledge and the virtue of humility (de Bary 1991; Hsu 1992). Another reason is that, as indicated by Jin and Cortazzi (1993), solutions are available. If one looks at Schumann's (1978) Acculturation Model, it is clear that only two-way acculturation leading to mutual adaptation — not assimilation — will create the right conditions for second language acquisition but this, of course, presupposes that in-group and out-group boundaries are reassessed. This solution would also favour designs whereby group work for learning and training as well as cooperative exchanges would be given more prominence than individual work. Mutual acculturation may take a long time but it is a possible (if long-term) solution.

Thirdly, we need to be aware of the reasons why we have difficulties in capturing the concept of autonomy. The concept has been hijacked by the 'enterprise' culture discourse (Fairclough 1993) which is part of the cultural engineering that has taken place in Britain. It can be demonstrated in the following way:

If one looks at the following three sentences and tries to fill in the blank space, the word *autonomy* will come immediately to mind.

1. ... means an acceptance of personal responsibility and a confidence and desire to take action to improve your own circumstances.
2. ... encompasses flexibility, innovation, risk-taking and hard work.
3. ... meets people's needs. (Fairclough 1993)

In reality, these quotes come from speeches made by Lord Young, the former UK Minister of Employment, then Secretary of State at the Department of Trade and Industry, renamed Department of Enterprise in 1987. The word *enterprise* should fill in the three blanks.

In this fashion, gradually what I would call the 'Robinson Crusoe Culture' has come to replace Bunyan's 'Pilgrim's Progress Culture'. Here I should like to remind the reader that Robinson is not only a story of survival and self-management but above all a story of ruthless intervention into the language-learning process to assert power:

> In a little time I began to speak to him, and teach him to speak to me; and first, I made him know his name should be Friday ... ; I likewise taught him to say Master, and then let him know, that was to be my name; I likewise taught him to say yes and no ...

A lot of confusion about autonomy arises from confusion about the values underpinning the concept. As shown by the examples above, the spread of 'Newspeak' makes it difficult to disentangle what is pedagogically innovative and valuable for language learning from what is purely ideological.

Conclusion

In its attempt to provide for increasing numbers, higher education is faced with the prospect of increasingly standardized language-learning systems, neatly packaged in increasingly sophisticated software and hardware. If this happens, the educational benefits of language learning — cognitive flexibility and deeper understanding of other societies — will be diminished and impoverished. Indeed, language learning will be emptied of its content to become language skill training where no engagement of the learners' cognitive abilities and social responsibilities is required. I do not think this is compatible with the support of autonomy in higher education, or in education in general. On the other hand, I would like to conclude that it is up to us to shape the way in which the concept of autonomy is interpreted. It is the authenticity of our own social identities as language educators which is at stake, as users and not consumers of languages.

4

Learner culture and learner autonomy in the Hong Kong Chinese context

Herbert D. Pierson

> *The sages from the Eastern sea have the same mind and reason as the sages from the Western sea; the sages of centuries ago have the same mind and reason as the sages of centuries to come.* (Lu Hsiang-shan, 1139–1193)

> *Learning without thinking is blind; thinking without learning is vain.* (Confucius, The Analects)

Introduction

One concern about introducing an instructional innovation such as autonomous language learning into the Hong Kong educational environment is that it could be antipathetic to established educational traditions and practices. This is especially true when the innovations might be seen as something imported from the outside. The purpose of this chapter is to discuss some fundamental cultural and pedagogical issues as educational institutions introduce autonomous language learning into traditional pedagogical settings such as Hong Kong. By examining the current understandings of Hong Kong Chinese learners, I hope to examine some of the obstacles we might expect to encounter. I will balance these understandings with the research that is being done on the learning approaches of Hong Kong Chinese learners, and then briefly juxtapose Chinese cultural traditions — some ancient and some contemporary — relevant to the debate over suitability of autonomous language learning. Finally, I will mention the Independent Learning Centre (ILC), one attempt to concretize the principles of autonomous learning in the Hong Kong Chinese educational context.

Learner autonomy

A fundamental principle of autonomous learning is that the *locus of control* is in the hands of the individual learner. This emphasis on learner control puts independent learning at variance with ordinary instructional practices in Hong Kong, and surely practices in many other places. According to Boud (1988), learner autonomy can be approached in several ways. First it can be seen as a goal of all academic study and in that sense it is applicable to all the disciplines of knowledge. Secondly, learner autonomy can be used to describe certain deliberate instructional practices. Some good examples would be those educational programmes whose formal goals are to encourage students to be responsible for what they should be studying and how they should be studying. Thirdly, the tendency towards autonomy must necessarily be part of any normal learning effort. In any course of study learners must make certain decisions for themselves. It is not practical to think that teachers desire or are able to guide every aspect of student learning.

Let us consider the first approach, learner autonomy as a goal of all academic learning. This notion is attributed to ancient Greece where it was used in a political context. A feature of the ideal state was the capacity for self-government or self-rule. By analogy, this concept could refer to a feature of the ideal learner "to be an independent agent, not governed by others" (Boud 1988: 18). In this context, a succinct definition of autonomous learning is provided by Dearden (1972), who states that a person has autonomy:

> ... to the degree, and it is very much a matter of degree, that what he thinks and does, at least in important areas of his life, are determined by himself. That is to say, it cannot be explained why there are beliefs and actions without referring to his own activity of mind. This determination of what one is to think and do is made possible by the bringing to bear of relevant considerations in such activities of mind as those of choosing, deciding, deliberation, reflecting, planning and judging. (p. 461)

A stronger notion of learner autonomy is provided by Gibbs (1979), who states:

> ... an autonomous individual must have both independence from external authority and mastery of himself and his power. He must be free from the dictates and interference of other people, and free also from disabling or lack of coordination between elements of his own personality. He must have the freedom to act and work as he chooses and he must be capable of formulating and following a rule, pattern or policy of acting and working. (p. 119)

One portrait of the Hong Kong learner

Although it is not politically correct to generalize about any cultural/ethnic group, patterns do emerge as result of cumulative anecdotal evidence and empirical research. For years, data has suggested that the typical Hong Kong Chinese learner is passive, reticent, and reluctant to openly challenge authority, especially teachers. Hong Kong learners are reported to be inclined to favour rote learning over creative learning, dependent on the syllabus, and lacking in intellectual initiative (cf. Biggs 1991). A Hong Kong-based university lecturer (Murphy 1987) has written that :

> ... Hong Kong students display unquestioning acceptance of the knowledge of the teacher or lecturer. This may be explained in terms of an extension or transfer of the Confucian ethic of filial piety. Coupled with this is an emphasis on strictness of discipline and proper behaviour, rather than an expression of opinion, independence, self-mastery, creativity and all-around personal development. (p. 43)[1]

Some researchers (Balla et al. 1988) argue that the passivity and rote-learning behaviours reported among Hong Kong students can be attributed less to cultural factors and more to structural elements which have resulted when British colonial education bureaucracy is mixed with the residual elements of traditional Chinese culture transmitted by the family. This hybrid educational culture conditions Hong Kong students very early, making it exceedingly difficult for them to change their learning habits. It is a learning behaviour which is exacerbated by the socio-economic reality that primary and lower secondary classes in Hong Kong are typically quite large, with well over 40 students in an ordinary class and with many teachers possessing little or no formal teacher training or certification.

Locus of control is another element which contributes to the static, sometimes dysfunctional education system in Hong Kong (see Yee 1989). Students as well as teachers have very little power over what happens to them during the process of schooling. Academic curricula are devised by a centralized educational authority and learner achievement is assessed by the results in public examinations over which school authorities and teachers have minimal influence. The public examinations, although administratively convenient, fair and efficient, reinforce a more didactic, expository mode of instruction. Under these conditions, the most favoured learning model is simply one where the teacher transmits knowledge to students. By properly reproducing the transmitted knowledge in public examinations, students signify they have acquired the knowledge. The increasing number of secondary school students who attain a place in university find that the instructional mode has little changed.

Evidence that this is an enduring cultural element in Chinese learning behaviour is suggested when it is reported that Hong Kong learners, even when uprooted from the local environment, exhibit similar learning behaviour. In Canadian schools many Hong Kong-born students stand out in contrast to other ethnic groups. An investigation of Hong Kong immigrant children in Canadian schools by Chan and Hui (1974) has suggested that:

> ... Chinese students were polite, but more quiet and shy than other students ... some of the schools felt that these Chinese students are overly submissive to authority in that they regard the teacher as the authority and do not challenge him sufficiently. (p. 16)

A report from the Toronto Board of Education (1969) indicated that Hong Kong Chinese students do not readily value the freedom that Canadian education promotes. The report said: "Sometimes freedom doesn't help ... the amount of freedom in Canadian schools may be a bit of a shock" (p. 31). In addition, studies of Hong Kong undergraduates in Canada (Exum and Lau 1988; Waxer 1989) have noticed that Hong Kong university students seeking counselling therapy prefer a more direct approach in contrast to an indirect approach to counselling, the approach preferred by their non-Chinese counterparts. In short, the Chinese learners, no matter where they are, seem to exhibit similar learning behaviour. They seem to want to be told what to do, show little initiative, and accordingly have difficulty in dealing with autonomy.

Furthermore, a questionnaire research study on general autonomy (Feldman and Rosenthal 1991) indicated that Hong Kong students acquire behavioural autonomy at an age comparatively later than their Australian or American counterparts. The same study also revealed that Hong Kong Chinese youth had delayed expectations for autonomy and placed less value on individualism, outward success and individual competence.

The general picture of the Hong Kong Chinese learner that emerges so far points to an individual who is conditioned by a pattern of cultural forces that are not harmonious to learner autonomy, independence or self-direction. Learning is perceived as something static and directed by others. The teacher functions as a transmitter of correct knowledge to learners and the school is the setting where students absorb *the knowledge*. The student is viewed as the passive recipient of knowledge. Whatever happens in the school is termed learning. The teacher decides what is correct and little room is given for the students to exercise personal initiative in the context of traditional Chinese learning culture.

Learning Approach Theory

To gain another perspective, it is profitable to examine Hong Kong students in light of recent theoretical approaches to learning (see Marton and Säljö 1976; Pask 1976; Biggs 1979, 1991, 1992; Entwistle and Ramsden 1983). These current theories identify three distinct processes that could go on when an individual approaches learning tasks. The approaches are *surface, deep* and *achieving*. These approaches are determined by learner motivation and orientation, and the tactics and strategies the learner uses when dealing with learning tasks. What follows below is a summary of these three approaches based on the work of Gow, Balla, Kember and Hau (in press).

The *surface* approach to learning is linked to extrinsic motivation. The student sees his/her learning efforts as moving towards some specific goal — for example, getting a good job. Fear of failure in attaining this goal and working over-diligently on the task are balanced by the learner in this approach. The learner concentrates on those elements of the task which will get him/her through the course of study. This usually means focusing on the literal and concrete components of learning tasks, emphasizing words rather than meanings. Such an approach encourages reproducible, rote learning. The student has very little personal involvement in and commitment to learning and is fearful of academic failure and what that will do for future wage-earning prospects.

The *deep* approach suggests that the learner has significantly more involvement in and commitment to the content of the learning task rather than attainment of short-term occupational and failure-avoidance goals. This approach implies intellectual curiosity towards study. Maximum effort is expended to satisfy that interest and curiosity. The learner is personally engaged in the subject matter and, by means of his/her own initiative, seeks to integrate more information by reading and discussion through every available intellectual avenue. The student is intellectually challenged and passionately engaged.

The *achieving* approach is one that follows from the ego-enhancement and pride that come from visibly achieving good grades or results. This approach, according to Biggs (1991), is not concerned with the content of the learning task as much as the context of the task. This would include such elements as time management, personal discipline, working space and the most efficient ways to cover the syllabus. The learner is motivated by the sense of achievement that comes from success and the part it will play in his/her future achievement and advancement.

Biggs (1987) believes that Hong Kong learners are more likely to assume a surface approach to learning because they are facing an excessive amount of syllabus material to be learned, very little choice and control over content and method of study, an assessment system that requires reproduction of what has been learned, and a learning environment where independence and individuality are neither nurtured, valued nor required. A deep approach to learning would be achievable if the students were given time to digest, contemplate and to discuss what they are learning. Such an approach to learning might be viable if the public examinations concentrated on understanding principles rather than the reiteration of facts and procedures. In summary, it seems likely that the didactic, expository type of school teaching that is common in Hong Kong schools, a function of overcrowded classrooms, lends itself to more surface approaches to learning.

Research on the learning approach of Hong Kong learners

In contrast to what has been represented so far, research by Kember and Gow (1991), in which Hong Kong post-secondary students were compared with a similar Australian cohort, have indicated that Hong Kong students have a relatively strong achieving approach to learning rather than a surface approach. Similar research on Hong Kong undergraduates, however, has yielded less congruent results. In a longitudinal study of Hong Kong undergraduates, Gow and Kember (1990) and Gow, Kember and Cooper (1994), discovered that tertiary education was not so successful in sustaining deep and achieving approaches to learning. This study indicated that deep motivation and an achieving strategy declined from the first year to the final year. A similar longitudinal study (Balla et al. 1991) indicated a significant drop in deep and achieving motivation over a three-year course of studies at a tertiary institution in Hong Kong. Students tended to limit their study to what was specifically taught in the course and showed little motivation to do outside work. Perhaps this was a response to the heavy workload demands of tertiary level courses. Garner (1990) suggests that learners follow primitive study strategies, ignoring more enriching time-consuming study skills if these primitive strategies provide them with a practical way to get though a course. However, a more encouraging note comes from a comparative study (Gow, Kember and Cooper 1994) of Hong Kong and Australian undergraduates, which indicated that the stereotype of excessive reliance on rote learning at the expense of autonomous learning was not confirmed in Hong Kong undergraduates.

What has emerged from this discussion is that the determining role of

Chinese culture, as represented in the stereotype of the passive rote learner, might not have the effects as originally postulated. Also, we should note that the stereotypical representation of the Chinese learner is not wholly a product of culture. We must consider the total context in which the Hong Kong Chinese learner functions. There are of course the expectations of the parents and family, which, it can be argued, form part of the residual cultural influences on the learner. However, we should not ignore the structure of the present colonial education system with its excessive workloads, centralized curricula, didactic and expository teaching styles, concentration on knowledge acquisition, examinations emphasizing reproductive knowledge over genuine thinking, overcrowded classrooms, and inadequately trained teachers. All these local structural and environmental elements might contribute more to sustaining and fostering a surface approach to learning to a much greater extent than the thousands of years of Chinese culture.

Traditional and contemporary Chinese viewpoints on learning

Much has been said about the influence of traditional Chinese learning practices, which, because of their relationship to the imperial examination system, are represented as sterile, uncreative and based on memorizing ancient texts. For this reason, I will briefly examine some authoritative voices, both traditional and contemporary, which, in my opinion, touch on the subject of learner autonomy in the Chinese context. It is hoped the insights of these writers will alter some popular beliefs about traditional learning behaviour and make people realize that there is an ancient Chinese pedagogical tradition congruent and consistent with the best practice of autonomous learning.

According to the Ming Dynasty scholar Wong Yang-min (1472–1529), pure memory training in education is a lower type of schooling. Emphasis on memory is a degenerate form of traditional Chinese education instead of the conscious effort of serious educators. Wong attacked the existing elementary schools of his period because of their emphasis on memory training and training in the formal essay, suggesting that by these means "the true teachings of the ancient sages were lost" (Chiang 1963: 87). However, even earlier than Wong Yang-min, we find that there is a preference for thinking over memory. For example, the Sung Dynasty scholar Ch'ingtsze (1032–1107), in discussing the method for studying history, stated that:

> ... it is not sufficient merely to memorize facts; it is more important to understand the causes. (ibid.: 86)

Another Sung Dynasty scholar, Lu Tung-lai (1137–1181), reinforces this notion when he states:

> The youth who is bright and memorizes a large amount of information is not to be admired; but he who thinks carefully and searches for truth diligently is to be admired. (ibid.: 86)

For Lu Tung-lai, memory is not an end in itself, but a means to an end. To understand what is in books without reference to personal needs or experience is of secondary importance. For him, the most important thing is to *digest* thoroughly what one gets from books so that it becomes an integral part of one's own experience.

Chu Hsi (1130–1200), also a Sung Dynasty scholar, came close to expressing ideas about what we now understand as autonomous learning. For Chu Hsi, true knowledge must be obtained for and by the learner himself. To gain knowledge is similar to eating. When one is hungry, one eats. Nourishment concerns the individual only. If one studies in this way, according to Chu Hsi, one will learn. To learn is to satisfy one's mental hunger. This is up to the individual, not others. To learn well, one must want to learn, not because his parents or teachers want him to learn, but because he is eager to learn. Moreover, Chu Hsi suggests that if one studies because his parents and teachers want him to, and he does it for their sake and not for himself, the result will be bad: as he puts it, "One must learn by himself" (ibid.: 90). In short, Chu Hsi advocates learner autonomy when he states:

> If you are in doubt, think it out by yourself. Do not depend on others for explanations. Suppose there was no one you could ask, should you stop learning? If you could get rid of the habit of being dependent on others, you will make your advancement in your study. (ibid.: 90)

Finally, one of the most important elements in the method of teaching and probably the one most emphasized by all the philosophers of the Confucian school is the doctrine of individual differences. Confucius, both in theory and practice, recognized that the intelligence of the individual differs, so that teaching cannot be extended uniformly, i.e. lockstep, to everyone. Confucius believed that the highest class of men are born with knowledge; the next acquire knowledge through learning; the next, although slow, acquire it through a persevering application to learning; and the last are stupid and are incapable of learning (ibid.: 109).

There are also indications that scholars and institutions in contemporary China value and encourage autonomous learning. In an address by the

President of the prestigious Shanghai University of Technology, the following was said (Qian 1985: 23):

> Since the pace of development of scientific research and cultural learning is too fast, it is quite impossible to complete the learning of a particular discipline within four years. Higher education should make full use of its four years to motivate a man into a scholar of initiative. Under this direction, the transmission of knowledge in the classrooms can be eliminated to those of the most crucial value and the core of the required expertise only. It is only through this way that professional training can be completed within four years. Moreover, it is very likely to produce students of higher initiative in self-studying. The problem of knowledge aging can be tackled. Practically speaking, besides classroom teaching, the functions of a library must be stressed in order to initiate self-study.

In addition to this, we have the official voice of the Chinese government which runs the 'State-Administered Examinations for Self-Learners in China'. This office administers examinations to hundreds of thousands of candidates who have learned through various self-study programmes that have been established throughout China. In the foreword to its most recent annual report, this institution's rationale for independent learning is made clear (*The State-Administered Examinations for Self-Learners in China* 1992: 1):

> ... while an independent learner cannot benefit from the culture and nurture of a university and from the direct contact with faculty members and from the stimulation of one's peers ... (H)owever, an independent learner does have some advantages over a full-time college student in that the former may achieve a better integration of theory with practice, a better understanding of the knowledge acquired, and may be in a position to find immediate application of the knowledge and skills learned, and to play a positive role in work or production.

Conclusion

Taking into account the present state of the Hong Kong Chinese learner and guided by the principles of autonomous learning, my colleagues and myself at The Chinese University of Hong Kong have been able to set up an autonomous language-learning facility, called the Independent Learning Centre (ILC). The ILC, as it has now evolved, has two stated pedagogical goals:

1. to enable individual language learners to assume more responsibility for their continued language learning; and

2. to motivate language learners to continue to enhance their language proficiency in a variety of ways.

After two years of operation, the ILC now possesses a modest resource bank of language-learning materials through a full range of media, from print to CD-ROM technology. In the ILC learners can be advised and guided by language counsellors on how to improve their language skills with increasingly less teacher intervention and dependence. In other words, the staff of the ILC is counselling learners on how to attain autonomy.

The ILC strives to conform to the principles of autonomous learning. Notwithstanding the already reported dependency and passivity of Chinese learners, my colleagues and I embarked on this course because of the increased awareness on the part of many experts that *all* language learners, no matter what their culture is, are individuals with their own set of needs and preferred learning styles (Holec 1981; Riley 1985). Autonomous learning has been made more attractive by advances in computer and A/V technology, which allow students to deal with many aspects of language learning, under different conditions, on their own, and at their own pace. However, in planning the ILC, it was not our intention that technological innovation be equated with autonomous learning. Technology is a motivating accessory to autonomous learning, but not its essence. Autonomous learning is rather a deeply held attitude and conviction. We intended that the spirit of autonomous language learning, as concretized in the ILC, would increasingly complement and enhance the learning that arises from more dependent, traditional modes of classroom learning.

The ILC is now set up on campus and with the help of interested language-teaching colleagues, is developing a resource bank of self-learning material. This material is being made available through a full range of media, from print to multimedia. However, even more important, the ILC is a place where learners can seek advice and guidance from language counsellors or advisers on how to improve their language skills with increased autonomy by using the ILC facilities. It is hoped that as a result of these interactions, the traditional Chinese language learner will become less dependent on teachers and formal classroom instruction, conscious of the paradoxical situation noted by Little (1991) that the teacher, and only the teacher, leads the learner to freedom and autonomy.

Note

1. It should be noted, however, that juxtaposed to this unflattering portrait of the typical Chinese learner is the enviable portrait of the brainy, academically inclined undergraduate and graduate student who predictably excels in Mathematics, Science, Engineering and Architecture.

II

The learner and the learning process

This section reports on projects in which teachers/helpers interact with learners or organize a learning experience with the aim of increasing learner control over the learning process and developing learner autonomy. Similar projects, involving the use or creation of language-learning materials, are reported in later sections; here the focus is on the capacity of learners to develop new ways of learning through training or counselling or through the provision of opportunities for the practice of self-directed learning.

One type of help that can be provided is strategy training (see also the chapters by Nunan, Esch and Sinclair). In Chapter 5, Diana Simmons reports on the effect of strategy training on the cognitive and metacognitive skills of four adult ESL learners enrolled on a six-week Independent Learning Program. Using a combination of quantitative and qualitative research methods, Simmons found that learners used a greater number and wider range of strategies at the end of the training period.

Simmons's study focuses on the reported and observed learning strategies of individual learners. In Chapter 6, by contrast, Chihiro Kinoshita Thomson looks at learners as members of cultural and linguistic groups. Within the context of a self-directed/self-assessed project run with a mixed group of learners of Japanese, she noted that self-ratings and confidence in the ability to learn without direction from a teacher appeared to be affected by native language and gender. Given a group of diverse cultural backgrounds, it would seem that including self-ratings as part of the course mark can be problematic, unless there is considerable preparation beforehand. The question of assessment is examined again in Chapter 9, but in the context of a culturally homogeneous group of learners.

Clearly, the learner is central to the development of learner autonomy. This does not mean, however, that the teacher should be marginalized, whether the reasons are educational, political, or financial. As Thomson shows, if learners are to take more control over their learning, they will need a lot of assistance along the way, particularly if their previous experience has been overwhelmingly teacher-directed.

This point is further emphasized in Chapter 7, in which Rena Kelly turns the focus to the skills required by *teachers* in the development of learner autonomy. Kelly argues that in order to help learners undergo a transformation in their beliefs, teachers need to develop the helping skills of one-to-one therapeutic counselling. She outlines the macro- and micro-skills of counselling and the humanistic values that underlie them; and shows how they can be applied in the context of helping learners to control their own learning with reference to the type of counselling offered at various stages during individual projects. She also provides extracts of consultation sessions to exemplify how learning strategy and language awareness can be developed.

A very different way of promoting learner autonomy is presented in Chapter 8. In this chapter, Peter Voller and Valerie Pickard describe a conversation exchange scheme in which there is minimal teacher involvement, and in which learner autonomy is developed, not through training or therapeutic dialogue, but through experience. Voller and Pickard consider the factors that can lead to success in such learner exchanges, and make recommendations for future exchange schemes.

The final chapter in this section focuses on *peer* assessment, one of the features of learner-centred approaches mentioned by Nunan in the first chapter. This might seem to veer away from the focus on *self* that is a central feature of the book. But, as Lindsay Miller and Raymond Ng point out, taking control of an aspect of learning that takes place in the classroom is an important prerequisite for taking responsibility for learning outside the classroom.

In the chapter, Miller and Ng describe a project in which groups of undergraduate students designed and conducted tests to assess their peers' speaking ability. Although attitudes to the process and reliability of peer assessment were on the whole not positive, the marks given by the peers were close to those given by the teachers, and Miller and Ng suggest that with more time and preparation, student perceptions would become more positive. Other advantages of the project were increased language awareness and an awareness of the benefits of negotiation.

5

A study of strategy use in independent learners

Diana Simmons

Background to the study

This study arose out of the concerns of teachers on the Independent Learning Program at Macquarie University about the lack of preparedness of our students to negotiate their own learning programs.

In 1991 the first Independent Learning Program was carried out at the National Centre for English Language Teaching and Research at Macquarie as part of the government-funded Adult Migrant English Program (AMEP) conducted there. There were 18 participants in the initial course which was designed to provide opportunities for people wishing to continue studying English, but who for various reasons were unable to attend the mainstream courses. All had expressed a willingness to work independently, and originally the program was conceived as one which would give as much autonomy as possible to the learners. During the first semester, however, it became evident that most of them were unable to negotiate their own learning contract effectively and relied on the teacher to direct their personal study programs on a weekly or fortnightly basis.

At the beginning of the second semester, a study awareness session was held for all the participants in the program; the format of the original diary was changed and the learners agreed to write this up each week. While these measures proved successful in helping them monitor their learning experiences, they all tended to record what they had learned, rather than what processes had been useful, and once again they did not make much progress in taking the initiative in planning their learning contracts.

Since independent study was a major objective of the course, it was decided to give future participants a short period of intensive one-to-one learning strategy training with an emphasis on the metacognitive strategies of monitoring, evaluating and planning learning. It was hoped that raising awareness about these processes would lead to more successful outcomes both in terms of actual learning, and in the autonomous planning of individual programs. With the opportunity to make their own decisions and assess the effectiveness or otherwise of a particular strategy, students could well gain more confidence in their ability to manage their own learning.

Another concern of the Independent Learning Program was for some measurable outcomes. In the prevailing climate of program budgeting in 1991 and because of the preference of funding providers for quantifiable gains, Brindley (1991) pointed out the necessity for explicit and systematic assessment practices in evaluating programs. Thus an exploratory study was undertaken in 1992 whose purpose was to look at the effects of learner training in cognitive and metacognitive skills on four adult learners enrolled in the Independent Learning Program. After a training period of six weeks, the students were monitored to see if there had been an increase in awareness on their part of learning strategies, and if they applied any new and more effective strategies which they had been exposed to.

The scope and methodology of the study

Scope and limitations

This study's orientation is ethnographic rather than experimental, intending to document, examine and analyze what occurred in the Independent Learning Program. Grotjahn points out that an investigation such as this one employing exploratory-interpretative methodology "strives for understanding" (1987: 66). Thus the content analysis of the diaries aims for a systematic description of the information, so that it is not just an impressionistic account of the events and strategies used. The descriptions and explanations treated in the discussions of the results, on the other hand, attempt to give from a variety of perspectives an understanding of those events by looking at not just the facts, but also the circumstances surrounding them.

Because of the small size of the group under investigation and the shortness of the training period involved, any findings cannot be generalized beyond this situation. My intention was to describe carefully what happened during the training period and to refine the procedures already put into practice in the Independent Learning Program, so that further investigation on a larger scale could then be carried out.

The participants

The participants were four AMEP clients, two men and two women, who were enrolled in the Independent Learning Program and who volunteered to take part in the study. Their proficiency level had been assessed according to the Australian Second Language Proficiency Ratings (ASLPR) at 2(+). This indicated they were above minimum social proficiency (able to satisfy routine social demands and limited work requirements), but had not yet reached ASLPR 3 (minimum vocational proficiency) (cf. Ingram and Wiley 1984).

Methodology

As their teacher, I saw the learners for half-hour sessions on a regular basis which was at least once every two weeks, but more usually once a week. The interviews were "individual" and "non-directive" (Holec 1987: 147) to give the opportunity for me to present strategies and for the learners to decide how much self-direction they wanted to undertake.

In 1991 some data was collected from the student diaries over a 13-week period which revealed the need for further research and refinement of procedures. Accordingly, Oxford's (1990) Strategy Inventory for Language Learning (SILL) questionnaire was administered to the four 1992 participants at the beginning of their period of strategy training. I administered it again at the end of their six-week training session in order to compare the results and obtain some quantitative data of the type of number of strategies used. Oxford's system was chosen because it offered a comprehensive and manageable system for the classroom situation. Of particular interest too was the information in her book about affective factors not dealt with in such depth by other researchers.

My field notes and the students' diaries from both the 1991 and 1992 groups were the other sources of data on the strategies used. A content analysis was carried out on the diaries and notes using Krippendorff's (1980) procedure (cited in Bailey 1991). Two independent observers were also asked to categorize the data which was then subject to interpretative commentary.

There was a *Reflections* section of the diary forms which was designed to elicit information about affective factors such as attitudes to the program and the learners' management of their learning. Any strategies mentioned were included in the content analysis, but essentially the aim of this section was to gain further insights into strategies and strategy training from the learners' perspective.

Constraints on data collection and analysis

Classification of strategies

Although the two observers were asked to classify the data independently when doing the content analysis, their lack of experience in the area of learning strategies meant that they occasionally had difficulty in assigning them to categories. They followed Oxford's (1990) classification system, but occasionally sought my opinion to confirm their ideas.

Another concern was the fact that other researchers have used different typologies. If used, these would clearly have led to different results. Rubin (1987), for instance, identifies only cognitive strategies in the direct category of mental processes, whereas Oxford draws a distinction between these and memory strategies.

Furthermore, my definitions for two of the strategies ('evaluating' and 'organizing') differed slightly from Oxford's. For me, 'evaluating' included assessing the usefulness or otherwise of a particular strategy or learning activity, in addition to monitoring of progress made. I extended 'organizing' to mean not just "organizing one's schedule" (Oxford 1990: 139), but also to include any unplanned activities and program management strategies which the learners reported they carried out.

Inclusion and omission of strategies

Some strategies which the learners reported using were included in the organization category even though evidence of their use was not directly observable. I would argue that it gives too narrow a picture of the learners' activities if all the reports are discounted, when in any event they were able to demonstrate their awareness of management and/or learning strategies. An example of this is a diary entry (Week 5) from A.R. where he stated "I have splitted my daily time for reading, listening [...] and recently writing."

On the other hand, the instances where learners reported in their diaries that they had learned something have not always been included, where there was not time for me to observe the outcomes directly myself. The limited time in the interview sessions often left no opportunity for 'checking up' on what had been undertaken, and the learners did not always choose activities like vocabulary extension which were readily testable by a third party.

While every effort was made to include all the strategies discussed in the interviews, I was concerned that some might be left out in the often lively and involved discussions. A tape recorder was tried on one occasion, but the learners were much more restrained than they had been on the previous occasion we had met. Since there was often talk on personal matters as well, and I felt recording them was adversely affecting two students' participation in the course, I decided to rely on taking notes of the strategy use.

Results and commentary

Strategy use: data from the field notes and diaries

Examination of the field notes shows that the learners reported using nearly three times the number of strategies at the end of the training period (65) than at the beginning (23). (See Figure 1.) The growth was not steady, however, and there was a drop to 32 strategies in week 4 and 42 in Week 5 from 49 identified in Week 3 of the course, reflecting the greater demands on their time that two of the participants were experiencing because of work commitments.

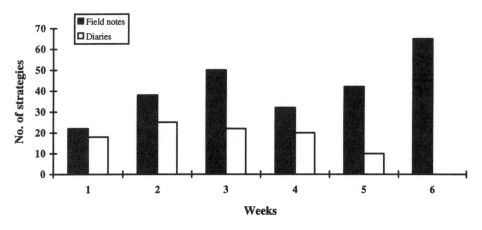

Figure 1: Number of reported strategy uses*

* Includes all strategies discussed by participants, even if not used by them.

A greater variety is also evident, from 4 different strategies used at the beginning of the training to 13 reported at the final interview. (See Table 1.)

Table 1: Range and number of strategies used

Strategies	Week 1		Week 2		Week 3		Week 4 (2 students)		Week 5		Week 6	
	Field notes	Diaries	Field notes	Diaries (3 Ss)	Field notes	Diaries	Field notes	Diaries	Field notes	Diaries (3 Ss)	Field notes	Diaries
A	13	7	18	15	19	9	14	8	20	5	20	No diaries submitted
B	7	10	11	10	19	11	8	6	11	7	29	
C	2		2	1		1	1	1	1			
D			1						1			
E(i)			1						1			
E(ii)			1		1							
E(iii)					1	1					1	
E(iv)					1		1		1			
E(v)					1				1		2	
F					2	1	1	1	1		1	
G					1		1	1			1	
H					1		1	1			1	
I							1	1			1	
J												
K(i)							1		1		1	
K(ii)							1		1			
K(iii)			1						1			
K(iv)												
L(i)									1		1	
L(ii)									1		1	
M(i)			1		2		1		2		4	
M(ii)											2	
N(i)	1		2		1		1					
N(ii)												
N(iii)												

Key

A	Planning/organizing	E	Memory strategies
B	Evaluating	E(i)	Grouping
C	Practising	E(ii)	Writing down
D	Examples in use	E(iii)	Associating
		E(iv)	Reviewing
		E(v)	Repeating aloud

F	Predicting
G	Guessing in context
H	Skimming for gist
I	Timed writing
J	Analyzing

K	Compensating strategies
K(i)	Using synonyms
K(ii)	Confirming
K(iii)	Rephrasing
K(iv)	Getting help

L	Creating structure
L(i)	Note-taking
L(ii)	Highlighting
M	Affective strategies
M(i)	Sharing feelings
M(ii)	Encouraging self

N	Social strategies
N(i)	Clarifying/verifying
N(ii)	Asking for correction
N(iii)	Cultural awareness

It was clear from the start that the learners in this group were able to plan and evaluate their work quite competently because these strategies were in the majority each week. Again though, the increase was not steady, moving from 20 in all in Week 1 to 29 and 38 in Weeks 2 and 3 respectively, but falling again to a total of 31 in Week 5. A number of the other strategies were discussed in the interview sessions, and if, for example, a student used rephrasing to express an idea, I pointed this out as part of the awareness-raising approach. As indicated, all these strategies are recorded in Figure 1 and Table 1, even though they might not have been directly used in the students' work.

The participants found it hard to assess their progress in English *per se*, but they were able to decide whether or not a particular strategy was useful and appropriate for them. A.R. reported twice (Week 1 and Week 3), for instance, that he was not sure if he was making progress, but was quick to reject my suggestion that he try the keyword technique (a sound association with a word in his own language) to help with his vocabulary learning, saying "I prefer explanations in simpler language in English." Furthermore, not only were both he and B.K. dissatisfied with how the review strategies were working for them, but they were also able to suggest modifications to ways these could be carried out which would be more suitable for them. F.S. was also uncertain about whether her English was improving, but her diary entry of Week 3 showed insight into how she was managing her learning: "I've done too much at once therefore I didn't grasp much."

The predominance of planning and evaluating can be accounted for to some extent by the structure of the training program, where in the orientation session and initial interviews, emphasis was laid on the need for learners to take responsibility for the management of their individual programs. Nevertheless, it was a little disconcerting to find how well and how quickly they were able to put these ideas into practice, as I had thought that this would be a major area for strategy training. This meant, however, that there was more chance to present other direct and indirect strategies to the participants which they could try.

The format of the learner diaries taken from Helmore's (1987) handbook also encouraged planning and reflection, but the use of the journals fell very rapidly, and in the last week of the training period not one of the participants submitted an entry. Rather than increasing, there were fewer instances of strategy use reported in the diaries in the later weeks, and even though three of the learners wrote up their accounts in Week 5, only 12 strategies could be found. Moreover, while the learners talked about practising and predicting during the interviews, they often failed to write about them. Thus, instead of confirming the findings of the field notes, those from the diaries would appear to contradict them, and lead, as Cohen and Manion (1989) point out, to less confidence in the results. However, the reasons for avoiding the diaries that the learners gave were valid ones — particularly as, being independent learners, it was their decision whether to keep them or not. B.K., for instance, felt that it was "not a good use of time to keep writing the same thing every week", while A.S said that she believed it was more important to concentrate on teaching methodology and her Geography studies, and not spend her limited time writing about what she was doing. F.S., for her part, acknowledged that she would much rather talk than write and that coming to see me motivated her to study. This statement caused me some concern, as did the general reluctance on everyone's part to keep their own records, especially in the light of Rubin and Henze's (1981) findings that keeping a diary does help learners to evaluate their own strategies without recourse to the teacher.

Strategy use: data from the SILL questionnaires

While the learners' reactions on being shown the field notes ranged from a cursory glance to, at best, polite but uncritical attention, they were most interested to compare the two SILL questionnaires. These were administered at the first individual interview and at the end of the training period. Both F.S. and A.R. said they thought there would be some change before they completed the questionnaire, and the other two expressed the same view at the next interview before they saw the results, having asked (without being prompted) to compare the two sets of results.

Table 2 (see below) does show some inconsistencies in the results, indicating that the accuracy of learners' perceptions of their strategy use is not always reliable. For instance, in answer to a question from part A of the questionnaire (ways of remembering more effectively) which asked if new words were used in a sentence, B.K.'s score dropped one point, although this was a strategy he used most effectively. He in fact decided for himself that dictionary definitions were "no good", and that making up his own examples in sentences was "much better for remembering the meaning" (Week 5), demonstrating to me how well this and the review strategies were working when I tested him. However, his explanation for a lower score on another question in this group was that he had not fully understood what "physically acting out" new English words was the first time, but now realized what this meant and it was most definitely not a strategy he used. F.R.'s lower score on managing feelings can be accounted for by the series of setbacks to her plans she had received over the previous few weeks — advice not to proceed in a Master's course, and lack of success in getting any of the three jobs she had recently applied for — which left her feeling very demoralized and depressed. Looking behind the figures reveals, therefore, that not all of the apparent discrepancies in the learners' responses occur without good reasons. Moreover, all four of the second questionnaires showed that there had been an increase in organizing and evaluating strategies, and in overall strategy use, this last figure being in agreement with the findings recorded in the field notes.

Further insights were obtained from the comments of the learners themselves which support the findings that they did increase their strategy use, and were able to explain not just what they had learned, but also how they had gone about it, often giving their opinion too on the usefulness and appropriateness of the approaches taken.

Table 2: Change in strategy use between Week 1 and Week 6
(data from SILL questionnaires)

Student B.K.				
Strategy	Week 1 Total	Week 1 Average	Week 6 Total	Week 6 Average
A	21	2.33	17	1.88
B	36	2.57	33	2.35
C	16	2.66	24	4
D	27	3	32	3.5
E	10	1.66	18	3
F	19	3.16	18	3
Total	129	2.58	142	2.84

Student A.R.				
Strategy	Week 1 Total	Week 1 Average	Week 6 Total	Week 6 Average
A	21	2.3	24	2.66
B	45	3.2	54	3.85
C	26	4.3	24	4
D	38	4.22	42	4.66
E	19	3.16	19	3.16
F	24	4	25	4.16
Total	173	3.46	188	3.76

Table 2: to be continued

Table 2: continued

Student A.S.				
Strategy	Week 1 Total	Week 1 Average	Week 6 Total	Week 6 Average
A	21	2.33	24	2.66
B	41	2.9	50	3.57
C	23	3.83	24	4
D	35	3.88	37	4.1
E	18	3	20	3.33
F	24	4	24	4
Total	162	3.24	179	3.58

Student F.S.				
Strategy	Week 1 Total	Week 1 Average	Week 6 Total	Week 6 Average
A	17	1.88	24	2.66
B	43	3.07	44	3.14
C	18	3	20	3.33
D	34	3.7	40	4.44
E	21	3.5	15	2.5
F	24	4	25	4.16
Total	157	3.14	168	3.36

Key to Oxford's (1990) Strategy Inventory for Language Learning (SILL)

Strategies covered		Frequency		Overall Average
A	Remembering more effectively	High	Always or almost always used	4.5 – 5.0
B	Using all mental processes	M/H	Usually used	3.5 – 4.4
C	Compensating	Medium	Sometimes used	2.5 – 3.4
D	Organizing and evaluating	M/L	Generally not used	1.5 – 2.4
E	Managing emotions	Low	Never or almost	1.0 – 1.4
F	Learning with others			

Numbers of learning activities in relation to strategies used

As sources of information about learning activities, I found the diaries of the participants in the 1991 program were even worse than the second group's. In order to find a similar number of diaries from four people to analyze, I had to take what they had written from over 13 weeks, more than twice as long as the 1992 training period. This lack of material is as much a reflection of my ideas and training methods at that time as their reluctance to write, and was one of the changes implemented in the second program. Although any comparisons of the two sets of diaries have to be treated with caution, there are some interesting insights to be had in examining them both.

Table 3 shows that for the 1991 participants' 119 learning activities which were recorded over the three months, 24 strategies were used. Of these, 13 were evaluating, four each social and affective, and three practising, strategies. As well as a smaller number of strategies being used, only four different kinds were identified, although the learners had been exposed to a greater variety of these in the training session they had had at the beginning of their course. Twenty-seven instances of planning were counted in the journals, but there was no procedure in place for checking if the plans had been carried out, and this was another of the changes made for the new course.

Table 3: Comparison of strategy use by the 1991 and 1992 groups*

	1991 group: diaries		1992 group: diaries		1992 group: field notes	
Week	Activities reported	Strategies reported	Activities reported	Strategies reported	Activities reported	Strategies reported
1	17	4	23	10	19	10
2	10	0	16	11	11	20
3	12	3	15	14	12	30
4	10	0	10	12	6 (2 students)	18
5	5	1	17	7		22
6	4	2	No diaries	submitted	13	45
7	No diaries	submitted			11	
8	13	8				
9	12	5				
10	7	0				
11	12	0				
12	10	0				
13	7	1				
Total	119	24	81	54	72	145

* Does not include any planning strategies. Only includes those strategies directly related to the activities reported.

The 1992 participants recorded 81 activities in their diaries over 6 weeks and the number of strategies directly related to these was 54. Evaluating strategies accounted for most of the ones used once more (43), but there was also a wider range: three practising, two predicting, and one each of associating, guessing from context, timed writing, sharing feelings, asking for correction and skimming for gist. Thus the data from the diaries indicates that these students who had on-going exposure to learning strategies, employed them more frequently and used a greater variety of them than those in the first group. Information from the field notes also bears out the range and frequency of strategy use by the 1992 group, as can be seen from the shaded part of Table 3, where again, in contrast to Table 1, only those directly related to the activities have been recorded.

Execution of plans

There was also a check kept on whether or not the second group carried out their plans, and an examination of the field notes as shown in Table 4 reveals that of a total of 70 planned activities, 50 of these were carried out in such a way that the participants were able to demonstrate their fulfilment to me. Predictably, the diaries showed fewer planning activities, and total numbers dropped as fewer diaries were written, but their completion rate was even higher, with 30 of the 36 plans being carried out. In the case of the field notes, there was not the large growth that was evident in strategy use as a whole over the course of the training period, so that 7 planned and completed activities recorded at the beginning of the training period, increased to only 14 planned and 10 completed for the final week. However, as indicated before, I counted just those which I was able to document myself and there was often not the opportunity in the interviews to confirm with the participants whether or not they had been able to carry out their intended activities.

Table 4: Execution of planned activities*

	Data from field notes		Data from diaries	
Week	Planned activities	No. carried out	Planned activities	No. carried out
1	7	7	7	7
2	13	7	11	8
3	14	10	8	6
4	8 (2 students)	7 (2 students)	7	7
5	14	9	3	2
6	14	10	No diaries submitted	No diaries submitted
Total	70	50	36	30

* Includes only plans made by the participants themselves. No teacher suggestions.

Success in learning and understanding

Concern for observable behaviour also limited the number of instances to six where the participants were able to demonstrate to me that they had successfully carried out learning, and testing new vocabulary provided the only opportunity for this. Furthermore, even success in this could have been the effect of practice on the task. Vocabulary extension was not on F.S.'s agenda, but the other three tried a range of strategies which I had suggested to them, including reviewing. All three performed very well on two separate occasions, achieving on average a score of 14 out of 15. Moreover, the second time I tested B.K., he had not recently had the chance to review the words he had learned a few weeks previously, but was still able to get them all correct, bearing out how helpful his adaptation of the "spiraling" technique was for him in making new material "more or less automatic" (Oxford 1990: 66).

Although there were so few instances where I could get quantifiable evidence of learning, Tyacke (1991) and Holec (1987) argue that quality of learning is equally important — as Montaigne put it in 1588, "Mieux vaut tête bien faite que tête bien pleine"[1] (cited in Holec 1987). The structured training period which I had originally envisaged with readily testable tasks to assess the effectiveness and appropriateness of strategies did not eventuate because of the nature of the learning activities that the learners chose. However, Tyacke (1991) cites Entwistle's (1987) recommendation that training should encourage "deep" learning, so that the student can reach understanding as opposed to increasing knowledge or simply performing tasks. Understanding was also perceived by the students to be important. "I don't know all the rules yet, but I'm beginning to get to grips with the structure of English; that's good" (F.S., Week 3). "It's good to understand how to learn. I can use prediction strategies for watching the news as well as for reading" (B.K., Week 5). On the other hand, they also expressed frustration sometimes when they felt they were not making progress, and tasks producing concrete results like the vocabulary tests helped to boost their morale when they did well in them.

Success in learning independently

The participants' remarks also reflect their reactions and attitudes to learning independently, and although B.K. stated at the beginning of the course that he was confident about this, he admitted at the end that he hadn't been quite so sure:

> I thought I should say that because it was an independent learning course!

> But now I feel I can make my own plans. It's good to be able to do what I need to do.

A.R. and A.S., who had also said at the beginning that they felt "quite confident" about managing for themselves, remained positive about the "independent way" and noticed an improvement in their management of their work.

> I like this way. Now I feel better about deciding for myself, and having plans is good because I'm motivated to do what I said I would do. (A.S., post-course interview).

When asked at his post-course interview to comment on the strategy training, A.R. said:

> I think it's been very useful. I'm more aware of different ways to learn and they're very helpful. Because of these I think I manage my study better now.

F.S. was the least confident at the beginning, saying openly that she wasn't sure if the Independent Learning Program was the course for her. She was pleased that the SILL questionnaire showed her using more strategies at the end of the training period, saying "At least I'm learning something", but was still rather reliant on her visits to the Independent Learning Centre to "keep going" (Week 5). Although she seems to be the least independent of the four, she still surprised me on many occasions with work that she had planned and carried out on her own initiative, such as deciding to read a book on study strategies for mainstream rather than ESL students (Week 6). Nor was she the only one to admit that the thought of coming to see me was an important incentive to study! None of the participants was quite sure how they would manage if left entirely to their own devices at this stage. They expressed in similar words to A.S. that they felt they still needed to come along "for another two or three months at least" (post-course interview) for support as much as for help with their English. As Oxford points out, learner self-direction is not something which happens overnight, but is often "a gradually increasing phenomenon, growing as learners become more comfortable with the idea of their own responsibility" (1990: 10).

Summary and review of the study

It is not possible to draw incontrovertible conclusions from the information in the field notes and diaries because of the subjective nature of much of the data. As has been mentioned, even the questionnaires and quantification of the strategies are open to challenge, for other researchers (e.g. Ellis and Sinclair 1989; O'Malley and Chamot 1990; Wenden 1991) have different classification systems which would have affected the results. Moreover, Oxford herself acknowledges that individual researchers "often classify a particular strategy differently at different times" (1990: 22).

However, the aim of the Independent Learning Program at NCELTR was to promote learner independence in order to enable participants to continue their language development in English and take increasing responsibility for managing their own programs — to take on, as Tyacke (1991: 45) says, "more 'ownership' of the process." This study was undertaken to see if training in learning strategies could help in this process. The findings show that although there were few opportunities for measuring actual learning because of the nature of the program, the students did use a greater number and variety of strategies at the end of the training period. The instance of their use was much higher than for the previous group who did not receive ongoing strategy training. The 1992 group was also more aware of which strategies suited them. They felt too that their learning and management of their programs had improved at the end of the course, even though they began by using many more planning and evaluating strategies than expected, and did not receive as much training in this area as originally envisaged.

Strategy training does not guarantee increase in motivation and confidence in the learners, nor that they will continue to use the strategies they have learned, but by making the learning process more transparent, the learner is "empowered to make his or her own changes" (Tyacke 1991: 50). This empowerment should also, as Holec (1987) says, leave the learners free to decide whether they want to direct their own learning or let others do it for them. However, in order to be in a position to exercise this choice, to make decisions about the management of their learning, he argues they need to know how to learn, and this was the goal of the strategy-training program at NCELTR.

Note

1. Loosely translated: "Better a good head than a full head."

6

Self-assessment in self-directed learning: issues of learner diversity[1]

Chihiro Kinoshita Thomson

Introduction

I would like to claim that we are born self-directed learners. My own experience in child rearing and a number of casual observations of other children tell me that the young ones know how to take charge of their own learning. Recent developments in psychology support this notion (Hatano and Inagaki 1990).

However, by the time they have grown up, they have changed. When they come to our university classes, many have 'unlearned' most of their skills as self-directed learners. All come with preconceived ideas on how learning should occur, and this often excludes self-directed learning opportunities. Many like to be directed by teachers and find themselves at a loss when they are thrown into a learning opportunity which requires them to be self-directive. It is wrong to assume that adult learners are equipped with study skills and learning strategies (Galloway and Labarca 1990). Their beliefs and attitudes about learning in general, and more specifically about self-directed learning, appear to be influenced by their cultural, educational and developmental backgrounds.

The focus of this chapter is to discuss the impact and implications of the introduction of self-directed learning on a group of great diversity. The chapter first discusses the goals of a project that promotes self-directed learning and a learner-centred curriculum, then describes the project that was run with the third-year Japanese language learners in the University of New South Wales in Sydney. The chapter then discusses the project results and issues that relate to the learner diversity.

Project goals

The term 'self-directed learning' is used differently by different researchers. The following definition is used in this chapter.

Self-directed learning refers to learning in which the learners themselves take responsibility for their learning. Self-directed learners in foreign language learning are those who can:

1. set up a favourable climate of learning for themselves by collaborating with peers, instructors and resource persons;
2. diagnose their own needs realistically;
3. translate learning needs into learning objectives;
4. select and utilize tasks and effective strategies to achieve the objectives; and
5. assess their own achievements for feedback on how to improve the next cycle (adopted from Knowles 1973, 1975, 1980; Dickinson 1987).

In the Japanese language programme at the University of New South Wales in Sydney, the following is stated as one of the overall programme goals:

> To nurture self-sufficient learners who can demonstrate autonomy in learning and who can continue learning on their own.

The Japanese programme believes that language learning is by nature a life-long endeavour. The degree programme, which requires three years of language study, is by no means sufficient to equip the students with all the Japanese language skills they will need in all possible situations they may encounter. However, the programme can help the students become self-directed learners who are able to continue their study of Japanese autonomously even after they have left the programme.

An example in reintroducing self-directed learning — a self-assessment project — will be discussed in this chapter. Our third-year Japanese language and communication course included a self-assessment project as a part of the course requirements. In the self-assessment project, learners assessed their weaknesses at the beginning, their performances during, and their achievements at the end of the project. Performance on the project, assessed entirely by the students' own self-ratings, made up 10% of the total course marks.

The self-assessment project was brought in to introduce self-directed learning to the students. However, it served another significant purpose. It supported the overall course in coping with the diverse backgrounds of the student population. In a tertiary language course, the assessment procedure is typically bound by university rules. In the case of the University of New South Wales, heavy weight is given to the final examination. This demands a tightly organized syllabus and clearly drawn course objectives which are tested at the final exam. Such a syllabus can cause problems when trying to cater for the needs and interests of a diverse group of students and make the course more learner-centred. The self-assessment component of the course aims to give the learners freedom to study what they feel necessary in the manner they feel fit, thus aiming to make it more learner-centred.

Project implementation

The Japanese language programme at the University of New South Wales offers a core sequence of 7 levels ranging from novice to advanced. A beginner will be placed at Level 1 and complete Levels 1, 2 and 3. A student with previous experience in learning Japanese will be placed at a higher level after a placement test, and will complete three consecutive levels from that point.

The self-assessment project was conducted with Level 3 students in Sessions 1 and 2, 1993. This study looks at the project in Session 2. The student number was exactly 100, and the course was taught by a team of three teachers.

The self-assessment project had three major stages: a planning stage, a monitoring stage and a review stage. In the planning stage, the students assessed their Japanese language and communication skills, drew up learning objectives and planned their learning activities and their assessment measure. They turned in their planning sheets and received comments from one of the instructors. The planning sheet became a learning contract between the student and the instructor. In the monitoring stage, the students assessed their progress and made adjustments to their plans. They met with their instructors for consultation if they felt it was necessary. In the review stage, the students reviewed their objectives, learning activities and progress and rated their performance on a scale of 0 to 10. Thus, the project involved self-assessment in all stages.

At the end of the course, a feedback survey (see Appendix) was given to the students, and the project was evaluated using the student assessment and student feedback, as well as the instructors' observations.

The learners

This self-assessment project was innovative for the large number of learners and the diversity of the learner population. Each learner approaches a learning project with a unique set of expectations and assumptions, and preferred mode of learning (Nyikos 1990). Wenden (1991) discusses the following seven factors that influence learner attitudes towards autonomy: socialization process; conflicting demands; complexity of roles; lack of metacognitive knowledge; learned helplessness; self-esteem; and self-image.

In the student population, there were five notable variables that could have had a significant influence on the execution of the self-assessment project. The first variable was gender. Although pedagogy tends to ignore the question of gender altogether (Sanguinetti 1992–93), evidence of gender differences in the socialization process, role expectations (e.g. in terms of occupational opportunities), language-learning strategies etc. is over-whelming (e.g. Nyikos 1990; Kelly 1991; Bacon 1992; Baker and Jones 1993; Oxford 1993).

The second variable was mother tongue or culture. The student population was mainly composed of three large native language groups — English, Chinese and Korean. Their mother tongue or rather the culture that their mother tongue represents also seems to have a major influence on socialization process, role expectations (e.g. teacher and learner roles), and language-learning strategies (Sato 1981; Sinha and Kao 1988; Kumaravadivelu 1990; MacCargar 1993).

The third variable which relates closely to the second, was the students' experience with Chinese characters or Kanji. Students who received Chinese language education in places like Hong Kong, Taiwan and Singapore, and some of the Korean students who had formal education in Korea, came with knowledge of Kanji. This is a big asset in learning Japanese in comparison with those with no such background.

The fourth variable, which has curriculum implications, was their entry level. Some students started their Japanese study at Level 1; others had five years of high school Japanese before directly entering Level 3; others had no formal instruction in Japanese but had lived in Japan for various periods. They all had different Japanese language learning experiences, knowledge bases and skills.

The fifth variable was their maturity. Most of the students were traditional university-age students. However, as the programme offers classes at night, it attracted some mature students. Some worked for Japanese companies in Sydney, some were high school Japanese teachers. The working students often suffered from conflicting demands on their time. Of the traditional university-age students, because of the varied entry levels, some were fresh out of high school and some were already near graduation. They all had distinct life experiences and diverse interests and needs.

Each student represented a unique combination of the above five variables.

Project results

Out of the 100 students, 98 students completed the project. The course was characterized by a very high percentage of women and Asian students. Among them, 75 were female and 23 were male. Thirty-five students reported that their native language was Chinese (Cantonese, Mandarin, Hakka, etc.), the majority being Cantonese speakers from Hong Kong. Ten students were Korean speakers, followed by three Indonesian speakers. Forty-five English native speakers included a few ethnic Chinese and Koreans. There were also three Indonesian speakers, and one native speaker each of Arabic, Hebrew, Persian, Spanish and Tagalog (see Table 1).

Table 1: Distribution of students by native language and gender

Native language	Female	Male	Total
English	31	14	45
Chinese	31	4	35
Korean	7	3	10
Others	6	2	8
Total	75	23	98

As shown in Table 2, the students showed an overall positive attitude to the self-assessment project on a scale of 1 (negative) to 4 (positive). (Note that responses to the survey statements listed in the Appendix were scored as: Strongly Agree = 4, Agree = 3, Disagree = 2, Strongly Disagree = 1. However, for Statement 9 the values were reversed to: SA=1, A=2, D=3, SD=4.) The attitude towards and acceptance of the self-assessment project, according to the survey results, does not seem to differ by gender, native language, age or previous achievement in the subject.

Table 2: Overall rating of attitude to the self-assessment project by native language and gender

Native language	Gender	Mean (overall attitude)
Chinese	Female Male	3.0 3.0
Korean	Female Male	3.0 2.8
English	Female Male	3.1 2.8
Others	Female Male	3.5 3.5
All	Female Male All	3.0 2.9 2.9

Examination of the marks the students gave themselves showed that they gave their performance in the self-assessment project 7.3 points out of 10 on average. The self-rating scores show only a moderate correlation with the marks for this course and the previous course marks.

Table 3: Self-rating score on the performance of the project, compared with the overall course final mark by native language and gender

Native language	Gender		Self-rating score out of 10	[Rank]	(SD)	Course mark out of 100	[Rank]
English	F M Total	(n=31) (n=14) (n=45)	7.7 7.1 7.4	[2] [5]	(1.1) (0.8)	64 62 63	[3] [5]
Chinese	F M Total	(n=31) (n=4) (n=35)	6.9 7.3 7.1	[6] [4]	(0.5) (0.4)	64 62 63	[3] [5]
Korean	F M Total	(n=7) (n=3) (n=10)	7.5 8.3 7.9	[3] [1]	(0.7) (0.7)	70 65 68	[1] [2]
Others		(n=8)	7.7			65	
All		(n=98)	7.3		(0.9)	64	

A close examination of the self-rating score by native language group and gender reveals an interesting trend (see Table 3). Korean male students rated themselves by far the highest of the six groups. Chinese female students rated themselves lowest, even though the course marks given to them were average. Comparison between the rankings for the self-rating scores and course marks suggests that Chinese and Korean female groups rated themselves lower than they should have, and that Chinese and Korean male students rated themselves slightly higher than they deserved, as did English-speaking female students. English-speaking males were the only group whose ratings reflected their course marks. Of course, we should not read too much into these figures. They represent small samples (especially for Chinese and Korean males), they are measuring performance in two different areas (self-assessment project and overall course marks), and the course marks are very close together. However, they do suggest some tendencies that would be worth investigating further.

As shown in Table 4, analysis of responses to Statement 6 ("I am confident in planning, managing, and assessing my own study and I consider myself as a self-directed learner") does not reveal a great difference in the learners' perceptions of their self-confidence and ability to direct their own learning and they all have a positive attitude towards self-directed learning on a scale of 1 (negative) to 4 (positive). However, it is notable that the English-speaking female students rated their self-directedness higher than did learners from any other group (apart from those in the 'Others' category).

Table 4: Attitude towards Statement 6 by native language and gender (Statement 6: I am confident in planning, managing, and assessing my own study and consider myself as a self-directed learner.)

Native language	Chinese		Korean		English		Others	All
Gender	F [n=31]	M [n=4]	F [n=7]	M [n=3]	F [n=31]	M [n=14]	[n=8]	[n=98]
Strongly agree [No. (%)]	1 (3)	0	1 (14)	0	6 (19)	0	3 (38)	11 (11)
Agree	19 (61)	3 (75)	4 (57)	2 (67)	19 (61)	11 (79)	4 (50)	62 (63)
Disagree	11 (35)	1 (25)	2 (29)	1 (33)	6 (19)	3 (21)	1 (13)	25 (26)
Strongly disagree	0	0	0	0	0	0	0	0
Average	2.68	2.75	2.86	2.67	3.00	2.79	3.25	2.86

Discussion

The self-assessment project was received fairly well by the students. It was successful in introducing the students to self-directed learning, and in making the course more learner-centred. To this diverse group of students, the self-assessment project gave opportunities to learn what they felt they needed to learn. Activities the students selected varied a great deal and included Kanji review, diary entries in Japanese, creation of grammar notes, activities in the language laboratory, viewing Japanese videos, and writing letters to Japanese pen pals. Although the course was delivered in the otherwise traditional mode of lectures, tutorials and uniform testing, the project gave students the opportunity to be themselves. From reading their reports and looking at the support documents they submitted, I believe that the project served an important function in making the course more learner-centred. The students also agreed. In the survey, Statement 7 ("The self-assessment project was a good complement to the overall subject") received the average value of 3.0, which corresponds to "Agree", while responses to the first four statements — those related to awareness of strengths and weaknesses in language ability; awareness of their own learning patterns; awareness of their ability to take initiative in language learning; and awareness of learning opportunities outside the classroom — were similarly positive, averaging 3.0, 3.1, 3.0 and 3.2 respectively. (See the Appendix.)

As discussed earlier, the learner population presented a great diversity involving many variables. This complexity of the learner population has raised some issues concerning attitudes to assessment, selection of objectives, activities and assessment measures, and the students' self-esteem.

Attitudes to assessment

In the self-assessment project, the students were engaged in three types of assessment, i.e. needs assessment, continual assessment and final assessment. The students lacked confidence in all areas of assessment, especially in assessing their performance without the assistance of their instructor. Many commented that they wished they had had more support and guidance from their instructor and they wanted the instructors to correct their written work. Many agreed or strongly agreed with Statement 9 ("I would like to have had more guidance on the self-assessment project"), as can be seen in Table 5. (Note that here this was calculated using the values: SA=4, A=3, D=2, SD=1.) This was true for all types of students, but particularly so for the group of Chinese students.

Table 5: Attitude towards Statement 9 by native language and gender
(Statement 9: I would like to have had more guidance on the
self-assessment project.)

Native language	Chinese		Korean		English		Others	All
Gender	F [n=31]	M [n=4]	F [n=7]	M [n=3]	F [n=31]	M [n=14]	[n=8]	[n=98]
Strongly agree [No. (%)]	2 (6)	1 (25)	0	0	3 (10)	2 (14)	0	8 (8)
Agree	23 (74)	2 (50)	4 (57)	2 (67)	12 (39)	4 (29)	5 (63)	52 (53)
Disagree	5 (16)	1 (25)	3 (43)	1 (33)	14 (45)	8 (57)	3 (37)	35 (36)
Strongly disagree	1 (3)	0	0	0	2 (6)	0	0	3 (3)
Average	2.84	3.00	2.57	2.67	2.52	2.57	2.63	2.66

Assessing one's own performance formally was something that few students were used to. Although they continuously assess their own performances internally in classrooms and in real-life interactions, they are seldom aware of it or have rarely externalized it. Many students had the pre-set idea that assessment in all forms, whether needs assessment for planning a course or final assessment for giving course marks, was the responsibility of the teacher. Many learners are comfortable with this type of teacher-centred arrangement (Tarone and Yule 1989). The students were conditioned by their many years of experience with traditional school culture which did not promote student responsibility in assessment.

This might also be reinforced by some of the students' native cultures which strictly divide the responsibilities of teacher and disciple. For many of the Asian students, taking the initiative and responsibility in learning means stepping over the line drawn between the teachers and learners (Ballard and Clanchy 1991; McMullen 1993). MacCargar (1993) reports that ESL students in his study in the USA, which included Chinese and Korean students, expected a more teacher-oriented environment than did their American teachers, and that both Chinese and Korean students respected authority highly.

It also may have affected the group of younger students who entered Level 3 right after high school. The group of younger students, who were not yet used to the university's learning environment which demands more initiative from the students than in high school, might have had an adjustment problem. One Year 1 student commented that he understood this was a university course and he knew he was expected to be more self-reliant, but he felt lost with the degree of freedom given and wished for a somewhat more structured project.

Identifying objectives and choosing activities and assessment measures

Lack of adequate skills in needs assessment and continuous assessment showed up in inappropriate selections of objectives and activities.

From observation of the overall performance of the students, I saw the weakness of the Chinese students in speaking and listening, particularly in pronunciation, while non-Chinese students lacked skills in Kanji. However, Chinese students did not necessarily identify their weakness in speaking or listening, but many chose Kanji-related areas. They chose tasks such as vocabulary building and grammar review in the form of writing down sentences. Even for those who recognized that their weak areas were in speaking and listening, the tasks chosen to overcome the weakness were written ones, such as writing down a conversation from the textbook. This could be due to the Chinese preference for individual work over group work (Melton 1990), as a conversation is difficult to perform in an individual study setting.

Similarly, non-Kanji background students did not necessarily concentrate on improving their skills in Kanji, which is their typical area of weakness. They tended to choose oral interaction-related activities, such as getting a Japanese conversation partner. I have observed that relatively low importance seems to be given to written language and written communication in the Australian society in comparison to some Asian societies. I speculate that different degrees of value given to written communication may have influenced the students' activity choices.

In spite of the list of suggested activities given in the beginning of the course, which included many unconventional tasks, the selected activities tended to be traditional ones that the students were used to getting as class assignments.

The assessment measures adopted by the students were also rather traditional. They were often self-imposed written testing in which the students themselves acted as pseudo-teachers. Reality testing was rarely used as a valid measurement. Native speaker friends were used in some cases to practise the language, but not in the assessment of either spoken or written work.

This reflected the students' previous educational experiences. In their previous experiences in learning a foreign language, they probably didn't think about learning objectives and their relationship to learning activities. They may have tended to concentrate on mastering small skills one by one but lose sight of the overall picture which mapped the relationships of all the small skills with their surroundings. Possibly written tasks were assigned often and assessed often, but spoken tasks rarely assessed formally, because speaking tests take tremendous manpower when the enrolment is large. Probably only a few students were aware that they could delegate the assessment tasks to their native Japanese friends, that they might go to see the instructors when they wanted a particular performance evaluated, or that a record of reality testing would serve well in assessing one's performance.

Self-esteem

For a self-assessment to be objective, participating students need to be self-confident as learners (Wenden 1991; Bacon 1992). Lack of self-esteem would contribute to the formation of a negative attitude in the learner towards his or her capability to learn autonomously (Wenden 1991).

A Chinese female student wrote after her comment, "P.S. I hate rating myself." Another commented, "I wish you wouldn't make us rate ourselves." It appeared that the group of Chinese female students was uncomfortable with the task of giving themselves a mark and it reflected in their self-rating, which was the lowest among the groups. Although there were only two such written comments, many could have felt the same way, and could have obeyed the instructor's command and rated themselves. It is conceivable that they could not express dissatisfaction against the instructor, unless they added it after the overall comment as a postscript, or unless they used an extra polite expression (e.g. *I wish you wouldn't*).

A similar trend, although weaker, was seen in the group of Korean female students. In Japanese language courses, in my observation, Korean students on average always outperform other students, due to the similarity of Korean language and social rules to those of Japanese. At Level 3, which was typically their third year of studying Japanese language, this group should have been well aware how proficient they were compared to other students. Even so, they rated themselves conservatively, much lower than their male counterparts.

The trend of Asian female groups rating themselves low and the reverse trend of Asian male groups, notably the Korean male group, rating themselves high, although the sample population was small (Chinese males: n=4, Korean males: n=3), may possibly be a reflection of their upbringing.

The cause may conceivably be traced to their self-esteem. It is well known that traditionally, boys are valued more than girls in Asian cultures. Confucian ethics, which is widespread among Chinese, Koreans and Japanese, teach a girl to obey her father, her husband, then her son. This is not a myth of the past. Singapore's Senior Minister Lee Kuan Yew, one of Asia's most prominent leaders, stated in his speech in Sydney recently, "The Asian male does not like to have a wife who is seen to be his equal at work who may be earning as much if not more than he does." and "You cannot change deeply-rooted values and behaviour and standards, patterns of conduct." ('Jobs or husbands?', 1994). Although I do not believe all Asian men feel the same way as Mr. Lee, it is quite understandable that the female group's self-esteem is low, and they do not feel worthy of giving a mark, not to mention a high mark, to themselves. In contrast, the relatively high self-rating of the Asian male students reflects the high value placed on males in Asian cultures. The widespread currency of such cultural values suggests that the Asian males in this study, although a small sample, are probably not unrepresentative of Asian males in general.

However, although this project indicates that the group of Asian female students are prone to rating themselves low due to their low self-esteem, further literature review suggested that it could be a larger trend encompassing females in many other societies. It should be noted that patriarchal values exist outside of Asia to a variety of degrees. Oxford (1993) and Hyde and Linn (1986) state that males are more aggressive than females, females are more likely than males to show a continuing need for approval and desire to please others, and females are more cooperative and less competitive. Bacon's (1992) study on American university students of Spanish reveals that men are generally more confident than women. Marsh et al. (1988) state that women are forced to have a lower level of self-esteem than men.

Further thoughts

Although counter-evidence of the validity of learners' self-ratings (Davidson and Henning 1985) is documented, value of self-assessment cannot be denied (LeBlanc and Painchaud 1985; Boekaerts 1991). Self-assessment procedures, if applied well, will make the learners the "architect" (Galloway and Labarca 1990) of their own learning. Self-assessment procedures involve learners to a much higher degree in learning than any prescribed learning opportunities can offer. Positive learning experiences, especially those in which effort and accomplishment are rewarded, such as the self-assessment project, help learners establish adequate internal standards and develop identity as a successful learner.

Projects involving self-assessment, as shown in this chapter, are valuable and strongly recommended to foster autonomous learning and promote a learner-centred curriculum. However, this examination of the project makes me wonder if it is fair to use the learners' self-ratings as a part of the course mark when their gender, cultural, educational and developmental backgrounds are so diverse and self-ratings across the groups may differ significantly. On the other hand, who is to say that any assessment cannot be influenced by certain backgrounds of any assessor. How can we cope with a seemingly unlimited number of culturally and pedagogically bound sets of rules regarding the use of a language and its assessment?

In spite of the fact that there was disparity in self-ratings across groups, it is interesting to note that this diverse group of students, which includes sub-groups of Chinese, Korean, English and other speakers, sub-groups of males and females, and sub-groups of traditional university-age students and older students, uniformly had a positive attitude towards the self-assessment project.

For a self-assessment project such as this one to work even better, I believe that classroom teachers and curriculum planners need to create day-to-day instructional settings that nurture and reward self-direction. Thomson (1992), for example, discusses a curriculum in which learners themselves contribute to the creation of the classroom tasks that they carry out. Perhaps, in- and out-of-classroom counselling may be necessary for certain groups to increase their ability to take on responsibility for their own learning.

In order to address learner diversity more seriously, we should examine it from many angles. Grouping students into Asians and non-Asians may not be the best way to gain insight into learner diversity. Other dimensions such as gender differences, and sub-grouping for Chinese individual preference (Melton 1990) vs. Korean collectivism (Sinha and Kao 1988) should also be considered.

This study categorized learners by their native languages. However, the cultural context of the instructional act is also an important consideration (Young 1987). In the multicultural Australian context, native English speakers carry many different cultural heritages. A further study may be needed in the area of diversity within the native English-speaker group concerning the execution of the self-assessment project. In learning Japanese in Australia, many of the foreign students, such as the Korean and Chinese students, are coping with three cultures: their own, the Australian, and the Japanese. Some of those students seem to experience difficulties in dealing with the third culture while they are still coping with the second. We need to take note of the complexities involved in this situation. In this regard, length of stay in Australia also seems to be a meaningful variable to be studied in relation to acceptance of self-directed learning.

The self-assessment project, which aimed to cope with learner diversity, had a diverse impact on different groups of learners. This sounds like an impossible paradox. However, I would like to believe that a study such as this one brings us one step forward in the teaching and learning of a language and the development of autonomy in learners; and I hope that a study of diversity will not remain to be a listing of differences, but will help us raise our awareness of diversity and serve all learners equally well with respect to all the differences.

Note

1. I would like to thank Sumiko Iida and Fusako Oosho who taught the course with me and assisted me in many ways, especially in running the self-assessment project. I would also like to thank Hiromi Masumi-So and David Thomson and others for their assistance in writing this paper. Acknowledgement is also due to the editors who made many meaningful suggestions for improving my original paper.

Appendix

Survey Statements

1. The self-assessment project helped me understand my own strengths and weaknesses in Japanese.
2. The self-assessment project gave me an opportunity to think about my own learning patterns.
3. The self-assessment project helped me further understand my role as a learner who takes initiative in my own learning.
4. The self-assessment project made me realize that there are learning opportunities and learning resources outside the classroom.
5. The self-assessment project helped me find a direction in my future study in Japanese.
6. I am confident in planning, managing, and assessing my own study and I consider myself as a self-directed learner.
7. The self-assessment project was a good complement to the overall subject.
8. I would like to apply the concept of self-assessment in studying for other subjects.

9. I would like to have had more guidance on the self-assessment project.
10. The list of recommended activities handed out in the beginning of the term was helpful in planning my study.

7

Language counselling for learner autonomy: the skilled helper in self-access language learning

Rena Kelly

Introduction

Self-access language learning (SALL) is widely acknowledged as a leading innovation in TESOL. Many tertiary institutions in Asia have established self-access centres within the last five years (Miller 1992). Focusing on the needs of the individual language learner can be seen as an outcome of curriculum evolution that originated in the needs analysis protocols of early ESP (Munby 1978), and of a humanistic person-centred approach to course design and classroom teaching (Nunan 1988). SALL is also an expression of technological innovation, particularly with regard to computer applications to language learning. The underlying theory of SALL, to the extent that there is one, can be traced to humanistic concepts of autonomy and self-direction (Harding-Esch 1976; Holec 1981), and to theories of adult learning (Knowles 1975).

The visible face of SALL is defined by the growing number of self-access centres: the layout, the materials, the technology. Self-access practitioners tend to be preoccupied, at least initially, with the configuration of self-access resources, which is perhaps an expression of the demanding technical process of setting up a centre and coping with budgetary decisions. The responsibility for 'getting it right' and making a self-access centre work is daunting as there are few established reference points to steer by in the domain of self-access learning.

However, the secret to making a self-access centre succeed requires more than technology and the right configuration of resources. Creating a self-access centre does not in itself enable learners to become self-directed.

Learners need to undergo a considerable transformation of their beliefs about language and their role as learners in order to be able to undertake independent learning effectively. This process of reorientation and personal discovery is directly or indirectly an outcome of learner training. To facilitate this process, the teachers who work in a self-access centre need to develop new ways of interacting with learners.

This chapter proposes that the competencies that self-access helpers need to acquire derive from a counselling model of one-to-one helping, and argues that language counselling is a valid application of counselling within education, as much as is career counselling, academic counselling and study counselling. Counselling is essentially a form of therapeutic dialogue that enables an individual to manage a problem. It is particularly effective when personal choices have to be made, and when acquired beliefs about oneself and the world need to be changed.

It is not difficult to conceptualize the transition to self-directed and self-managed language learning as a problem for the learner, requiring decisions that are based on a new understanding of self-responsibility and self-help. Language counselling is just one example of what Egan (1986: viii), a leading counsellor-trainer, calls a "problem-solving or problem-management approach to helping".

The skills of language counselling

In this chapter I propose a split-level classification of the skills of language counselling, into macro-skills and micro-skills.

The macro-skills category describes particular strategies by a self-access helper that can facilitate learner self-management of a self-access project. Forms of language counselling include initiating, goal-setting, suggesting, supporting etc., as listed in Table 1 below. Some of these counselling strategies can come into play at any time during the cycle of a learner's project; others, such as concluding, are triggered by the learner's stage in the project process.

The macro-skills relate to stages in the process of a SALL project, and the top-to-bottom sequence in Table 1 below suggests a cycle, from initiating to concluding. However, an 'initiating' intervention by a helper could occur at any point during a SALL project when it becomes apparent, for example, that the learner needs to branch off and consolidate an aspect of grammar or text cohesion in order to improve his/her academic writing.

Whereas the macro-skills can be seen as strategies that are sequenced and based on the process stage of the learner's project cycle, the micro-

Table 1: The macro-skills of language counselling

Skills	Description	Purpose
Initiating	Introducing new directions and options	To promote learner focus and reduce uncertainty
Goal-setting	Helping the learner to formulate specific goals and objectives	To enable the learner to focus on a manageable goal
Guiding	Offering advice and information, direction and ideas; suggesting	To help the learner develop alternative strategies
Modelling	Demonstrating target behaviour	To provide examples of knowledge and skills that the learner desires
Supporting	Providing encouragement and reinforcement	To help the learner persist; create trust; acknowledge and encourage effort
Giving feedback	Expressing a constructive reaction to the learner's efforts	To assist the learner's self-awareness and capacity for self-appraisal
Evaluating	Appraising the learner's process and achievement	To acknowledge the significance of the learner's effort and achievement
Linking	Connecting the learner's goals and tasks to wider issues	To help establish the relevance and value of the learner's project
Concluding	Bringing a sequence of work to a conclusion	To help the learner establish boundaries and define achievement

skills of language counselling are component behaviours that come into play in a variable way during any interaction with a learner. For instance, a helper will always try to fully 'attend' to a learner (give the learner their undivided attention), and will always be striving for empathy (identifying with the learner's experience and perception). Similarly, the skills of reflective listening (restating, paraphrasing, summarizing, reflecting feelings) will always be in action during communication with a learner.

In order to avoid oversimplification I should point out that the micro-

Table 2: The micro-skills of language counselling

Skills	Description	Purpose
Attending	Giving the learner your undivided attention	To show respect and interest; to focus on the person
Restating	Repeating in your own words what the learner says	To check your understanding and to confirm the learner's meaning
Paraphrasing	Simplifying the learner's statements by focusing on the essence of the message	To clarify the message and to sort out conflicting or confused meanings
Summarizing	Bringing together the main elements of a message	To create focus and direction
Questioning	Using open questions to encourage self-exploration	To elicit and to stimulate learner disclosure and self-definition
Interpreting	Offering explanations for learner experiences	To provide new perspectives; to help self-understanding
Reflecting feelings	Surfacing the emotional content of learner statements	To show that the whole person has been understood
Empathizing	Identifying with the learner's experience and perception	To create a bond of shared understanding
Confronting	Surfacing discrepancies and contradictions in the learner's communication	To deepen self-awareness, particularly of self-defeating behaviour

skills in Table 2 above are, of course, made up of yet other behaviours that counsellors and effective communicators acquire. Take the micro-skill of 'attending': you attend to someone by implementing a subset of attending behaviours, such as orienting your body to them, turning your face to them, maintaining comfortable eye contact, and by pausing and being silent so that the other can speak. Take 'empathy': you show empathy by nodding, smiling in recognition and acknowledgement of what has been said, and by responding in encouraging ways — "Yes, I see. I understand. Really? Uhuh? Mmm." Bolton (1987) describes these verbal and non-verbal responses as "Following Skills", using labels such as "Door Openers", "Minimal Encouragers", "Infrequent Questions" and "Attentive Silence". There are yet other essential counselling attributes that I can only indicate briefly here, such as 'trust'. Attending to the other and showing empathy helps to create trust, which is an essential feature of a therapeutic dialogue.

Foundation values of counselling

Underlying the macro- and micro-skills outlined above are a set of humanistic values that motivate and inform person-centred counselling. These foundation values include unconditional positive regard, genuineness and empathic understanding. For instance, the behaviour of attending fully to the learner in respectful listening not only allows the learner to speak openly, but is also an expression of the counsellor's unconditional positive regard for that person.

Unconditional positive regard, or 'non-possessive love', or 'caring' as it can also be called, is one of the foundation values of Rogerian, person-centred counselling. The other two foundation values are 'genuineness' or authenticity, and "accurate, empathic understanding" (Bolton 1987). Empathy, genuineness and positive regard constitute the trinity of counselling values. Other counselling theorists have added values such as "client self-responsibility" (Egan 1986). We can see that counselling behaviours are not just techniques. They are the expression of a comprehensive attitude to the integrity of the student-client, based on a set of values which I believe are particularly compatible with self-directed learning.

If we want to explore the origins of counselling a little further, continuing to look beyond the techniques and the values that underlie them, we discover in educational and counselling theory a model of the person, which has been elaborated in the humanistic psychology of Maslow (1954) and May (1967), and which affirms the primary need of an individual for autonomy and self-responsibility. Counselling acknowledges the difficulty individuals experience in achieving their autonomy and self-direction and has developed helping techniques to facilitate personal growth. The astute language teacher will be saying by now "But models of the person are culturally relative. If counselling, like western education, is based on notions of individuality and self-responsibility, it may not apply to non-western cultures where different theories of the person are embedded in social practice."

That is a very valid point to make, and one that preoccupies the many counsellors, psychologists and educationists around the world who work in the fields of cross-cultural communication, intercultural training, cross-cultural psychology and cross-cultural counselling. From my own perspective, self-access language learning requires language counselling assistance for learners precisely because of the difficult cross-cultural adjustment that a move to self-directed learning requires. However, making a cross-cultural adjustment to a 'foreign' or different learning style can happen within cultures (between subcultures) as well as across cultures, for instance in the shift from secondary school to university.

The context for language counselling

How, then, does language counselling work in the context of an individual learning project? I will now illustrate how it can be applied in a particular self-access centre, in this case the Centre for Individual Language Learning (CILL) at Temasek Polytechnic in Singapore. CILL opened in August 1993, and before that we faced all the usual planning challenges: Self-access for which students? What kind of materials in what categories? What items of equipment, how many and where? As well as the really big question: How do we get learners started? Behind the latter question lies all the anxiety of wanting to prove that the centre is viable.

At CILL we decided almost from the start that we would put most of our energy into a structured project approach to SALL, where individual students would be assisted to undertake a planned, contracted, time-limited and assessed language development project. This did not mean that we excluded other pathways for students into CILL. In effect there are now three pathways to CILL-based learning at our Polytechnic:

1. Self-referral (for browsing, recreation, or sustained study);
2. Lecturer-referral (obligatory or optional, for specific remedial assistance); and
3. CILL Project.

Language counselling plays a role in all of these pathways to SALL, but becomes particularly instrumental when a learner is embarking on a CILL Project. Let us take for example a project option for Engineering students, where the first year students with the weakest English proficiency (as assessed by the Language and Communication lecturers in the School of Engineering) were given the option of undertaking a self-improvement project in CILL that would be assessed for credit and thereby enable them to increase their overall grade-score for their first year. The learner pathway for this project is illustrated below:

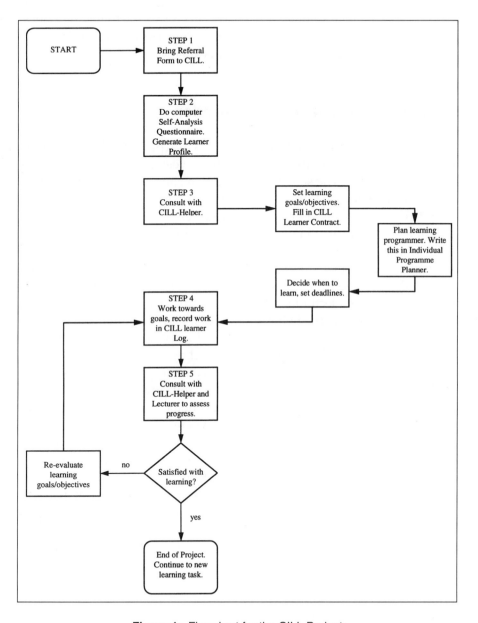

Figure 1: Flowchart for the CILL Project

Language counselling can occur at any point of contact between learner and helper during a CILL project but there are key points in the pathway where the learner needs help with decision-making. Therefore, the greatest opportunities for counselling assistance occur during the following stages: needs clarification; goal-setting; contracting; programme planning; monitoring; self-assessment; and project evaluation.

Language counselling skills in action

I will now describe some of the stages in the CILL project pathway in more detail, starting with the first consultation between learner and self-access helper. We call this 'The start-up consultation', and think of it as the most important stage for the learner. This consultation introduces the learner to a new person (the helper), new resources, new processes and responsibilities, new documents, and a new form of assessment.

In practice, of course, we would not inflict such a high volume of novelty on a young student in one encounter. We too believe that self-access learning starts in the classroom: all our student-clients have been introduced to the idea of SALL by their lecturers, and many have participated in an orientation to CILL and have met the helpers, or at least know who they are. But the most important psychological first step has been taken by the learner: they have made a choice to take up a CILL project option.

We also cater for learners who have been referred and who have not made a personal choice to attend CILL. Compulsory SALL poses an uncomfortable contradiction for self-access helpers, as do all compulsory referrals for counsellors and helpers anywhere. However, the only truly compulsory referrals to CILL concern foreign students who have been admitted to the Polytechnic without the standard English language proficiency grade. Their continuing admission and their academic success depends on improved English proficiency. So far, such students have welcomed the opportunity to study in CILL and seem to really appreciate the assistance they receive from CILL helpers.

The start-up consultation

The start-up consultation between the learner and a CILL helper has the following objectives and steps:

1. review of the purpose of the project option (how it fits into the learner's academic programme);

2. overview of the CILL project pathway, using the flowchart in Figure 1;
3. needs analysis, goal-setting, completing a learning contract and anticipating final assessment;
4. individual programme planning; and
5. project record-keeping (learner logsheets and other working documents).

Needs clarification

To best illustrate the role of language counselling, we can enter the start-up consultation at the point of learner needs analysis for goal-setting. CILL helpers use the CILL Referral Form (see the Appendix) as a platform for self-needs analysis with the learner. CILL helpers have suggested to language lecturers in the Schools of the Polytechnic that they allow the learner to assess his/her strength and weakness in the skills categories on the referral form. The role of the CILL helper at this stage is to explore and clarify the learner's perception of their main needs for language development. This process requires the counselling micro-skills of attending, restating, paraphrasing, summarizing, questioning, interpreting, reflecting feelings and empathizing.

Goal-setting emerges from learner self-needs analysis, so during this stage the helper will be clarifying the learner's assessment of his/her strength and weakness in relation to the broad language proficiency categories that are listed on the CILL Referral Form.

Here is an extract from a needs clarification and goal-setting dialogue between helper and learner:

(The helper (H) is going over the learner's (L) referral form.)

H: Now, to get this main goal we'll go back to your referral form, which Margaret, your lecturer, has filled in ... Umm, these ticks here show that you're average in these areas and weak in these areas. Did you ... are these weaknesses that you identified?
L: I identified.
H: You identified them did you? Right. Can you tell me a bit more about why you've ticked these areas?
L: I think that my spelling is very poor. When I do a composition or something I keep stopping and ask my ... how to spell that. It's a real problem for me.
H: Is it? Right. Is it a problem that you've always had? (yes, I've always ...) It's always been a difficulty, has it?
L: Because in Primary School I don't really have a basic ... not in spelling. I learned and forgot ... So I find I'm having a problem here.
H: OK, so you think that part of the spelling problem is forgetting the words?

(yes) You learn how to spell them and then ... (I forget) ... you forget. Could I just ... I'll just put what you say to me (OK) here, and say, um "learns how to spell" (yeah, I even get high marks) "and even gets high marks" (and you forget it) and then forgets, yeah ... So it could be a sort of a memory problem, couldn't it? (mm) OK. And tell me a bit more about the other writing weaknesses.

Here is another sequence with the same learner, where she is being helped to define her needs in relation to vocabulary and pronunciation:

L: So, vocabulary, I use quite simple words. I don't use ... like for 'fast' I don't use another word for 'fast'. More difficult words I don't use. Those type of more, um, more ... I normally use *fast, happy*, and all those simple words.

H: So you feel that your vocabulary consists mainly of simple words? (yeah, right) And ... you'd like to have more words to choose from, (yeah) is that right?

L: So my compo will not be so dull, using all the 'happy' simple words for my paper.

H: Are you saying too that you'd like to have some more academic words? (yeah, right) To widen your academic vocabulary for your writing here at the Poly? (yes) OK. And I notice you've ticked two areas of speaking (vocab and pronunciation) Mm, can you tell me a bit more about that?

L: Pronunciation is quite a bit weak lah. Um, at first, I can't ... I tend to speak very fast, so ... Like the words seem to go wrong. Like, how to pronounce something, I pronounce wrong, totally different. I think I need to improve on the pronunciation. So, if I get nervous lah, I speak totally out of control.

The outcome of the needs clarification dialogue is that out of all the language weaknesses the learner has identified one or two main goals will be selected for self-development. These are then written into a learner contract as main goals and sub-objectives.

Contracting

At CILL we encourage learners who undertake a project to sign a learner contract, as we believe that contracting helps a learner to see the concreteness, the discreteness and the personal ownership of their individual learning project. Language counselling continues to be important during this stage as the helper needs to check the learner's willingness to commit time to his/her project, which may entail reviewing other commitments and demands on the learner's time, and defining the relative priority of this project in his/her academic and personal schedule. Another important feature of the contracting stage is to help the learner anticipate completion (goal attainment) by focusing on goal achievement and a form of self-assessment at the end of their project. The kind of questions that are helpful here are "solutions-oriented" questions (O'Hanlon and Weiner-Davis 1989), which are illustrated in the sample exchange below:

H: So, how do you think you will know that you have achieved your goal at the end of this project?

L: (*Silence, puzzled look*) Umm, what do you mean?

H: Umm, how will you know you have improved?

L: Uh ... you mean my lecturer will give me a grade?

H: No. How will you yourself know that you have improved — that you have learned something in this project?

L: Oh ... I could write a good summary and ... you ... will you tell me if it's OK lah?

H: Well, yes, I could go through it with you. And maybe I can help you see why I think it's good or not so good? I can also give you some other summaries to look at, so you can compare your work with them.

Programme planning

In this stage the helper will help the learner translate his/her goals and objectives to a 'Project Programme Planner', which will span a period of four to six weeks. The purpose of the Programme Planner is to help the learner plot a pathway for the project, to see it as finite and manageable within the near future and to see the weekly time commitment as a regular requirement. The Planner also translates goals into chunks of work. By this stage in the CILL project start-up consultation the helper is becoming more of a guide than a counsellor, as the learner now needs to be connected with the resources that are available in CILL, particularly the materials that could be most relevant for their programme. 'Suggesting' is the macro-skill that most comes into play during programme planning. Until the learner knows the centre better he or she cannot make informed choices about which folders, videos, CD-ROMs and other resources could be suitable for their learning goal.

Managing project documents: from start-up folder to project portfolio

The remainder of the start-up consultation is directed at orienting the learner to other project documents, including the learner logsheets that record and evaluate every piece of work, and reviewing the project flowchart. Advice is given on how to keep all these documents in a project portfolio, on how assessment will be handled and where the relevant self-access folders and other resources can be found. This is definitely a more directive stage of project induction. All the project documents that we provide for the learner in the start-up consultation are designed to become working documents that help the learner to manage his/her project. What starts out as a folder of start-up documents becomes a project portfolio, where the learner places all learner logsheets and the pieces of work (drafts, notes, summaries, exercises) that go with them. The project portfolio then becomes the basis of assessment at the end of the project, which comprises process assessment (how well did the learner manage the project?) and product assessment of a final piece of work.

Counselling throughout the CILL project: the counselling-tutoring-helping continuum

During the process of an individual learner project there will be many opportunities for language counselling assistance by the self-access helper. For instance, we find that learners frequently lose sight of their original goals, and may become confused or want to re-contract; they may lose motivation and need encouragement, or to review the relative priority of this project for them; they may need to detour into grammar consolidation; they will definitely seek feedback on their work in progress. All of these encounters between helper and learner are opportunities for a range of helping behaviours that include, but are not restricted to, counselling: affirmation, encouragement, guidance, suggestion, direct tutoring, humour and storytelling. Through an affirmative relationship with a self-access helper a young learner can gain a new sense of his/her individuality, autonomy (the importance of the choices they are making), and dignity as a person. They can also directly and indirectly learn how to learn, an outcome that I will illustrate in the next section.

The self-access helper is constantly attempting to elicit learner choice and insight at every stage of the learner's individual learning cycle while trying to avoid being directive and prescriptive. This kind of learner-focused dialogue can be a startling experience for young learners, and so the interaction needs to be non-intrusive and managed in respectful non-verbal ways: not staring, allowing pauses, using soft voice and an 'inquiring' tone, creating a space for learner self-expression and adjusting proximity; above all by showing interest in personal disclosure by the learner ("Oh, that's interesting. Can you tell me more about that? I'm really interested in the way you see that"). Showing interest and empathy will help to create rapport and trust between the helper and the learner.

So, the overall applications of language counselling in a self-access language learning project, at least in our Centre, can be summarized as:

1. Needs clarification;
2. Goal-setting and programme planning;
3. Monitoring;
4. Guiding;
5. Self-assessment and helper assessment;
6. Project evaluation; and
7. Reflection and forward planning.

Other applications of language counselling

I can imagine that some self-access practitioners will not recognize their own self-access centres in the structured, individual-project model that I have outlined in this chapter. Other centres will have different SALL pathway options, some more structured and some comparatively unstructured. However, language counselling can play a role in any SALL setting in helping learners to manage their own learning. Counselling is, above all, an enlightening process for the client; it can illuminate aspects of personal experience that, without dialogue, may not become conscious or meaningful.

Hence, language counselling is a particularly useful process for learner development for autonomy: for learning about learning. The language counselling extracts that follow are taken from sessions with learners who are independently developing their competence in a foreign or second language. William, a Chinese student in the second year of his Polytechnic diploma course, is independently maintaining and developing his proficiency in Mandarin. Naoko is a Japanese woman, married and a part-time teacher of Japanese, who has been learning French through an individualized programme for a year.

I am not fluent in French, and I speak no Mandarin, but my aim as their language counsellor is to support their independent learning by helping them to develop:

1. learning strategy awareness: What do they do to learn and is it effective? Are there alternative strategies?
2. language awareness: What working knowledge are they developing about French and Mandarin?
3. learner self-management: What happens when they use their second or foreign language? How do they manage their anxiety and cope with limited knowledge?

This kind of strategic awareness constitutes what Oxford (1990) and others

(Wenden and Rubin 1987; O'Malley and Chamot 1990; Wenden 1991) call metacognition: an articulate awareness of how one learns, what one knows and how one uses that knowledge. Metacognition is a form of self-knowledge that marks the difference between a passive learner obediently following a teacher and a reflective, self-aware learner who is creatively using and developing their language resources. Learning strategies and language awareness can also be acquired through training (Ellis and Sinclair 1989), but language counselling carries the special advantage of turning personal experience into learning through reflective dialogue.

Learning strategy awareness

In this extract the helper is focusing on William's strategies for in-dependently practising Mandarin. William attended a lecture given in Mandarin by a visiting academic from mainland China, and was pleasantly surprised by his (William's) ability to understand and enjoy a long monologue in Mandarin. The helper is trying to surface the significance of this experience in a more general sense. If it was good, can it be replicated?

> W: But the consolation is I've been doing a lot of Mandarin speaking with my classmates, and last week there was a professor from Fu Xian University, who was here to give a lecture in Mandarin. And I stayed through the whole lecture and I was really amazed by myself. Everyone else was confused as to what he was saying, but I understood everything. Although I couldn't reply and couldn't formulate my thoughts in Mandarin, I could understand and I could jot down notes.
>
> H: That must have been so satisfying, (it was, it was) because that's kind of high-level, serious, academic ... talking, isn't it ?
>
> W: It was ... I don't know, I think I'm used to it. It was something ... well, I used to do it in secondary school, and at home, so I'm not exactly ... This particular style of Mandarin is not exactly new to me.
>
> H: It's not new to you ? (no) So, had you been out of contact with it?
>
> W: I guess I had been, yeah.
>
> H: And this experience last week, with this visiting professor from Fu Xian, it put you back in contact with it?
>
> W: Exactly, yeah.
>
> H: And that felt ..?
>
> W: Really good. Very good. It was really enjoyable because he was speaking ... everything was so beautiful. The language sounded so nice. (did it?) It was, a really nice accent, and intonation, it was lively, he wasn't dull ... but he was lively and engaging. So, it was a very fun three hours.
>
> H: Three hours?
>
> W: Three hours ... sitting through. (that's a long time!) It was, non-stop, he just

went on and on and on, non-stop. I really wondered how he did it at first. Very, very enjoyable.

H: So, it sounds as if he was a good speaker, who brought the language to life for you? (yes) And you felt pleased with yourself for being able to follow it? (mm) Yeah, gosh. Does it make you wish there were more opportunities like that, to listen? To a good native speaker?

W: Yes, definitely. A good native speaker for me to practise my language with.

In the next extract Naoko is telling the helper about her recent trip to France, and how puzzled she is by the feeling of disappointment she now feels about her competence in French. The helper is attempting to clarify the origin of the disappointment and to reframe it as an opportunity to learn how to get more out of French language contact situations generally.

H: Tell me a bit more about the anti-climax feeling.

N: I don't know what it is, but I just didn't have this right situation. The things I learned. Because, um, Level 1, I did, I forgot about those sentences, and 2, again, was more office language — and just didn't come. I could have made a lot of things. I could reserve by telephone. But I didn't dare. I could have. And then changing the date. I wasn't prepared to do that. Umm ...

H: So, was it an anticlimax because you felt ... inhibited? Or was it an anticlimax because the opportunities weren't there?

N: I think a little bit of both.

H: If you were able to do that all over again, how would you do it?

N: Umm ... maybe I will ... I think probably I will go through the same ... speech. I will make sure I can use ... I wasn't quite sure. And after ... a couple of weeks I didn't use, didn't listen to French, at all, in England. And that makes it sort of ... That didn't help.

H: Pushes it to the back of your mind?

N: Maybe if I kept practising up to the day before, and then going better prepared. But ... I was doing something else in England, in London ... um.

H: So, if you were doing it all over again, you're saying that you'd do more practice (mm) up to the point of leaving (yes). What else would you do, if you were doing it again?

N: I'm not quite sure, but I'd try to make more ... um, try to create the situation, maybe ...

H: Uhuh? How could you do that?

N: Ah, for instance, you can, maybe you can talk to the receptionist a little bit more. Uh, for instance you can, you can explain your situation, like "I've just come from somewhere else". Maybe you can, and get over that ...

H: Just try to widen that (a little bit, yes) opportunity (stretch it a little bit) Take that initiative (mm) to open that up? (mm) Right. (yes, mm) Would that mean having more confidence, to do that? (yes) Mm. You're saying that it's not that you don't know the phrases; it's a case of having the confidence to use them? Is that it?

N: No, I think I have some stock, but it's not very ... it's not perfect. So I ... yeah, not enough confidence. (confidence?) Yes, mm. I know, sometimes, you know, talking about weather, you mix it up, and not sure really. So, that sort of thing.

Language awareness

In the following extract, William is comparing his experiences of speaking to native speakers of two languages that he himself uses (English and Mandarin). He is becoming aware that knowing a language does not guarantee mutual comprehension with a native speaker, and that cultural differences in usage and meaning have to be managed through checking and clarifying. This is an important stage in his developing awareness that language is more than words: language is also culture.

W: It's the same situation I have with Peter now [*Peter is a visiting student from a university in England*]. I don't understand him very well. And sometimes he doesn't understand what I'm trying to tell him. And I think it's the same with the Chinese. The expressions we use in Singapore is very different from what is being used ... uh, down in China. I've already experienced that when I was in China, years ago. When we say things, it's something else to them, and when they say something, we don't understand.

H: What do you do, in situations like that, when you realize that's happening?

W: I would ask, I would clarify ...

H: Mm, how would you do that?

W: I would ask them "Do you understand what I'm talking about?" And I ask them to give me feedback as to whether they understand me — whether they know what is needed, so they tell me, and I tell them they haven't understood.

H: So you're quite aware now (yes, I am) of these differences in usage — same language but um, differences ... Can you give me an example of a difference?

W: A difference? I can't think of any offhand.

H: Phrases? Names of things?

W: Names of things! Yes! Um, in China they call potato 'e-gwa' — the fruit from the ground. But in Singapore we call it 'ma-li-su' , which is something else, totally different. When I was in China we had 'kow-te-gwa' , which is basically heating this potato up in an oven, and we were curious as to what this thing's all about. They were telling us about it "Hey, it's very nice. You must try this specialty. This is really good. Let me buy you some." And we were wondering what's this thing all about? And then when we saw it we said "Oh gosh, but that's ma-li-su". They said "What's that again?" That kind of thing.

H: Uhuh, yeah, so different terminology (that's right) different names? (different names) Right ...

W: Intonation.

H: Intonation?

W: Intonation — very different accents.

H: Uhuh? Does that often lead to confusion?

W: Not to confusion, but I think it's more amusing. Well, they do understand us. We do understand them. But the Chinese, the native speakers, they have to make a real conscious effort to slow down and to articulate — usually they mumble and go "Ba-ba-ba-ba" among themselves. And when they speak to us they have to speak very slowly. And they have to say it word by word.

H: And this is native speakers of Mandarin to Singaporean speakers of Mandarin? So the difference is quite enormous?

W: Exactly.

H: And you're experiencing this process of adjustment? Clarifying, checking comprehension, sameness. (right) Uhuh. And this is something that you've learned over the last couple of years?

W: Yes. When I travel, especially when I'm in China.

H: But it's interesting. You're also experiencing it in the case of another shared language, when you talk with Peter. (exactly) And are you clarifying and checking with him?

W: I try to. But sometimes, I think I understand what he's saying, but in reality I don't. I perceive it incorrectly. He wants to tell me something but I see it as something else.

H: And you realize afterwards?

W: Exactly. When we have to do things. When I have to go and do that particular thing, that particular task he has told me to do. It's like "He told me to do that" and "Yeah, I thought you understood".

H: And you say "Oh, I didn't know you meant that".

W: Exactly.

H: Can you think of an example?

In the following extract Naoko is recounting how a weakness in her mastery of the pronoun-verb form system in French really limited her ability to participate in a conversation in French, in France.

N: Yes, another thing I can't do, is change the ... Uh, for instance, when you learn 'vous' form, then I change 'tu' form, is very difficult. And now I try to make it, if I have to say it in 'tu' form, I have to say this and that. And that sort of thing. I didn't do it earlier on, so it has to be the right person to talk to. And that's difficult.

H: So that mattered more when you were in France?

N: Yes, and like I say 'I' , but I like to say 'we' did this and 'we' did that. But that again is changing ... difficult.

H: Because you're talking about the family? (yes) So all of your practice about 'je' and 'tu' had to change because you're now talking about 'nous' to 'vous'? Is that right?

N: Yeah. 'Nous' and 'tu', I have to practise. 'Vous', it's in my textbook.

H: But the 'tu' form you aren't so familiar with? (no) And that's situationally dependent, isn't it? (yes) It depends on who is with you ...

N: That's right. Yes. Because I was talking to my, uh, husband's friend, who spoke French, and I wanted to talk to him. But that was too formal, so I wanted to ...

H: So you wanted to become ... to be able to use the 'tu' form?

N: Yes, but I couldn't. So, it's very hard.

Learner self-management

In this extract William is beginning to realize what initiatives he can take to make use of the Mandarin native speakers he has access to, and that this will require effort, effort that he is not yet ready to make.

W: Well ... um, but on the other hand, they visit us very often, and I always meet people from China. My father has guests from China all the time. So, it's not that bad.

H: So, you think the opportunities for you to have conversation are still there? (mm) To take advantage of this opportunity, is it going to take some planning? To develop your own Mandarin through conversation? Is it just going to happen automatically? Or are you going to have to do something to make it happen?

W: I would have to make a conscientious effort to calm down, and say "OK, I'm going ... on Saturday evening I'm going to visit this person and speak to him, and I'm going to practise my Mandarin." Yeah, I need to do that. But not now. I will only speak and practise as and when the chance arises. Like, when a visitor comes along. Or, I meet and entertain my father's clients.

H: So it would be kind of accidental (uhuh) practice (exactly). And it may not be talking about a topic where you want to learn the vocabulary? It might just be whatever happens? (mm) So, it may not meet your needs in any developmental way?

W: ... (long pause) ... No, it won't. Not specifically ... But I think all this interaction is essential, should I want to go to China, to study one day. I think all this contact, all this communication and interaction will come in very handy.

H: Tell me more about that. How will it help you?

In this extract Naoko recounts the extensive rehearsal that she undertook before initiating an exchange with the manageress of the hotel she stayed at in Paris. She is realizing that her level of confidence is an important factor in being able to communicate, and that her confidence depends to some extent on her role in the foreign language situation:

> N: And one time I wanted to leave the luggage in the lobby. But it took 30 minutes to have this courage to say that "Is it alright after the checkout time, um, leave my luggage here?" So then I did it in a few words — not the proper sentence. But she understood. (and you were preparing) Preparing.
>
> H: What did you say?
>
> N: I can't remember.
>
> H: And who did you have to say it to?
>
> N: To the madame of the hotel.
>
> H: And she understood what you wanted to do? (mm) That must be satisfying?
>
> N: Yes, but it took a long time ... (preparing for it?) Yes, it wasn't preparing the sentence but preparing my ... (courage? confidence?) Confidence. That means I didn't have the confidence — that's why.
>
> H: That's interesting. When you talk to the helpers here, all that confidence is there, but facing the madame ... (yes, it's a totally different ...) Yes, what is the fear, do you think?
>
> N: Because here ... the role ... I'm a student. So therefore I can make a fool of myself. But there ... again I'm a foreigner so I can make mistakes. But it's somehow different.
>
> H: So, the risk of embarrassment is higher? (yes ...) Of making a fool of yourself? (mm)
>
> N: But, on the whole, I enjoyed it.

We can see in these extracts how language counselling can help a learner develop a more holistic awareness of language and learning. Such helping is not a form of teaching and does not depend on the language knowledge of the counsellor. In this sense, language counselling skills can enable a knowledgeable language educator to help any student who is undertaking language learning, whether in a self-access centre or through a conventional classroom programme. By helping learners to become reflective and self-aware we are empowering them to make conscious choices and hence to take greater responsibility for their learning.

The teacher-helper-person continuum

Finally, we need to remember that "counselling situations are not separate and distinct from our everyday activities" (Belkin 1984: 64). As Carkhuff (1969: 42) further elaborates, "the same dimensions which are effective in other instances of human encounters are effective in the counselling and therapeutic processes". In the light of these statements we can see that what primarily makes us effective as self-access helpers is what we are as persons rather than what we are as practitioners. At the level of foundation values that is certainly true; it is also true that few of us can develop unassisted the skills of effective listening. Like all aspects of communicative competence these skills need to be consciously learned and consciously applied before they become automatic. We learn the language of counselling as a way of being more effectively genuine, understanding and respectful with our students, and in order to help them become self-directed, self-responsible learners. Developing skills in language counselling enlarges our competence as language educators and enables us to set up self-access centres where technological and human helping can creatively interact to foster learner autonomy.

APPENDIX

CILL REFERRAL FORM

Name of student:_____ No: _____

School:_____ Course and Year: _____

Name of Lecturer: _____ (Ext no:)

SKILL	Strong	Average	Weak
Listening: academic social			
Academic Writing: spelling punctuation grammar paragraph struct. organization style vocabulary			
Speaking: pronunciation intonation vocabulary			
Academic Reading: speed comprehension finding info inferencing			
Other:			

CILL-Engineering Upgrade Project
Referral Form - Version 1.0

8

Conversation exchange: a way towards autonomous language learning

Peter Voller and Valerie Pickard

Introduction

The path towards learner autonomy can be characterized as learning how to learn in order to take greater control of one's own learning. There are differing points of view on how best to achieve this — for instance, by teaching learning strategies, by raising language awareness, by de-institutionalizing learning, or by a combination of such approaches. However, the literature on learner training and learner development does agree on five or six characteristics that will help learners to become more independent and take them further along the road to full autonomy. These have been summarized as identification of needs, definition of objectives, selection of appropriate materials and study techniques, organization of appropriate times and venues, and self-monitoring of progress (Riley et al. 1989: 53).

The purpose of this chapter is to see how one particular type of language-learning scheme — conversation and study exchange — helps to promote these characteristics of learner development. After reviewing earlier studies of such exchanges, we shall describe a conversation exchange that has been operating from the self-access centre of the University of Hong Kong for the past two years. Data was collected from users both when they joined the scheme and when/if they reported back, and more recently from a follow-up questionnaire which was sent to this academic year's participants in the scheme. The analysis of this data suggests that users are often capable of controlling their own learning with minimal intervention from a teacher-helper. We shall conclude by making some recommendations on how best to organize such learning exchanges.

Historical development of language exchanges

Peer teaching and learning, at least in the field of language learning, has gone through a number of stages of development. Like the idea of autonomous learning itself, peer teaching and learning is a concept that has been adopted into applied linguistics from adult education. Particularly influential in this regard has been the work of Allen Tough who, in *The Adult's Learning Projects* (1971), described in great detail an approach to learning that relied on 'helpers', ordinary people from all walks of life whom learners could approach, usually on a one-to-one basis, in order to be taught what the learners wanted to learn. This approach to teaching and learning has influenced later writers on self-directed language learning such as Leslie Dickinson (1987). In his discussion of sources of support for the learner in self-instruction, Dickinson lists the following possible human sources of assistance: helper-counsellors, native speakers, peers and learning exchanges. He sees learners supporting one another through self-help groups (as did Tough) and 'study buddy' arrangements. He continues:

> Furthermore, it may be possible to fix up learning exchanges, in which, for example, a speaker of English who is learning French works with a speaker of French who is learning English. Finally, native (or competent) speakers of the target language can provide very valuable help in supplying language input, talking with the learner and, maybe, assisting the learner in self-assessment. (1987: 102f.)

This quote suggests that there are two different approaches to peer teaching and learning: one where there is a *mutual* learning exchange going on, and the other where a native speaker acts as an *expert informant* (a surrogate teacher) for the language learner. Dickinson goes on to describe a number of peer teaching schemes that had been set up in British universities in the 1980s, such as the Cambridge Sound and Video Library experiment (Harding and Tealby 1981: 104) where language learners were put in touch with native speakers through a counsellor associated with the library, and the Assisted Self Tutoring Scheme at Aston University where the learner had access to a native speaker informant (Ager et al. 1980: 21). Dickinson suggests that there may have been problems with these projects, with learners seeing the informants as substitute teachers, and then being disappointed by their lack of knowledge of grammar and correct usage. This is perhaps an oversimplification of the problems involved. It could also be surmised that they were less than successful because of the roles of the participants and the lack of autonomy evidenced by the learners. Were the native speakers being forced to play surrogate teacher roles when they expected friendship? Were the learners unable to view the native speakers as anything other than teachers and informants?

More successful have been attempts to set up mutual learning exchanges. Dickinson describes Dalwood's (1977) learning exchange, which she called a 'Reciprocal Language Learning Course' where groups of French learners of English travelled to Britain and worked for a few weeks with groups of English learners of French. Müller et al. (1988) describe a one-to-one language-learning exchange at the University of Fribourg, the Uni-TANDEM project, which was organized between speakers of German and speakers of other languages who were brought together by means of an intermediary from the German Language Institute at the University. The methodology employed had originally been developed in the late 1970s by a group of teachers in Madrid who had named their project TANDEMadrid. This was a more formalized learning context, involving the exchange of contracts, and the alternation of teaching and learning roles. Feedback from questionnaires at the end of the Fribourg programme indicate that there were no problems provided the partners got on well with one another, and used the time for learning through communication, not for learning about the target language. This suggests another point to bear in mind when developing peer learning exchanges: not only must they be *mutual*, but they should also emphasize that successful language learning is about the negotiation of meaning, about *procedural* rather than declarative *knowledge*.

A number of other language exchanges have also been reported. Most have been set up in universities. CRAPEL has experimented with both 'peer matching' and giving learners access to native speakers (Henner-Stanchina 1985). Murphey (1991: 107-8) reports some success with one-to-one language exchange programmes at the University of Florida in the late 1970s and then at the University of Neuchatel. Little (1988a) describes how a language exchange developed out of the self-directed learning scheme at Trinity College, Dublin. A number of conversation and learning exchanges have also been reported on e-mail from North American universities (Beatty 1994; Eveland 1994; Harris 1994; Taxdal 1994). Finally, the University of Minnesota runs a language exchange programme (called TANDEM) where ESL students are encouraged to sign up for conversation partners, English speakers who want to study the ESL student's native language. Partners are matched "according to interest, gender preference and schedule". The programme is deemed successful, with around 100 participants per term (Bare 1994). This programme sounds very similar to the scheme we have been running at the University of Hong Kong, which we shall now describe.

Conversation exchange at the University of Hong Kong

When we were setting up a consultation desk in the self-access centre of the University of Hong Kong in September 1992 we decided that one of the services we were going to offer was a conversation exchange. We decided to call it a *conversation* exchange rather than a language or learning exchange in order to publicize its informal and non-academic features. We anticipated that we would be constrained by a number of variables and took these into account when tailoring the scheme. These were:

1. the preponderance of native Cantonese speakers among the student body (over 95%);
2. the fact that at the University of Hong Kong the official language of instruction is English; and
3. the limited availability of native speakers of languages other than Cantonese, most being staff or students on non-degree courses in Mandarin and Cantonese.

We therefore anticipated that most of our applicants would be Cantonese speakers seeking to practise English, and so made it clear to users that we could not guarantee a native speaker partner of their target language, and that most of them would have to be satisfied with partners who spoke the same first language. Most applicants accepted this constraint though an effort was made to recruit native speakers of English by means of a publicity campaign targeting learners of Mandarin and Cantonese. We decided to follow the suggestions made by Murphey, and our first application form and *modus operandi* were adapted from the samples he provides in *Teaching One to One* (1991: 125-6).

    As analysis of our initial application form will show (see Appendix 1), we requested only the most basic information about users of the scheme, leaving decisions about partner selection wholly in the hands of the self-access consultants. Apart from first, other and target languages, the information requested covered age, sex, academic field and general interests. If a suitable partner was already on file, the applicant was immediately given his or her contact telephone number and a set of instructions and suggestions for initiating the conversation exchange (see Appendix 2). These now seem both over-prescriptive in terms of what to do and talk about and naive in that they do not make any attempt to suggest that different partners may have different objectives in using the service. If no partner was immediately available, the applicant was placed on file until a suitable partner joined. Most applicants were given a contact telephone number within a week. In the first year of operation, a total of 89 people signed up for the conversation exchange service and 22 of these spoke a language other than Cantonese as their first language. It was possible to provide conversation exchange with native speakers of languages as diverse as Hungarian, Burmese, Thai and Japanese as well as English. All participants were paired up with at least one other partner. Although participants were asked to report back to the consultation desk, only eighteen did so, and in most cases this was because they wanted to be put in contact with a new partner. Verbal feedback from these participants was generally positive: they had met and talked to their partners, who had, however, "got too busy to meet again".

In the second year of operation the major innovation was the reformulation of the application form (see Appendix 3) to address both the requests users had made during the scheme's first year and the difficulties consultants had faced in finding appropriate partners. We added questions about the applicant's role in the university (so as to avoid pairing up first-year undergraduates with staff), and about place of residence and best time for meeting a partner in an attempt to ameliorate reported problems with fitting exchanges into users' busy schedules. We also added an extensive section about partner preferences in order to give users more control over the choice of partners. This was not wholly successful, however, because it greatly increased the number of applicants who requested a native speaker of the target language, which greatly increased the length of time that some applicants had to wait for a partner.

Evaluation of the conversation exchange

The number of participants in the academic year 1993-4 was almost identical to the previous year. Eighty-eight participants (30 male and 58 female) from eight language backgrounds (Cantonese, English, Mandarin, Japanese, French, German, Korean and Danish) registered for the conversation exchange and partners were provided for 77 of them. As in the previous year, very few participants (11) reported back on their progress. It therefore became necessary to find other means of finding answers to the following questions:

1. which participants are actually meeting and exchanging language skills?
2. which languages are they exchanging?
3. where, how often and for how long do they meet?
4. what are they doing when they meet, i.e. what techniques and materials do they use?

5. what do participants consider a successful conversation exchange and how do they achieve this?
6. how can the system be organized to optimize language exchange?

In order to answer these questions, a questionnaire (see Appendix 4) was mailed to 78 participants, and 27 (35%) were returned. Eleven of the 27 respondents had had an exchange with one another. It may be significant that returns from Cantonese L1 speakers comprise 25% of the total returns while they constitute approximately 55% of the scheme's participants. Very few questionnaires were returned by Cantonese speakers who had been paired with other Cantonese speakers for English conversation exchange. Indeed, the only feedback we received from this category was from three members of a group of five students (including one Japanese student) holding a weekly discussion group. The lack of response from Cantonese-Cantonese partners is worrying and warrants further investigation to find out whether such pairings have been successful.

Eighteen (67%) of the 27 participants who returned questionnaires had met their partners. Twelve had exchanged languages successfully, four felt that they had experienced some success but were not totally happy with the experience, because they felt their mastery of the target language was insufficient, or because of time constraints, while two had been unsuccessful due to either a problem with pairing (a personality clash) or a lack of time. Of the nine participants who did not make any contact with partners, five had received no calls, two had had no time to contact their partner and two were unable to establish contact (one was abroad when her partner rang and one was unable to communicate in Cantonese so couldn't leave a message). Nevertheless, seven of these respondents still expressed the desire to use the conversation exchange again. The problem of failure to make contact has been reported in other schemes and has been attributed to a failure to understand the degree of commitment required by a learning exchange (see Murphey 1991: 107-8; Eveland 1994).

Organization and conduct of conversation exchanges

Data from the 18 participants who met partners show that they have usually developed independent learning strategies in order to carry out the conversation exchange. Of the five or six characteristics that learners need to develop in order to become autonomous learners (referred to at the beginning of the paper) our data shows that all the participants (not surprisingly) could organize appropriate times and venues for meeting.

Table 1: The total number of meetings held by partners

Number of meetings	Number of respondents
1 – 2	2
3 – 4	5
5 – 9	4
10 – 14	1
15 – 20	4
20+	1
Total	17

Table 1 summarizes the number of meetings held up to April 1994, though many of the exchanges continued after this date. The most common meeting arrangement was once a week (13 respondents) for one hour (see Table 2) though one pair had been meeting for 4-5 hours on four consecutive Sunday mornings and the respondent felt this was so useful he had requested a further partner for midweek meetings! All of the meetings took place on campus, mostly in the self-access centre or student halls and canteens. A few respondents mentioned the lack of suitable venues, and it would be interesting to know whether partners meet in the self-access centre through lack of alternatives or through preference for a less informal study setting. Likewise, would students elsewhere be so conservative in their choice of meeting places, or is this specific to Hong Kong's spatial and cultural milieu?

Table 2: The average length of meetings

Length of meetings in hours	Number of respondents
1	11
1 – 2	4
2 – 3	2
3 – 4	0
4 – 5	1
Total	18

Table 3 shows the nature of the language exchange taking place between respondents. It should be noted that all but four of these exchanges are between native and target language speakers.

Table 3: Languages exchanged by respondents

Languages	Number of respondents
English — Mandarin	10
English — English	4
English — Cantonese	1
Cantonese — French	1
Cantonese — Japanese	1
Cantonese — German	1
Total	18

Apart from organizing appropriate times and venues, participants have also demonstrated their ability to negotiate the procedure of their language exchange. The only guideline given to them suggested that they spend half their time talking in each other's language. Eleven respondents reported having a 50/50 language exchange within each meeting. At least three definitions of '50/50' appear to be operating, however. For some it means that the first half of the meeting is in one language and the second half is in the other language. For others it is a 'mutual exchange' where each partner asks the other about idiomatic expressions and how to use them, while for one pair it means that each person speaks only in the other's language. Though consultants had tended to recommend alternate meetings in each language, only three respondents organized meetings in this way. This again suggests that *autonomous* learners are able to make their own choices in spite of contrary advice from 'experts'. For the respondents meeting in a group (three Cantonese and one Japanese), 100% of meeting time occurs in the target language.

Likewise, our findings suggest that with regard to setting objectives and selection of appropriate materials and study techniques, our respondents are well on the road to autonomy. Though the methods and materials used for exchanging languages vary greatly, *chatting* figures prominently, with most pairs having it as some component of their meeting. In two cases textbooks were used for the beginner partner but chatting for the intermediate/advanced partner. Other activities which have been reported are: discussion of (prepared) newspaper and magazine articles; answering of prepared questions; correction of, and feedback on, written work; help with, and discussion of, homework.

A further characteristic of autonomy is a capacity for self-assessment, or self-monitoring of progress. A number of our participants were able to identify what they felt they had learned from the exchange and what they still needed and wanted to learn. Perhaps not surprisingly, respondents reported improvements in the productive aspect of language: six mentioned increased fluency and confidence in expressing ideas in conversation, while three mentioned pronunciation and four colloquial phrases and vocabulary. Grammar, listening comprehension and reading have also been mentioned by individual participants.

On the other hand, four participants expressed disappointment that they were unable to learn as much as they had hoped to — areas they cited were accent, pronunciation, slang, vocabulary and writing. However, it would be interesting to know whether the partners of these participants agreed with their negative self-assessment, for, in at least two instances, respondents reported improvement in their partner's language, in contrast to their own perceived lack of progress.

Factors influencing successful language exchange

If there was a perceived lack of success in any given conversation exchange, it was usually attributed to one of three factors:

1. learning organization ("a lack of structure to meetings"; "she's not teaching me, we just chat");
2. language skills ("my language skills were not good enough to make the sessions useful"; "my partner had better language and dominated"; "lack of proper monitoring as we are not native speakers"); or
3. time ("it takes a long time"; "too busy to arrange meetings").

The comments made by respondents suggest that the factors leading to failure could be minimized by some initial learner training to show participants the diverse possibilities for conducting language exchanges, by asking applicants to specify more clearly their learning objectives, and by stressing that a certain degree of commitment is necessary for successful language exchange.

What makes the exchanges successful is very closely linked to explanations for why the exchange has been enjoyable. Of the 18 respondents who met partners only one did not enjoy it as there was a personality clash. Indeed, a major factor affecting both enjoyment and success is the personal nature of conversation exchange. At least 12 references were made to this aspect: participants were very pleased with the pairing, got along together well because they were the same age, or had the same interests, or the same level of commitment to learning; some also thought this was a friendly way to learn and a good way of making friends. These comments emphasize the importance of affective factors for successful language exchange.

Other comments highlight two further aspects of 'good language learning' apart from the importance of the affective domain: the need to build language confidence and the relevance of intercultural communication for meaningful language learning. Participants stated that they enjoyed the opportunity to speak and increase their confidence, to learn grammar and pronunciation from a native speaker, to learn how to be polite in another language, and to learn about a different culture and discuss interesting topics. A participant from the group reported that "it's a real-time learning and everyone tried to speak out and get involved".

Based on their own experience of the conversation exchange, respondents were asked to give advice to other students joining the conversation exchange in the future. The kinds of advice they gave can be categorized into the following three areas:

1. Selection of an appropriate partner — this will help to ensure an equally beneficial exchange (participants' perceptions of equality of exchange vary according to their language level, their perceptions of language learning and their personality). The following comments are taken from questionnaire responses: "be careful in screening prospective partners"; "find a good one"; "find one with a better language standard than yours"; "don't let your partner's desire to learn and practise overrule your needs"; "girls speak clearer"(!); and "take advantage of the variety of nationalities and languages spoken here".

2. Meeting organization and commitment — comments included: "meet frequently and regularly"; "insist on one meeting each week"; and "have a one-hour session".

3. Self-direction and language-learning organization — comments included: "make a plan and discuss it with your partner"; "you need to have a clear idea of what you want to learn"; "make the topic interesting"; "try to speak out and be relaxed"; and "be patient, one doesn't learn a language in a month".

Recommendations

The following recommendations, based on our observations, analysis of the data and responses from the participants, are intended as pointers for others who may be considering setting up conversation exchange schemes.

1. The exchange should be reciprocal. Even if there is a difference in language levels, maturity or personality, the partners need to perceive each other as participants in a *mutually beneficial* exchange. They also need to be made aware, from the beginning, of the need for negotiation: of learning objectives, of study techniques and materials, of the time, place and organization of their meetings.

2. Though many participants are capable of making their own choices regarding the organization of their language exchange, some will benefit from guidance as to the possibilities for various kinds of learning implicit in the scheme. Apart from designing an application form that will help learners to clarify what they want to get out of the conversation exchange, consultants could also provide a more detailed set of written guidelines for participants. An indication of the various factors which have led to successful exchanges in the past may be helpful in this context.

3. Participants need to be made aware of the importance of providing feedback to their partners during the exchange. It should be stressed that they need to encourage their partners and let them know in what ways they are improving. Respondents' comments show that partners *are* aware of their partners' improvement but not of their own. However, we do not know whether they ever verbalized this to one another.

4. In order to have a large pool of participants to ensure a high probability of matching applicants, publicity for a conversation exchange needs to be as wide as possible and as high profile as possible. Within the context of Hong Kong tertiary institutions, for instance, this could mean making the scheme available to non-Cantonese-speaking members of the expatriate business community as well as ensuring that new, non-Cantonese-speaking members of staff within the institution are made aware of the possibility of language exchange for learning Cantonese.

5. Both applicants and consultants need to be aware of the need for compatibility at a personal level as well as at the level of learning objectives and commitment. One of the unanswered questions that arises from our respondents' comments is why people failed to contact

the consultants when nobody contacted them or when they got an inappropriate partner, even though all applicants were asked to report back if there were any difficulties. In this context, we feel that a conversation exchange scheme could be improved by periodically bringing together participants in larger groups, for example in conversation exchange 'parties' and discussion and feedback sessions, so that new exchanges could be initiated spontaneously and existing ones could be developed. There is also a case for organizing orientation workshops both to facilitate the partner selection process and to give some learner training to those who need it.

Conclusion

The responses to the questionnaire show that, for those who met, the conversation exchange scheme has been largely successful. However, there is obviously still room for improvement, both to ensure that participants make initial contact (for instance in group orientation sessions) and to improve feedback mechanisms so that consultants can guide more participants to more successful exchanges. In terms of research, we need to find out whether those who are not paired with native speakers of their target language have been able to get as much out of the scheme as those who responded to the questionnaire. What their responses demonstrate is the mutual, reciprocal and equal nature of successful language exchanges, a process in which there is negotiation, not simply of meaning in the target language(s), but also of learning objectives, of study materials and techniques, and of the mechanics of meeting. They show that autonomous learning is possible and is already being practised by some. Moreover, a carefully planned language exchange scheme can help make others more aware of how they too can attain as high a level of autonomous learning as the best of our respondents.

APPENDIX 1: The Application Form for 1992–3

The Conversation Exchange Form

Do you need conversation practice in English or another language?

The conversation exchange programme puts students together who wish to practise conversing in English, or in other languages. If you want to practise different languages, then speak the one language for half the time, and the other for half the time. You and your partner are completely free to arrange where, how, and how long you meet, or to stop meeting. All the consultation desk coordinator does is give you a suitable partner's name and number.

Name: _____ Age: _____ Male/Female: _____

Department: _____ Contact phone number: _____

First language: _____ Other languages spoken well: _____

Desired language to practise: _____

Interests/Hobbies/Sports: _____

THE CONVERSATION EXCHANGE RECORD

You have been paired with _____ Phone no: _____

Date: _____ Consultant's initials: _____

Reported back on: _____ Consultant's initials: _____

Comments: _____

APPENDIX 2: Instructions and Guidelines for Participants

The Conversation Exchange Contact Sheet

Partner's Name: ———————————— Phone No:————————

When you receive this please contact your partner as soon as possible to arrange your first meeting at a place you both know and at a convenient time. Describe yourself and what you will be wearing. The first meeting may be a bit difficult, so use the information on this sheet to ask questions about each other and to stimulate conversation. Good Luck.

P.S. After you have met your partner, please report back to the Consultation Desk. If you want a new partner, also let us know.

Conversational topics to ask your partner about (if you need them):

Talk about: your family, your home, your best friend(s), places you have been to, your favourites (books/movies/singers/actors/sports personalities/restaurants/etc).

What is on your agenda for the next week?

What have you done this past week? Today, so far?

What do you think of HKU? Your course? Your teachers?

Why do you want to practise another language?

What do you like about speaking another language?

How do you think one learns a language best?

What do you think about (something that has happened this week)?

Adapted from Tim Murphey: *Teaching One to One*, pp.125-6, Longman 1991.

APPENDIX 3: The Application Form for 1993-4

The Conversation Exchange Form

Do you need conversation practice in English or another language?

The conversation exchange programme puts students together who wish to practise conversing in English, or in other languages. If you want to practise different languages, then speak the one language for half the time, and the other for half the time. You and your partner are completely free to arrange where, how, and how long you meet, or to stop meeting. All the consultation desk coordinator does is give you a suitable partner's name and number.

Name: _____ ☐ Male   ☐ Female   Age: _____

Department: _____

Year (please √)   ☐ 1   ☐ 2   ☐ 3   ☐ PG   ☐ Staff

Place of residence: _____ Contact phone number: _____

First Language: _____

Other languages spoken well: _____

Desired language(s) to practise: _____

Partner preference (please √)

Gender?   ☐ male   ☐ female   ☐ either

How many?   ☐ one   ☐ two   ☐ three

Native speaker?   ☐ not important   ☐ yes, of _____

Faculty/Department?   ☐ not important   ☐ yes, of _____

Best time for meeting partner? _____

What are your interests? _____

Appendix 3: to be continued

Appendix 3: continued

THE CONVERSATION EXCHANGE RECORD

1. You have been paired with _____

Phone no: _____

Date: _____ Consultant's initials: _____

_ _

Reported back on: _____ Consultant's initials: _____

Comments: _____

_____

_____

APPENDIX 4: The Questionnaire

HKU Conversation Exchange

In order to improve our Conversation Exchange service we are conducting a survey to find out more about how it has been used. We would therefore welcome your feedback and would be grateful if you would kindly complete the following questionnaire. Please give as much information as possible.

1   Did you make contact with a conversation exchange partner/partners? (PLEASE CIRCLE)

   YES (please complete questions **3, 4 & 5**)
   NO (please complete questions **2, 5, & 6**)

2   What was the problem? (Please explain as fully as possible why no contact was made)

3   After the initial (phone) contact, did you have further meetings? (PLEASE CIRCLE)

   YES
   NO (if 'NO' please answer questions **2, 5, & 6**)

4   As everyone uses the conversation exchange in different ways please answer the questions below and provide any other information necessary to give us a clear picture of what you did after you had contacted your partner.

Meeting Organization

   Totally, how many times did you meet?
   How frequently?
   How long was each session?
   Where did the sessions take place?
   Any other comments about how you organized the meetings?

Learning Organization

   Which languages were you studying?
   YOU _____ YOUR PARTNER _____
   How did you divide the time spent on each language, e.g. 50/50 each session or alternate sessions of each?

What teaching/learning methods and materials did you use e.g. textbooks, videos, chatting?

Overall

Did you **enjoy** the conversation exchange? (why/why not?)
Was it useful/successful for your language learning i.e. what did you learn/what didn't you learn?
Can you account for your success or lack of success?
What advice would you give to another student joining the Conversation Exchange?

5   Would you use the Conversation Exchange again? (why/why not?)

6   How can the Conversation Exchange system be improved?

9

Autonomy in the classroom: peer assessment

Lindsay Miller and Raymond Ng

Introduction

Promoting learner autonomy in the classroom has taken on a new focus recently with the establishment of self-access centres in many institutes throughout the world. Self-access centres rely not only on well-planned implementation and good management, but also on the learners' ability and willingness to use them. Miller and Gardner (1994) point out that much more research needs to be conducted into self-access language learning for it to become a viable supplement to classroom-based teaching. The project described in this chapter reports on one way of preparing learners for the responsibilities of monitoring and assessing their own language skills. In so doing, learners can work more efficiently and effectively in an autonomous environment such as a self-access centre.

Involving learners in their own language learning is not a new idea. There are many ways in which learners can become involved in curriculum decisions. They can help to define the input of a language programme as in a negotiated syllabus (Clarke 1991), they can actively participate in course management as a course progresses (Littlejohn 1983), or they can be involved in assessment of their learning. This chapter discusses how learners can be involved in their assessment.

Background

Various studies have been conducted into learner involvement in assessment. The following examples from the literature show how learners can be involved at the initial stage when placed onto a course, while the course is in progress through peer feedback, and in negotiating final assessment grades.

Spaventa and Williamson (1989) demonstrate how learner involvement can take place at the beginning of a course. These authors describe their experience in changing the placement procedure of a language programme in a large American university. According to the authors, the old placement battery was replaced with a new procedure which incorporated an oral exercise to gauge face-to-face communication skills. In this "synchronous discussion exercise" the teachers place themselves under a sign for the course levels, from Beginner to Advanced. Individual students then go to talk with a teacher at the level they think they can cope with. If the teacher feels that the student is at the wrong level, he or she can recommend that the student talk to someone at another level, and the procedure is repeated until both teacher and student feel that the student is at the appropriate course level. In evaluating this procedure, Spaventa and Williamson (ibid.: 90) observe: "Teachers meet students first as walking, talking wholes, not as a series of number two pencil markings on Scantron scoring paper". They maintain that "... a placement process in which administrators, students, and teachers participate as subjects of their own learning is better than a placement battery in which they are passive executors and recipients of standardized testing measures" (ibid.: 75).

Learners can also be involved in their assessment as a course progresses through peer review or peer evaluation. The purpose here is to turn passive recipients into active participants on a language programme. Peer review / evaluation, whereby students comment on and/or evaluate each others' drafts, has become a popular activity in process writing courses. Many writers have commented on the value of these methods. Jacobs (1988: 74) remarks that peer review "can play a role in the development of writing ability by giving students additional perspectives from which to learn and apply writing skills". Mittan (1989) observes that peer evaluation provides students with an authentic audience, allows them to read their own writing critically, and helps students to gain confidence in their writing. An extra benefit of peer evaluation, according to Lockhart and Ng (1993), is that it promotes a high degree of interaction among students in a class. All of these are positive attributes that peer review/evaluation can bring to the language class.

It is easy to understand why involving students in reviewing or evaluating their work has mainly taken place in writing courses, where:

1. students can be taught how to use a marking system relatively quickly;
2. there is often a 'right' and 'wrong' way, in terms of subject-verb agreement, use of preposition, etc.; and
3. as much time as necessary can be devoted to analyzing the text.

Another study which uses writing as the mode of assessment is that of Haughton and Dickinson (1989). This study reports on collaborative post-writing assessment. Haughton and Dickinson describe how non-native students on an MA programme for English Language teachers at Moray House in Scotland evaluated their own written assignments and then negotiated the grade they finally received with their tutor.

Haughton and Dickinson set out to test nine hypotheses in their study. Five dealt with the practicability of their scheme, as follows:

1. students are sincere and do not use the scheme as a means of obtaining higher grades than they themselves think they deserve;
2. students are or become able to assess themselves at about the same level as their tutors, i.e. they can interpret the criteria in the same way;
3. students are or become able to negotiate with tutors on the appropriate level of criteria;
4. students are or become able to negotiate grades in a meaningful and mutually satisfying manner; and
5. the scheme does not result in a lowering of standards on the course.

The other four hypotheses dealt with the benefits of the scheme, as follows :

1. students perceive collaborative assessment as fairer than other (traditional) forms of assessment;
2. students benefit in enhanced understanding of and attitude towards assessment;
3. students become more self-directed as a result; and
4. the scheme demands more thoroughly worked out criteria of assessment and hence results in fairer assessment.

Haughton and Dickinson claim that to a large extent the scheme worked and that the students were able to assess their own work realistically. Generally, their assessments did not differ by more than one grade from those of the tutors. Similar reliability of results in self-evaluation was found by Bachman and Palmer (1982) who investigated the self-rating of communicative language ability of a group of general ESL learners in the USA whose ages ranged from 17–67, and Fok (1981) who looked at a group of university students in Hong Kong and found a high degree of similarity between the students' self-assessment and past academic records for Reading and Speaking.

The above-cited studies demonstrate that with careful planning and good administration, learner involvement in language programmes can yield positive results. The question now arises as to why it is not a more common feature in all language programmes. Part of the problem may lie in teacher uncertainty as to how students will react: will it be seen as an abdication of responsibility or as a positive step in learner involvement? Furthermore, as we have already stated, it is relatively easy to implement learner involvement as part of a writing course, but it becomes more difficult for the other language skills. The dearth of reported research in this area attests to this.

This chapter is a first attempt to involve learners in assessing their speaking skills. In this study, students in a BA TESL speaking skills proficiency course were given the opportunity to assess each others' oral language ablity. The results of the students' assessments were used as part of their final course grade.

The project

Forty-one students took part in the project described here. They were young adult learners studying in their first year at a university in Hong Kong. The students were mainly taking proficiency modules in English — one of which was Speaking. In this course it was decided to include an element of peer assessment as part of the programme. The students were first of all given a two-hour lecture on the process of preparing, administering and marking an oral test. As we had a large group of students and only two hours in which to sensitize them to the process of oral assessment, we used a conversational style, non-participatory mode of presentation. The two researchers talked about and gave various examples of how to prepare, administer and mark oral tests. Some of the areas covered were: who/why/ what to test, types of oral tests (preparation); timing, prompting, scoring (administration); and accuracy vs. fluency, standardization of marks, marking scales (marking). After the lecture the students formed groups in order to do the task. They were given a week in which to prepare their tests.

Each group of students was given 30 to 40 minutes to test another group from their class (each group had four members). A wide variety of testing activities were designed by the students, including picture description, reading dialogues, situational conversation, group discussion, job interview and describing feelings. Reading dialogues, picture description and answering questions regarding the picture were the most popular test types. These are common types of oral testing activities which our students have been exposed to while at secondary school.

Most groups aimed to test students on vocabulary, fluency and pronunciation. Again, our students' ideas will have come from their own experience as testees in secondary school. However, grammatical accuracy, also greatly emphasized in the secondary language curriculum in Hong Kong, received relatively little attention in the peer assessment. This lack of attention to grammar is perhaps related to the fact that fluency was the area that was most emphasized in the speaking skills course.

After the tests had been conducted, the students gave their test results to the tutor. The tutors had sat in on all the tests and conducted their own ratings of the students' performances. A comparison was then made between the peer assessment and the tutors' assessment.

Table 1: Peer and lecturer's assessment for class A

Students	Peer assessment		Lecturer's assessment	
	Grade	(Marks)	Grade	(Marks)
S1	B	(70)	B	(70)
S2	C	(53)	C-	(52)
S3	B-	(65)	C	(61)
S4	B+	(72)	C+	(64)
S5	C	(61)	B	(65)
S6	B	(68)	C	(61)
S7	B	(70)	B	(70)
S8	B-	(67)	A-	(75)
S9	A-	(75)	B+	(74)
S10	B	(70)	B+	(72)
S11	A-	(75)	A-	(75)
S12	C	(61)	C	(61)
S13	B	(68)	C	(61)
S14	B	(71)	B+	(72)
S15	C	(61)	C+	(62)
S16	B-	(65)	C+	(64)
S17	B-	(65)	C+	(64)
S18	B	(68)	C	(61)
S19	C+	(64)	B-	(65)
S20	B	(70)	B	(70)

Table 2: Peer and lecturer's assessment for class B

Students	Peer assessment		Lecturer's assessment	
	Grade	(Marks)	Grade	(Marks)
S1	B	(71)	B+	(72)
S2	B	(68)	B	(68)
S3	B-	(65)	B-	(65)
S4	A-	(75)	A-	(75)
S5	C-	(52)	B-	(65)
S6	C+	(64)	B	(68)
S7	C	(61)	A-	(74)
S8	C-	(52)	B-	(65)
S9	C	(60)	B+	(72)
S10	A-	(75)	B+	(74)
S11	A-	(75)	B+	(74)
S12	B-	(67)	B	(68)
S13	C	(61)	B	(68)
S14	B+	(72)	B	(71)
S15	B-	(65)	B-	(65)
S16	B+	(72)	B	(70)
S17	A-	(75)	B+	(74)
S18	B-	(67)	B	(68)
S19	C	(61)	B-	(65)
S20	B	(71)	B+	(72)
S21	B+	(72)	B+	(72)

As can be seen from Tables 1 and 2, the letter grades for peer assessment and the lecturer's assessment appear quite similar. For class A there were five grades that matched exactly, eight grades which differed by only one point, e.g. A- vs. B+, and seven grades which differed by two points, e.g. B- vs. C. In class B, six of the grades matched exactly, eight had only one point difference, two had two points difference, and four had more than two points difference.

A Spearman Rank Correlation Coefficient was used to compare the rank order of the numerical marks in Tables 1 and 2. For class A the correlation coefficient is rs = .68, while for class B it is rs = .8. Therefore, there is a relatively high level of agreement between the peer assessments and the marks given by the lecturers, particularly in class B.

Students' reflections

After completing the task of peer assessment, and before receiving any feedback from the lecturers, the students were asked to reflect on what they had done and to write some comments in response to the following questions:

1. Were you given enough time to prepare the test?
2. How did you feel about conducting the test?
3. How did you feel about assessing the candidates?
4. How did you feel about being assessed by your classmates? Do you think their scores on your oral ability are reliable?
5. Did you learn anything from taking part in this oral assessment?
6. Would you like more peer assessment?

Table 3: Student responses to the peer assessment task (n=41)

	Positive comments	Negative comments	Neutral comments
Question 1: Preparation	36	5	0
Question 2: Conducting the test	25	16	0
Question 3: Assessing the candidates	7	34	0
Question 4 : (a) Being assessed by your classmates (b) Reliability	16 7	25 28	0 0
Question 5: Did you learn anything?	35	3	3
Question 6: Would you like more tests like this?	18	20	3

Table 3 above shows the number of positive, negative and neutral comments made by the students in the evaluation questionnaire on oral peer assessment. The following is a summary of their views.

Preparing the test

Many of the students felt that the test was not difficult to prepare since they had taken a number of oral tests in secondary school in the past. They also thought that it was easy to find test material suitable for the level of their classmates. Some students suggested that working in a group enabled them to share and discuss a wide range of ideas concerning testing. This made the job of preparing the test easier and more interesting.

Conducting the test

The majority of students said that they had no trouble conducting the test, with some making reference to the fact that they felt well-prepared. However, a number of students did find conducting the test somewhat difficult. One reason was mistiming: "We wasted much time giving instructions to the testees", said one student. Another reason concerned the poor coordination of the testers, as evidenced in the following comment: "Sometimes, all of us wanted to ask questions, at other times no one spoke". There was also the problem of arousing or sustaining the candidate's interest in the test. One student reported that her group had difficulty in keeping the conversation with the candidate going.

Assessing the candidates

Students were in general very negative about assessing candidates. Some thought that this was a subjective task and that there was bound to be unfairness involved. Others found that it was hard to make discriminations because the candidates had similar standards. It was also pointed out that one often had to argue before reaching a compromise with the other testers in the group about the grade to award, thus making the job of peer assessment arduous and time-consuming.

Being assessed by peers

Many of the students did not like being assessed by their classmates as it was a situation they were not used to. One student put the matter very succinctly: "I can hardly imagine that I am the candidate and they are the examiners." Others who also felt uncomfortable being assessed by peers made comments to the effect of losing face in front of their classmates. One student remarked, "We are assumed to have equal status, but if I got the lowest mark in the test, I will be quite upset."

Over a third of the students, however, were positive about the experience of being assessed by their peers. They thought that the 'fun' element was an important aspect of this type of assessment. There were several comments like the following: "I find it quite enjoyable as I treated the test as fun."

Reliability of peer assessment

Most students were doubtful about the reliability of peer assessment. The most common reason cited was that they felt inexperienced as testers. They would much rather have had an examiner who was more qualified and proficient in English than they were themselves — in short, they preferred to be assessed by the lecturer rather than by their peers.

Oral testing as a process of learning

Many of the students recognize that peer assessment is an effective way of facilitating learning. The following two remarks highlight what they learned — how to prepare and administer an oral test, and how to work with others: "I learned how to conduct a speaking test, how to select and tailor testing materials. I learned to pay attention to people's pronunciation, accent and problems of speaking." "I learned to appreciate other's ideas even though they were different from mine. It was interesting to find that different people had different interpretations for the same question."

More peer assessment in future?

In answer to this last question, the students were divided in their responses, with about half of them in favour of more peer assessment and the other half against it. It should be pointed out that most of the students answered the question with a simple 'yes' or 'no'. But of the comments that were made, several reflect the idea that the students would prefer the test to be labelled differently: "... please don't mention the word 'test' or 'assessment' because I feel more comfortable and perhaps speak better in a natural environment rather than in a test centre."

Discussion

The results of this action research demonstrate that under certain circumstances language students are able to make a realistic assessment of each others' oral language ability. To be able to do this, certain conditions must be present:

1. the students must be high proficiency language learners;
2. the group should be homogeneous;
3. the group should have had some previous exposure to each others' oral language ability;
4. the tests must be conducted in an environment which is, as far as possible, unthreatening; and
5. the students should be given some assistance in preparing their tests.

As the A level English grades of our students correlate to TOEFL scores from 530–560 we can say that they have a high level of language ability. We can call our students 'sophisticated language learners' in that they have reached a high level of communicative competence, they are actively involved in pursuing their language studies further, and they demonstrated their ability to cope with a complex concept in a second language — testing.

To be able to assess their peers' oral skills, students must be able to access some implicit or explicit criteria. The researchers in this study did not give the students a set of testing criteria; rather, the students were required to establish their own. We believe that our students, because they are a homogeneous group, have an internal set of rules governing the use — and abuse — of English. These 'rules' are used whenever they hear English being spoken by another Cantonese speaker, or when they themselves use English. In this way, our students were able to establish criteria of acceptable language use. We do not know what the results would be if, say, a Cantonese speaker of English were to try to assess a Spanish speaker of English. As Spaventa and Williamson (1989: 78) point out: "... students who come from a Japanese background and students who come from a European background have different abilities in the traditional language skill areas".

To make a fair and reliable assessment of oral ability, the testers must either be trained in testing and have experience as testers, or be familiar with the testees' oral ability. By conducting the oral tests halfway through the course, we gave the students enough time (six weeks) to become accustomed to their peers' oral abilities before we asked them to assess each other. In this way, our students were better prepared for the task of judging their peers.

As all our students were familiar with each other, the tests were conducted under friendly circumstances. This ensured that the candidates were able to perform to the best of their ability. Jones (1985: 81) explains the importance of an examiner/examinee relationship and concludes, "... ease of elicitation in an oral interview is often affected by the social relationship between the examiners and the examinee. The factors can include age, race, social class, education and profession." As all our students had similar social profiles, we feel this was an important factor in their ability to assess each other fairly.

As lecturers we have substantial testing experience, both within the academic setting of our institute and as external examiners (International English Language Testing Service, Hong Kong Examinations Authority). It would therefore be unfair to compare an untrained tester's first attempts at oral assessment with our own assessments of the students. This is why we gave our students information and some help in constructing their tests, substantial time to put the test together and groups to work in when making their assessment. Without this help, our students may not have constructed such interesting tests and may have relied solely on intuition in making the assessments.

The construction of the tests and criteria for assessment were part of the learning experience we wanted to give our learners. However, this may be unrealistic with less motivated students. We believe that in other situations a teacher-generated test and set of marking criteria would work as effectively, if not better, than the method we used with our students.

Littlejohn (1983) demonstrated how relatively low-level language learners, coming from a traditional educational background, took some responsibility for course management decisions. How much more responsibility, then, should we give to high proficiency language learners? In the study presented here, we allowed the students to be responsible for 20% of the course mark — in other situations this could be as high as 100%, depending on the type of students involved and their learning environment. We were conservative in the amount of responsibility we gave to our students because we did not know how the students would react to the task, and we did not know if the students could realistically assess their peers. In the end, 20% peer assessment was probably about right in our situation as our students were able to complete the task, although some of their comments indicated that they felt their teacher's assessment to be more reliable.

There is an obvious reason for involving our students in peer assessment: many of them will eventually become English Language teachers and have to develop the skills of testers at some stage in their training. However, as Lublin (1980) points out, higher education ought to produce people who can take responsibility for their own actions and judgements. It is fair to say that any attempt at learner-centred methodology, such as the project discussed here, is a positive step in this direction, as it makes students more aware of their potential as learners who can affect their own learning.

Several of the hypotheses set out by Haughton and Dickinson (1989) can be tested in our study. From our results we can conclude that:

1. our students were sincere in taking part in this peer assessment exercise;
2. they demonstrated a similar level of assessment to that of the lecturers;
3. the scheme did not result in a lowering of standards; and
4. our students benefited in their understanding of and attitude towards assessment by taking part in this study.

One further point must be commented on. Two-thirds of the learners did not perceive their oral assessment of their peers as reliable. The learners commented on this point before they were aware of how similar their scoring was compared with the lecturers' scores. We feel that because this was our learners' first experience of peer assessment of oral skills, they lacked confidence in themselves. Some learner training in oral assessment during class activities may have been helpful, and we shall endeavour to implement this in future speaking skills courses.

Limitations of the study

The present study clearly affirms the feasibility of peer assessment of oral language proficiency. However, the study is not devoid of limitations.

The small sample of the study is obviously a constraint which makes interpretation of the results limited. The present study is exploratory in nature, and its results are therefore only indicative of the ability of the students within one specific group in testing one another's oral language skills. To generalize the findings to all Chinese students studying in Hong Kong would require a much larger sample size.

The subjects in this study were interested learners of English and were highly motivated throughout the peer assessment project. Their awareness of the practical nature of the job of testing each others' oral language ability in relation to the course and to their prospective career as language teachers contributed to the effective running of the project. It is uncertain whether such positive results would have been achieved if the subjects were non-TESL major students. Research with learners from different study areas is needed before we can extend the findings further.

The researchers of this study were obviously keen about peer assessment as a means of developing students' oral language skills. Yet, according to the students' reflections, there was apprehension about the task of assessing each other and a lack of confidence about the reliability of such a testing method. If the students had had the opportunity of increasing their self-confidence through practising peer assessment in other situations in the class before the oral test, the discrepancy between teacher and student perceptions of the validity of their assessment may have been resolved.

Suggestions for further research

As a result of the findings from the research reported on here, and as a consequence of the limitations of the study, there are several areas in peer assessment which are worth considering for future research.

1. In the current research many of the students reported that they did not think the evaluations by their peers were reliable. However, the results indicate otherwise. We should therefore investigate whether some form of pre-training in peer assessment might encourage the learners to view the results as more reliable. For example, opportunities in class to discuss with their teacher, and with each other, evaluation of speaking skills.

2. If students can assess their peers' oral language reliably can they also assess their own language skills? Much of the work in self-access centres requires learners to monitor their own learning. If it can be shown that learners are capable of doing this we may have more confidence in promoting individual study in self-access mode to our students.

3. This research investigated peer assessment in a highly motivated group of learners. We now need to do similar studies with groups of poor language learners, or non-language specialist students to see if they too can realistically assess their peers' language ability.

Conclusion

The study reported on here shows how the responsibility for testing students' oral language abilities need not rest solely with the teacher. The tests devised by our students and the results obtained indicate that high language level students of a homogeneous group with some experience of listening to each other in English and a little training in how to conduct an oral test can realistically assess each other's oral language skills.

As mentioned in the background section, peer review/assessment often plays an important role in writing courses. It has been well documented how the general ESL learner benefits from peer review/assessment of their writing (Jacobs 1988; Mittan 1989; Lockhart and Ng 1993) — the task now is to demonstrate how learners who are not language specialists can help each other in assessing their reading, listening and speaking skills.

Further research into peer and self-evaluation of oral skills in the classroom and in self-access centres is obviously needed. Until more research is conducted, and reported on, tutors and students alike will remain unsure of the learners' abilities in monitoring and assessing their oral skills. And the tutor will remain the focus for such assessment.

III

Materials

This section examines the design and use of materials for autonomous language learning. Chapter 10 focuses on learner-training materials from the point of view of the materials writer. Chapters 11 and 12 are concerned with the use of authentic materials, from the point of view both of the teacher and the learner.

In Chapter 10, Barbara Sinclair considers the question of explicitness in learner-training tasks. She finds that most activities in current ELT course books that are designed to promote learner autonomy are not presented in an explicit way, and are therefore not likely to develop language-learning awareness. However, as she points out, excessive explicitness can be equally problematic, and she goes on to consider questions of how much explicitness to include, how to present the information, and where to locate it. Sinclair then turns to materials in self-access centres and examines how to balance the need for learner training with the need to allow learners to make their own choices. She illustrates her points by showing the ways that the appropriate level of explicitness can be achieved in course materials and tasks designed for use in self-access centres.

In Chapter 11, Winnie Lee examines learner perceptions of authentic and pedagogic materials in a self-access situation. The findings from her study of self-access language learners shed light on the question of whether to use authentic or non-authentic textbook materials in developing learner autonomy. Lee concludes that authentic materials tended to be enjoyed more overall and to be preferred by higher proficiency students. However, they were in general not perceived to aid learning as effectively as textbooks, especially by learners of comparatively low proficiency; these learners sometimes feel bewildered and confused when faced with authentic material, lacking as it does the systematic organization that they are used to in ordinary textbooks. Lee suggests, therefore, that we should not avoid authentic materials, but rather help learners to use them more effectively. She ends with practical recommendations for making both the organization and the use of authentic materials more systematic, with the aim of gradually enabling learners to select and design their own tasks.

In Chapter 12, Elsie Christopher and Susanna Ho report on a self-access film discussion project, in which learners watched and then discussed (in groups) a series of movies. Generic and specific worksheets of the type recommended by Lee for use with authentic materials were provided as discussion catalysts. Christopher and Ho's data show that by the end of the project learners had become more confident in their speaking and participated more actively in discussions. The success of the project in this regard suggests that interaction in a non-threatening group situation can be a powerful way of building self-esteem — one of the preconditions for developing learner autonomy.

10

Materials design for the promotion of learner autonomy: how explicit is 'explicit'?

Barbara Sinclair

Introduction

This chapter considers the representation in published and self-access materials of the promotion of learner autonomy in language learning. Learner autonomy is by no means a new concept, but its promotion in the field of language learning through systematic learner development (most commonly referred to as *learner training*) is a relatively recent phenomenon. In particular, the design of tasks and materials which effectively promote such learner development has become a current issue of concern for materials writers and teachers.

Work in this field by Wenden (1987, 1991), Ellis and Sinclair (1989) and Oxford (1990) has highlighted the need for *explicit* learner training in such materials, i.e. an explicit focus on both the purpose of, as well as the strategies required by, language-learning tasks. Research (Brown et al. 1983; Duffy et al. 1986) has shown that this kind of explicitness is important for the successful promotion of learner autonomy. To what extent, however, is such an explicit focus on the learning process in English language materials possible? What is meant by 'explicit' and what should we be explicit about?

During the last decade publishers have increasingly become aware of the need to take account of learner autonomy in their English language course books. However, a recent survey (Sinclair and Ellis 1992) concludes that activities aiming to promote autonomy are often presented in an unprincipled and unexplicit way. It would seem that to achieve an explicit focus on learning to learn without overwhelming the language-learning aims of the materials or presenting the learners with additional hurdles, can be a difficult balancing act for materials writers.

In the light of the above, this chapter aims to raise some points for reflection by those involved in designing materials for the promotion of learner autonomy and to suggest some practical guidelines. Firstly, the chapter will consider briefly what is meant by 'learner autonomy' and 'learner training'. It will then focus on three issues:

1. the potential role of published language teaching materials in the promotion of learner autonomy;
2. the nature and degree of 'explicitness' in published language teaching materials; and
3. the implications of 'explicitness' for materials design for the self-access centre.

Learner autonomy and learner training

This chapter takes as its starting point the definition of learner autonomy provided by Henri Holec (1981: 3), which describes the autonomous learner as one who "is capable of taking charge of his own learning", i.e. "capable of determining objectives, defining contents and progressions, selecting methods and techniques to be used, monitoring and evaluating what has been learned". In other words, such a learner has the *capacity* to make informed decisions about his/her learning, but need not do so all of the time; the promotion of learner autonomy and the realization of individual potential are often cited as basic educational goals in our profession, and this humanistic view requires that teachers also accept that learner autonomy cannot be forced.

This chapter recognizes that a steady state of true autonomy is probably unattainable. Rather, this varies in degree in individual learners according to a range of variables or conditions, such as the learning situation they find themselves in, the topic of study and the type of learning task they are engaged in, as well as their awareness of task demands, their level of competence, degree of confidence and willingness, mood, motivation, reactions to the physical environment, and so on. One learner may well operate generally at a high level of autonomy outside the class, but tend to be completely dependent upon the teacher for direction for certain tasks while inside the class. Another learner may show great initiative in class one day and none at all the next. There may be times when a learner chooses to be dependent.

Holec's (1981: 3) view that the capacity and willingness to be autonomous in language learning is not necessarily innate has led to the development of techniques and procedures for helping learners learn how to learn, i.e. learner training. The term 'learner training' itself is sometimes criticized as not properly representing the processes of development which take place in the learner who is learning how to learn. Although the term 'learner development' is preferred by some working in this field, 'learner training' is, nevertheless, the label most commonly given. Learner training, as referred to in this chapter, ignores the narrow focus implied by the word 'training' and takes instead a broader, more educational view, as provided by the following definition:

> Learner training aims to help learners consider the factors which affect their learning and discover the learning strategies which suit them best, so that they may become more effective learners and take on more responsibility for their own learning. (Ellis and Sinclair 1989: 2)

The role of published materials in the promotion of learner autonomy

Anita Wenden (1991: 7) has suggested that teacher education is crucial for the successful introduction and promotion of learner autonomy, as it is for the management of any educational change. Certainly, the techniques and processes involved in learner training require teachers who are capable, motivated and informed. It can be argued that published language-teaching materials in which the promotion of learner autonomy is appropriately presented have a potentially important role to play in the creation and support of such teachers, as well as of more effective and autonomous learners.

Such materials can:

1. help teachers understand the rationale and procedures for learner training by providing direction and support, as well as direct examples of tasks; and
2. allow teachers to experiment with and reflect on learner-training practices and principles in their own teaching contexts and for an extended period of time — something teacher-training courses rarely provide.

The above points are important, for how many trainee or practising teachers actually have access to training courses on learner training? Furthermore, do such courses provide adequate training? One day in-service workshops, for example, are of limited help; the writer's experiences as a teacher trainer indicate that, while the concept of learner training may be quickly acquired, learning how actually to implement it in the classroom takes a good deal of time and practice. This practical application of the theory of the promotion of learner autonomy needs to be carefully addressed not only by teacher trainers and teachers, but also by materials writers.

There are now on the market a limited number of books intended to inform practising teachers and academics on the theory and research in the fields of learner autonomy, learner strategies and learner training (e.g. Wenden and Rubin 1987; Willing 1988, 1989; Ellis and Sinclair 1989; O'Malley and Chamot 1990; Oxford 1990; Wenden 1991). But how many English teachers around the globe actually have easy access to such handbooks or are even aware of their existence? How much of the expertise in these books can then be passed on in a practical way to the learners? Published *teaching* materials, however, are a resource made available to most English language teachers around the world in the course of their daily work. Although such materials are always subject to the interpretation of the teachers and the students, and may not be used in the manner in which they were intended or be used inappropriately, they can nevertheless be enormously influential; for those who do not teach their native language — a large majority of English language teachers in the world — they can be a vital source of information and support.

Publishers will continue to invest heavily in the promotion of their materials and to produce a wealth of new titles. Meanwhile, the competitive world of ELT requires publishers to keep abreast of the latest thinking and, at the same time, appeal to textbook buyers and teachers. The promotion of learner autonomy and learner training have, in the last ten years or so, become topics of interest for academics, teachers and materials writers and, as such, have now become saleable features of language course books. As a result, there has been a recent proliferation of English language teaching materials which purport to include these aims. Despite the current popularity of 'the promotion of learner autonomy', most course books do it rather badly, leaving the enormous potential of published teaching materials in this area, for the most part, unrealized.

Explicitness in learner-training materials

A recent survey of published language-teaching materials for both adult and young learners (Sinclair and Ellis 1992) aimed to investigate the ways in which these materials promoted learner autonomy through learner-training activities. The survey recognized that a number of interacting factors would determine how the learner training was presented and a set of criteria for assessing this was established.

One of the criteria focused on the *explicitness* of the learner training in the books, i.e. the extent to which the learner-training aspects of the materials were made obvious to the learners and the teachers, in Brown et al.'s (1983) terms, "informed" training, as opposed to "blind" training (training where the learner has no idea of the aim, focus or purpose of the learner-training task). Such explicitness is, perhaps, one of the most difficult things to achieve within the constraints set up by the act of publishing materials. However, experience of carrying out learner training indicates that it may be the single most significant feature of materials aiming to promote learner autonomy. As has been pointed out by Wenden (1987: 160), an explicit focus on learning to learn enables learners to focus on and evaluate strategies that they may be able to apply to different learning situations, to understand what they are doing and why.

There are a number of factors which influence the way in which learner training, and, hence, levels of explicitness, are incorporated into language-teaching materials, such as the target students' assumed ages, cultural backgrounds, levels, past learning experiences, expectations, attitudes, learning goals, motivation, as well as the length and type of course. However, once the writer has decided on the learner-training foci, the proportion and distribution of learner training in the course and the design of the tasks to be included, he or she has to wrestle with their presentation and the degree of explicitness to include.

It may be argued that, in order to carry out a learner-training task successfully, the learner should know the following about it:

1. that it **is** a learner-training task and its general significance in the scheme of the course;

    Learners who do not know in advance if their course is to focus on aspects of learner training may regard the time spent on such activities as time wasted; experience has shown that it is important that they should be informed of the aims of the learner training and its importance for their learning and developing autonomy. Learner-training tasks should be easily identifiable by the learners, possibly through the use of specific design features, such as colour coding, different typefaces, special headings etc.

2. the purpose of the task and its significance;

    Learners need to be aware of the learner-training focus of the task; for example, that a particular strategy is being focused on so that it can be practised and, if desired, later transferred to other learning tasks. To give another example, a task could enable learners to perceive that encouraging the exploration of individual attitudes towards specific aspects of language learning, such as pair work practice, is useful because attitudes can affect the way they learn and the progress they make.

3. what it requires the learner to do;

Learners need to recognize what the task demands of them, i.e. reflection, accuracy, risk-taking etc.

4. how to do the task;

Learners need to know how to attack a task. Such information is often included in the rubric.

5. whether it is a new type of task or one that is being recycled;

Clearly, task types which are novel to the learner need to be designed so that the information the student requires is clearly accessible. Task types which are being recycled for further practice may require less explicitness in their presentation, but learners may still need help in recognizing that they have already encountered such a task so that they can make use of previously tried and evaluated strategies.

6. the language with which to manage the task;

Some types of learner-training task may be carried out in the learners' mother tongue with no loss of learner-training benefit. However, most learners and teachers would expect to operate in the target language. Obviously, learners need to have the linguistic competence to do this and the language demands of the task need to be carefully considered. It may, for example, be useful for the text presented in a task introducing and raising awareness of skimming strategies to be at a level slightly below the competence of the learners, so far as this can be ascertained, so that linguistic difficulties do not interfere with the learner-training aims of the task.

Can a writer include all of the above information for each new learner-training task? A survey of most course books demonstrates that authors rarely try and that it is left to the teacher and learners to uncover the implicit. Research by Duffy et al. (1986), cited by Wenden (1991), demonstrated that when teachers explicitly informed learners of

1. what strategy they were learning,
2. how they should employ that strategy, and
3. in what contexts they should apply that strategy,

the students indicated a greater awareness of what they were learning and why, as one might expect. However, this research was concerned with *verbal* explanation. To what extent can a textbook writer rely on a teacher being able or willing to do this? This would imply the need to include notes or scripts for such explanations for teachers' use. Unfortunately, in practice, many authors do not include such extensive notes on learner training in their manuscripts, nor do many teachers make regular use of teachers' books accompanying course materials or have access to them.

Let us now consider more specifically some of the decisions which need to be made about learners' materials (see Figure 1 below). In doing so, it is necessary to recognize that decisions which favour the promotion of learner autonomy may conflict directly with the publisher's business constraints, such as the number of pages provided for, the design of the pages and the limitations imposed by layouts, and this can lead to materials being less effective than they might be.

In terms of providing the most explicit training for both learners and teachers, it may seem educationally and pragmatically more appropriate to focus the learner training entirely in the learners' materials. However, the constraints set up by publishing, such as page size, layout and number of pages, call for a compromise which places at least some of the learner-training information in the teacher's notes. The writer then needs to decide how much information about the learner training the teacher's notes should contain.

For example, which of the following should be included:

1. 'How to handle it in class' (step-by-step instructions)?
2. 'What to say' (a script for the teacher)?
3. Background theory (the development of and rationale for learner training)?
4. Theoretical rationales for each learner-training activity?
5. Recommended further reading on related issues?

Examples of a learner-training task

In order to consider in more detail the problems faced by a materials writer in making a learner-training task explicit, we can take as an example a very common classroom activity with a good deal of learner-training potential: helping learners guess the meanings of unknown words in a text from the clues provided by the text. If we were to view explicitness as a continuum, we would find a blind version of the task at one end and a highly explicit version at the other. Figures 2 and 3 present examples of such versions. In particular, note the differences in rubric content and length, as well as text content.

Figure 2 shows a task presented in its most common form in published

An introduction

Should there be an introduction in the learners' materials to induct the learners into the course content and approach, i.e. with a specific focus on the inclusion of learner training, or should this be in the teacher's notes, or in both?

Should this introduction be in prose or in the form of a chart or map, or both?

What language should this be in?

Should the introduction include a zero unit presenting tasks which exemplify learner-training principles? (For examples, see Geddes et al. 1986; Soars and Soars 1989.)

Headings / labels etc.

Should they be interesting and quirky to gain attention and motivate, or say exactly what the unit, task etc. is about?

e.g. "How's the dog?" versus "How to start a conversation with your neighbour".

Rubrics

How long can they be?

Should they explain to the learners or use a questioning approach?

How much metalanguage can they contain?

How much information should they contain? For example, should the aims of the task be stated? Should some of the task information be put in the teacher's notes? If so, how much?

What language should they be in?

If task types are recycled or regular features, how should this affect the rubric?

Figure 1: Some decisions to be taken about learners' materials

Guess the meanings of the words in *italics*:

Our holiday was wonderful. We stayed in a hotel *splunged* at the top of a *tronk*. The *poon* from our bedroom window was amazing. We could see the lake and the *slads* behind it. We watched people *wishwooshing* on the lake. Peter *noobled* how to windsurf. He wasn't very good at it. Dad went fishing and *flubbed* a large *goond*. The hotel chef *zicked* it for our dinner. It was very *ooby*.

Figure 2: An example of a 'blind' or unexplicit task

materials. Teachers and learners are left to uncover the purpose and significance of the task. In many classrooms there is merely a focus on checking answers with no further discussion as to how the learners made their guesses, and the learner-training potential of the task is ignored.

At the other extreme, Figure 3 below presents a task in which the level of explicitness is highly developed. While such explicitness may be useful, there is a danger that the rubrics and explanations may sound patronizing to many learners. Other issues to consider are the level of language in the rubrics and, thus, accessibility to the learners, and whether the target language or mother tongue should be used. Furthermore, the length of the task, as it is presented on the page, may have a demotivating effect on learners. Finally, for financial reasons, few publishers would find such a lengthy, page-consuming task acceptable in a course book. As already mentioned, a compromise might involve putting some of the explicit explanations and examples into the Teacher's Book with the intention that the teacher would encourage the learners to consider these factors. Relying on the teacher in this way, however, can be risky, as we have already noted, so it is particularly important for writers and publishers to be aware of the needs and levels of expertise of the teachers using the materials.

Another area for compromise might be in the design of the task itself, for example, by using a *questioning* approach which encourages reflection, discussion and a sharing of ideas, rather than a *telling* one. For example, "What do you do when you come across a word you don't know while you are reading?", instead of a paragraph explaining what "good readers" do. This kind of compromise is particularly beneficial if the materials are used by groups of students in a classroom setting where discussion can take place and where a teacher is confident about facilitating such learner training. In addition, a materials writer familiar with the target learners' cultural and educational backgrounds may be in a position to edit a highly explicit task so that it focuses on key issues relevant to those learners.

How to be a better reader: *guessing unknown words*

Good readers try to guess the meanings of words they don't know if they look important for understanding the text. Good readers depend more on themselves than on dictionaries.

(Adapted from Ellis and Sinclair 1989)

(a) Some words in the following text have been replaced by nonsense words. Can you guess what the original words could have been?

> Here's an example,

> "I missed the bus, so I *dibbed* home."

> *Dibbed could mean "walked" or some other way of transporting yourself.*

Sometimes you can guess from the meaning of the sentence.

> *You know what "to miss a bus" means, so the answer is logical.*

Sometimes you can guess from the word itself and from your knowledge of English grammar:

> *The word comes after "I" and ends in "-ed", showing that it is probably a verb in the simple past.*

You can use clues like these to help you guess the meaning of a word you don't know whenever you read a text.

(b) Now try it:

> The best way to learn new words and their meanings is by (1) *noobling*. By constantly meeting a word in its (2) *scrunge*, you will gradually understand more about the word's meaning. This is a much better way of (3) *squifferising* the meanings of words than using your (4) *liag* each time you feel (5) *boofed*.

(Adapted from Ellis and Sinclair 1989)

(c) Discuss your answers.

(d) How did you guess?

(e) Do you think you will use these strategies when you read? Why? Why not?

Figure 3: An example of a highly explicit task

To summarize, then, it is suggested that explicit learner-training tasks can play an important role in the promotion of learner autonomy by informing both teacher and learner. As we have seen, one of the more difficult aspects of achieving a desired level of explicitness in learners' materials concerns the use of rubrics. In addition, there needs to be an appropriate balance between information provided in the learners' materials and that given in the teacher's notes. The decisions which need to be taken by a materials writer can only be informed by a deeper understanding of the target students and their teachers. Inevitably, though, there will be compromise between the perceived needs of the learners and teachers and the business constraints faced by the publishers.

Implications for self-access learning

Having raised issues concerning explicitness in published materials, let us turn to materials for the self-access centre. What are the implications of the above discussion for the design of tasks for self-study?

Self-access learning poses its own dilemma; on one hand, the ultimate purpose of the self-access centre is to provide learners with the opportunity for self-direction; to allow learners to do what they like in whatever manner they like with whatever materials they choose, for a period of time specified by themselves. Learners must be allowed to make the materials their own and take from them whatever they wish. For example, left to themselves, different learners would probably approach the same written text in different ways and get from it different things; one might practise skimming, another might focus on new vocabulary, another might read the text purely for pleasure, and so on.

On the other hand, experience has shown that the average learner needs a period of guided induction and adjustment to the demands of self-directed learning, especially when it is presented in an institutionalized way in the form of a self-access centre. Without some kind of preparation for self-access learning, learners turned loose in a sea of collected materials, authentic or otherwise, generally tend to spend a lot of time in rather aimless activity, desperately seeking something interesting and useful to do, and end up feeling frustrated, even angry, and with a sense of wasted time. Indeed, according to a director of studies who runs a language school in Lyons in France which organizes its courses around a self-access centre, it takes, on average, some 30 hours of practice in a self-access centre before a new student feels satisfied that he or she is making good use of the facilities available.[1] Useful though such free experimentation may be in terms of learning about learning, most educational settings and most learners cannot afford this. It follows, then, that learners need help in order to get the most from a self-access centre in as economical a period of time as possible. In addition to such learner training, they also need, however, to have the freedom to choose their own pathways, to practise learner autonomy. The dilemma is how to provide both things.

There are two principal ways of dealing with this, which will be discussed below.

Learner training in the classroom

Perhaps the most commonly used approach is to provide explicit learner training in the classroom and a series of induction sessions as preparation for using a self-access centre. The learner training would, of course, be based on the needs of the learners, and would include increasing opportunities for self-direction. (For example, adult literacy and basic skills students taking the Communication Skills Programme provided by the British Council in Singapore in 1990-91 and who had had very limited experience of classroom learning found the concept of self-direction very difficult to accept.[2] They were regularly encouraged to choose practice and revision activities for self-study in the classroom under the supervision of the instructor. At first, the choice was between two alternatives and both were explained orally by the instructor before the students made their choice. It took some time for the students to accept that they had to choose one and not do both. Gradually, the choice was increased to three, then four, and so on. After some 240 hours of tuition, the students were happily doing self-directed learning in their lunch breaks, choosing from a wider range of materials and in the absence of a teacher.)

The induction sessions would focus students on the layout, systems and procedures in the self-access centre, provide them with opportunities to try working in it and to focus on experimentation and reflection. Learners would be encouraged to report back in class and to discuss their experiences, feelings and problems. They could also be encouraged to evaluate the strategies and materials they used and discuss these. Suggestions for implementing this kind of induction can be found in Ellis and Sinclair (1989: 56–61).

The disadvantages of this approach include the amount of time that needs to be spent in class on preparation. (While it is time well spent, it is not always recognized as such by learners or teachers with crammed syllabuses to follow.) Another is that this approach relies on the readiness and expertise of the teacher with regard to implementing such learner training in the classroom. As we have already seen, this readiness or expertise cannot always be relied upon in practice.

Learner training through self-access materials

Another approach would be to provide learner training in the self-access centre through the materials alone. As we have seen with the examples presented earlier, materials which aim to focus students explicitly on one or more aspects of the process of learning are directive, as are tasks which focus students on one or more linguistic points. However, autonomy can only be gained when students are free to focus on whatever they wish. Thus, it is suggested that there should be broadly two types of materials in a self-access centre, those which are directive and those which are not. *Directive materials* would include learner-training tasks, as well as language and skills practice exercises. *Non-directive materials* would consist of collections of authentic texts, both written and recorded.

Directive materials which provide language or skills practice are generally obvious to the learners. They may be labelled "Practice in the past simple", or "Comparatives" and so on. They may be colour-coded according to the skill they practise and the level of difficulty.

Directive materials which provide learner training need to be explicit in the ways discussed previously. This time, however, we cannot rely on the presence of a teacher for explanation or encouraging reflection. It is clear, then, that learner-training materials for the self-access centre do need more lengthy rubrics and explanations. The focus of the task needs to be explicitly stated, e.g. "Strategies for guessing unknown words in a text". Such rubrics might even need to be in the learners' mother tongue. A distinction may additionally be made between tasks which focus on different categories of strategies. For example, one category of tasks could focus principally on the development of metacognitive strategies, i.e. reflection about learning, such as thinking about how to learn, planning and evaluating learning. Another category might focus on a combination of metacognitive and cognitive strategy development, where cognitive learning strategies involve actually doing something with the language, such as predicting the topic of a text from its title or processing new vocabulary. A category of tasks with such a combined focus is important; practical experience of learner training suggests that the most effective learner development takes place when training combines reflection and experimentation, i.e. thinking about the learning, as well as actually doing it (O'Malley et al. 1985; Ellis and Sinclair 1986) .

Materials in a self-access centre could thus be organized hierarchically, as shown in Figure 4.

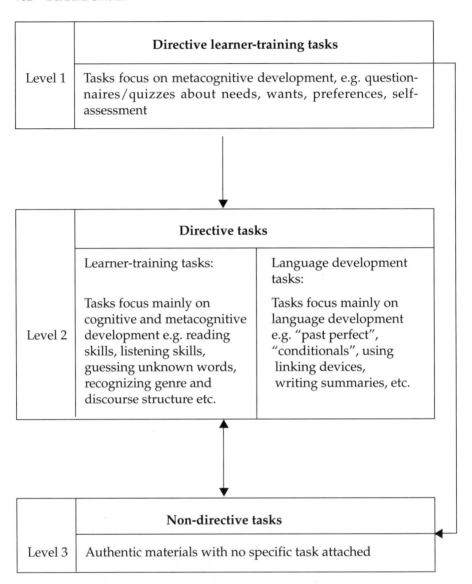

Figure 4: Suggested hierarchy of tasks for the self-access centre

Learners entering the self-access centre would be encouraged to work through one or more introductory tasks with a metacognitive focus at Level 1. These could be in the form of questionnaires, quizzes and exploratory tasks which would encourage learners to consider their needs, wants, learning preferences and styles, and provide opportunity for generalized self-assessment. Feedback would be given by these tasks which would direct learners to consider using either the directive materials at Level 2 or non-directive materials at Level 3. For example, for a learner who prefers to work on his/her listening skills, there would be suggestions which would guide him/her to look at the bank of directive learner-training tasks on developing listening strategies (Level 2), as well as directions for finding listening material to practise with as he/she desires (Level 3). Students preferring a greater degree of direction would be able to work for a longer period at Level 2 doing learner-training and language practice tasks before proceeding to Level 3. Others might opt to miss Level 2 tasks and go straight to practise at Level 3.

With self-access materials organized in this way learners should be able to follow their own paths through the directive materials to the non-directive materials. These paths will be varied and individual. Learners would be free to reject any suggestion for further directive tasks, yet, at the same time, have the opportunity for explicit learner training according to their needs and interests. As Holec (1981: 34) has suggested, there should be no question of forcing learners to be autonomous, only of developing their capacity to be more responsible for their own learning.

Figure 5 provides a suggested template for a directive learner-training task at Level 2 which incorporates the features of explicitness previously discussed. The headings in this template provide a focus for reflection, experimentation and evaluation. For example, the section on "Learner-training questions" (LT questions) encourages learners to reflect on their approach to the task and to build a greater awareness of their learning strategies and habits. "Self-assessment" focuses the learners on their own performance of the task. This may be presented in a variety of ways; as direct questions, as in Figure 5, as a chart or a scale, and so on. The learner's assessment can be recorded to provide monitoring of progress. "Task evaluation" aims to encourage learners to identify their learning preferences and is probably most effectively presented as a series of direct questions. The section on "Further suggestions" requires at least four alternatives, as suggested in Figure 5. These suggestions need to include precise references to actual materials in the self-access centre so that they can be easily located. Other suggestions may recommend directive tasks which focus on relevant language-learning activities, rather than learner training. It would be useful to provide a system whereby learners could log their responses to the different sections of the template and, thus, be in a position to monitor their development. This could take the form of record cards, special learning diaries or CD-ROM-based computer programs.

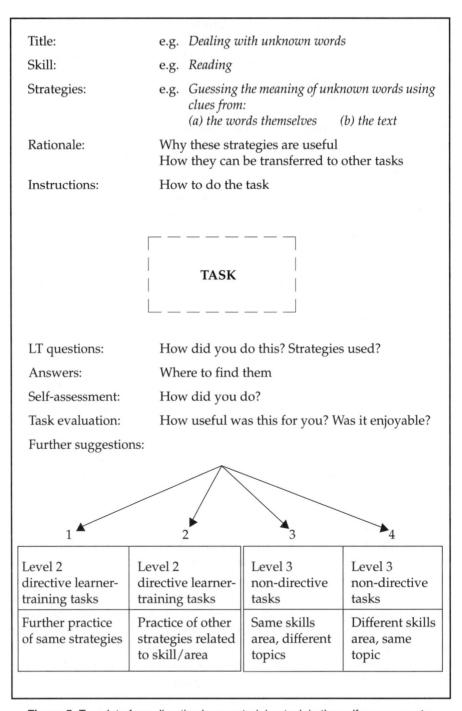

Title: e.g. *Dealing with unknown words*

Skill: e.g. *Reading*

Strategies: e.g. *Guessing the meaning of unknown words using clues from:*
                    (a) the words themselves   (b) the text

Rationale: Why these strategies are useful
                    How they can be transferred to other tasks

Instructions: How to do the task

TASK

LT questions: How did you do this? Strategies used?

Answers: Where to find them

Self-assessment: How did you do?

Task evaluation: How useful was this for you? Was it enjoyable?

Further suggestions:

1	2	3	4
Level 2 directive learner-training tasks	Level 2 directive learner-training tasks	Level 3 non-directive tasks	Level 3 non-directive tasks
Further practice of same strategies	Practice of other strategies related to skill/area	Same skills area, different topics	Different skills area, same topic

Figure 5: Template for a directive learner-training task in the self-access centre

Conclusion

It is the writer's belief that learner autonomy should be promoted in an explicit way. At the same time, it is acknowledged that achieving an appropriate level of explicitness is not easy to do. This chapter has explored issues relating to the nature and degree of explicitness in learner-training tasks in published language-teaching materials and has suggested guidelines for designing tasks for the self-access centre. However, there is one question which is largely still unanswered, and which probably has many different answers; how does a writer know that what he or she *thinks* is explicit **is** actually explicit to the learner? Can it ever be guaranteed that the materials designer's focus is the one the learner will take? Does it actually matter since all materials will be reinterpreted by the learner anyway? Perhaps further research is required into the perceptions of learners, teachers and writers of learner-training tasks. How far do writers have to go to be explicit? When learner-training tasks are published, how do we know whether they are explicit enough to promote learner autonomy or annoyingly patronizing in their tone? To what extent do explicit learner-training tasks in the self-access centre actually help promote learner autonomy? The answers to these questions will no doubt differ according to the individual learners and learning contexts examined, highlighting the need for materials designers to inform themselves as much as possible about their target learners. Ultimately, however, the multiplicity of learners' views concerning explicitness may lead us back to a situation in which the materials writer can only operate in the light of his or her beliefs and opt for the best possible compromise.

Notes

1. Pearson Brown of English International, Lyons, France, in a personal communication (1988).

2. The Communication Skills Programme (CSP) is a workplace literacy scheme set up in 1990 by The British Council in Singapore for workers at the SIA (Singapore Airlines) group of companies. It is estimated that some 4,000 workers will undergo training over a period of 15–20 years. Barbara Sinclair was CSP Project Director during the programme's development phase, 1990–1992. Further information about the CSP can be obtained from The Industrial Language Training Unit, The British Council, 30 Napier Rd., Singapore 1025.

11

The role of materials in the development of autonomous learning[1]

Winnie Lee

Introduction

In recent years there has been a good deal of interest in the development of self-access, self-directed and autonomous learning. It is now widely believed that in order to develop learners' responsibility for their own learning, they need to have some idea of learning strategies, and should know how to choose their materials and how to evaluate themselves. Consequently, much of the discussion relating to self-directed and autonomous language learning has focused on learner training and self-assessment (Allwright 1981; Blue 1988; Dickinson 1988; Blanche and Merino 1989; Ellis and Sinclair 1989; O'Malley and Chamot 1990; Oskarsson 1990).

Within this context, the question of materials design has received relatively little attention (Block 1991). Literature on the subject can be found: for example, Allwright 1981, Frankel 1982, Hill 1982, Hughes 1982, Sturtridge 1982, Dickinson 1987 and Sheerin 1989, 1991. However, empirical studies in this area are scarce.

Whether learners can maintain their interest in learning depends very much on whether they find the materials they use interesting and useful (Frankel 1982; Hughes 1982). This is especially true in the context of the development of self-directed/autonomous learning. There have been studies which indicate the importance of materials in this context (Allwright 1981; Sturtridge 1982; Aston 1993). However, there have been few studies on what makes effective materials for self-directed/autonomous learning.

In this chapter, the issue of effective self-access learning materials will be addressed. This will be examined through discussion of a rationale for self-access learning materials, material types and effective learning, and of a survey of 50 Hong Kong Polytechnic University students. The survey was designed to find out students' preferences as to material types used in a self-access learning context when using textbooks and authentic materials. It was hoped that through this, we can find out which material type can result in more effective learning.

A rationale for effective self-access learning materials

In a self-access learning context, materials function as a surrogate teacher, assuming the pedagogic role normally performed by the teacher in the classroom (Frankel 1982). However, this does not mean that materials will take over the teacher's role in dictating what and how learners are going to learn. On the contrary, what I would like to stress is that materials play a very important role in helping learners move towards self-directed/autonomous learning.

Sturtridge (1982) points out that self-access materials should be "learning" materials rather than "practice" materials. This is because 'learning' materials can help learners move towards learner autonomy as they allow learners to expand their knowledge of language and decide what they would like to learn while 'practice' materials are largely remedial and more geared to learners' practice needs. However, should all our self-access learning materials be 'learning' materials only? What actually makes good self-access learning materials?

The criteria effective self-access learning materials have to meet

One of the criteria is that they must be interesting and motivating. In a self-access learning context, the interaction between materials and learners is direct because of the absence of a teacher. Thus, materials have to play the role of sustaining learners' interest and motivation in learning (Frankel 1982; Hill 1982).

Secondly, the materials used in the early stages of the development of autonomous learning have to be well-structured, systematic and accompanied with clear and simple instructions/guidelines/answer keys. This is because most of the learners at this stage are not very familiar with this mode of learning and they need guidance so that they can work on the materials independently and confidently.

In addition, they should be 'good-quality' materials chosen or designed by teachers. This will give the self-access 'beginners' a taste for 'good' materials and indirectly prepare them to choose and design their own materials later.

Lastly, the materials should have the qualities of what Sturtridge (1982) terms "learning" (as opposed to "practice") materials. Aston (1993: 220) further elaborates Sturtridge's point by stating that 'learning' materials should allow learners to "invent their own infinitely varied learning pathways". In short, the materials should allow learners to develop their autonomous learning capacity. This is particularly true for those learners who are at the later stages of the development of autonomous learning. As they are becoming more independent, they have to be provided with more chances to practise their materials selection and adaptation skills.

To sum up, the kinds of functions assumed by effective self-access materials are both *affective* — increasing motivation in learning, encouraging the learners and making learning more enjoyable — and *cognitive* — providing comprehensible input, giving instructions for tasks, suggesting systematic learning routes, and providing learners with linguistic information and mechanisms for independent learning (such as how to set learning goals, decide on what to do with materials and carry out self-assessment).

Material types and effective learning

Our materials have to fulfil both the affective and cognitive functions mentioned above if we want our learners to establish what Widdowson (1979) claims to be an "authentic" relation with materials, which can then result in a meaningful autonomous learning experience.

What is authentic interaction?

According to Widdowson, "authentic" interaction is a proper interaction between materials and learners through which learners are able to give appropriate responses by recovering the intentions of the writer.

I believe his suggestion of "authentic" interaction can be used best to describe whether learning is effective because it is natural that learning will not take place unless there is interaction between materials and learners. However, I would like to expand his point to include learners' psychological responses to the materials (both cognitive and affective), that is, the learners' perception of the usefulness and interest of the materials. This is because learners' perceptions will also affect the learning outcomes (Bacon and Finnemann 1990; Clarke 1991). This is especially applicable to a self-access/ self-directed learning situation as learners' psychological responses will determine whether they have sufficient motivation to continue with their learning. The questions I am concerned with here are as follows:

1. Both textbook and authentic materials are popularly used in a self-access learning context. Which of these two types of material best fulfils the 'teacherly' roles — both affective and cognitive — and elicits positive affective and cognitive learner responses?

2. To what extent does material type determine whether learners can create an 'authentic' interaction with materials which results in effective learning?

Textbook materials vs. authentic materials

Authentic materials are regarded by Dickinson (1987), Block (1991), Glisan and Drescher (1993) and Richards (1994) as more interesting, up-to-date and realistic, but linguistically more difficult. Textbook materials, on the other hand, are well-presented, systematic and graded but not as up-to-date as authentic materials. This argument is also supported by a research study conducted by Bacon and Finnemann (1990).

It appears that the greatest danger with textbook materials is that the materials become too 'dogmatic' and slow down the learners' movement towards the development of autonomous learning. In an article on textbook use in language classrooms, Richards (1994) raises the concern that relying too much on commercially prepared materials may have the effect of 'deskilling' the teacher, as the materials assume much of the pedagogical decision making. The same danger exists in a self-access situation, where it is the learners themselves who are being 'deskilled' as they may come to rely on the pre-set format of the materials rather than developing the ability to select materials that are stimulating and relevant to their needs.

Authentic materials, on the other hand, seem to have greater potential to prepare learners for autonomous learning as they potentially possess the qualities of 'learning' materials. Unlike textbook materials, they do not have a systematic framework or a pre-determined syllabus. As a result, those who use them have to decide on how to use them and this experience indirectly develops learners' decision-making ability.

It seems that textbook materials, as Richards (1994) argues, generally perform the cognitive functions better by providing learners with systematic learning because the material contents are usually graded. However, authentic materials seem to fulfil both the cognitive and affective functions better because, as suggested by Bacon and Finnemann (1990: 459), in cognitive terms, "authentic materials provide the necessary context for appropriately relating form to meaning in the language acquisition process", while in terms of affect, "authentic texts are regarded as motivators and as a means to overcome the cultural barrier to language learning". However, the question is whether authentic materials can inherently fulfil these functions and establish an 'authentic' interaction with learners.

What leads to the occurrence of authentic interaction

As suggested above, whether authentic interaction can take place depends on appropriate learner responses and positive psychological responses towards the materials. Widdowson (1979) argues that simply exposing learners to authentic language data does not necessarily mean authentic interaction will take place. He makes a distinction between *genuineness* and *authenticity:*

> genuineness is a characteristic of the passage itself and is an absolute quality; while authenticity is a characteristic of relationship between the passage and the reader, and it has to do with appropriate response. (ibid.: 80)

This implies that whether authentic interaction can be established is a complex issue and we have oversimplified the whole issue if we attribute this to material type only.

It would seem that task plays a very important role in this respect because, in a learning process, learners usually have to interact not only with the materials but also with tasks. No matter what sort of material types they are using, they have to perform a task to practise what they have learned or check whether the process of intake has taken place.

To test the extent to which the above assumptions are justified in the Hong Kong context, a survey of 50 Hong Kong Polytechnic University students was carried out.

Hypotheses

Based on the above discussion, the following hypotheses were formulated:

1. Textbook materials perform the cognitive function better whereas authentic materials fulfil the affective function better.
2. Whether materials can produce a positive effect on learning will depend not only on material type, but also on the interaction between material type and task type.

Research methodology

Subjects

A total of 50 first-year Hong Kong Polytechnic University students, who were learning in a self-access context, volunteered to take part in this survey. They were divided into two groups. Group 1 students were following courses in Business, Accountancy and Chinese Translation and Interpretation and were considered to be of higher proficiency because they had obtained Grade D or above in their A level Use of English Examination. Group 2 students were doing courses in Applied Social Studies, Textiles and Clothing and Electronic Engineering and their proficiency was considered to be lower than that of students from Group 1 as they had obtained grade E or lower in their Use of English Examination.

Procedures and instruments

Students were asked to complete three sets of questionnaires and two language practice activities. These were completed one after the other in the order given below. The whole procedure of this survey took about two hours.

To test the first hypothesis, students were asked to complete the Material Type Questionnaire. The questionnaire consisted of two sections — students' background information sheet, and students' cognitive and affective responses to the use of authentic materials and textbook materials.

Students were asked to give their opinions on a five-point Likert Scale. They did not have to refer to any specific materials when doing the questionnaire. They simply gave their responses based on their past learning experience. It was hoped that from the results, I would be able to detect the function(s) each material type can fulfil.

To test the second hypothesis, the same group of students were asked to do two language practice activities which aimed to practise students' question and answer techniques. On the completion of these activities, they had to fill in the Activity Evaluation Questionnaires. The purpose of these was to find out students' cognitive and affective responses towards the activities they had completed. I hoped these could give me some insight into the relationship between materials and tasks.

A set of tasks was chosen from two textbooks, one set from each. They were basically different in nature. The first set was taken from *Communicative Grammar Practice* (Jones 1992) and it included communicative controlled practice, a game and a role play interview activity. As the activities required students to interact with each other and give their personal opinions, I would like to call them 'communicative' activities. The second set, from *English Grammar in Use* (Murphy 1987), included rules and traditional paper and pen grammar exercises. As they were exercises mainly practising students' grammar knowledge and no context was given in each exercise, I called them 'structural' activities.

Two sets of tasks were designed for a newspaper article, entitled 'She's my everything, says superstar Chow' (1993), which was about a popular local film star, Chow Yun-fat. As the article was quite long, students could choose to read only the parts which were marked if they wished.

The nature of these two sets of tasks was the same as those from the textbooks. Thus, the first set was also communicative and the second set structural. The types of activity in these two tasks were similar to those from the textbooks.

Students were randomly divided into two groups. Group A did the structural task from the textbook materials (*English Grammar in Use*) and the communicative task from the authentic materials; while Group B did the communicative task from the textbook materials (*Communicative Grammar Practice*) and the structural task from the authentic materials.

Students were given one hour to complete the communicative task and half an hour for the structural task. Within each task, they could choose the activities they liked and did not have to complete all the activities. They had to do the two tasks on their own without the teacher's involvement.

After completing the tasks and the questionnaires, a ten-minute retrospective interview was held between the teacher and students. The purpose was to give students a chance to express their opinions of the two tasks.

Statistical procedure

The statistical software SAS was used to analyze the data. The statistical procedures employed were:

1. Split-half analysis — this enabled us to establish the internal consistency of the questionnaires.
2. Frequency tables, means and standard deviations — this showed the distribution of the responses along the scale.
3. Chi-squared test — this showed whether students' responses were affected by a background variable.
4. t-test — this indicated whether there were statistically significant differences between the students' responses.

Results and discussion

I was satisfied with the results of the split-half analysis because the reliability coefficients are 0.77 for the Material Type Questionnaire and around 0.65 for the four Activity Evaluation Questionnaires. Thus I am confident that the results are reliable, even though they lack external validity due to the small sample size.

Hypothesis 1: Material Type Questionnaire

Table 1 shows students' affective and cognitive responses to the textbook and authentic materials. Due to the small sample size, all the students' responses on the five-point Likert Scale (Strongly Agree to Strongly Disagree) were changed to the three-point scale (Agree to Disagree: A = Agree; N = Neutral; D = Disagree). The purpose was to make the data valid for the chi-squared analysis.

Table1: Responses to Material Type Questionnaire

	Textbook materials			Authentic materials		
Affective items	A	N	D	A	N	D
I enjoy using ...	15	24	11	28	15	7
I find ... more interesting	6	23	21	33	7	10
I feel uncomfortable if asked to use ...	4	22	24	11	8	31
My interest in learning English is increased if I use ...	7	28	15	19	21	10
The content of ... is usually up-to-date	9	21	20	32	11	7
Cognitive items	A	N	D	A	N	D
I learn better when I have to use ...	22	21	7	14	30	6
I find ... easy	14	29	7	19	20	11
Using ... makes the learning of English orderly/systematic	30	16	4	9	29	12
... enable me to learn independently	29	17	4	11	27	12

Authentic materials

The results suggest that affectively students preferred authentic materials. Out of 50 students, 33 agreed that the authentic materials were interesting, while for the textbook materials only six said so. Moreover, 28 said they enjoyed using authentic materials while only 15 said so for textbook materials.

I performed a chi-squared test to check whether students' responses were affected by background variables such as sex, age and proficiency. The results show there was no significant relationship between their responses and the background variables as the probability levels shown in the chi-squared tests were all above 0.05, indicating that statistically, they were not significant at the 5% confidence interval. This suggests that most of the students in my survey, whether male or female, or of high or low proficiency, found authentic materials interesting and motivating to use. This supported part of my Hypothesis 1 that authentic materials perform better affectively than textbook materials.

Textbook materials

However, this does not mean textbook materials have no pedagogical value at all, because when asked to make judgements on the usefulness of both types of material, students gave high ratings for the textbook materials. In response to cognitive items 2 and 16, 22 students said that they would learn better with textbook material while only 14 said so for authentic materials; 30 students said they would learn more systematically if they used textbook materials but for authentic materials only nine agreed with this statement. And 29 students said they could learn independently with the textbook materials while only 11 said so for the authentic materials. This seems to indicate that cognitively, students preferred to use textbook materials. Based on these results, we could say that textbook materials fulfilled cognitive functions better than authentic materials.

I also performed a chi-squared test to see whether students' responses were influenced by their background variables. Out of 18 items, only items 16 and 13 showed that there was a strong relationship with the proficiency variable.

Item 16 is the statement, 'I learn better when I have to use authentic materials'. In Table 2, it can be seen that high proficiency students tended to agree with the statement. Of the 22 students from Group 1, whose members had scored grade D or above in their Use of English Examination, 10 agreed with the statement, whereas for Group 2 students, whose grades in the Use of English Examination were E or below, only four out of 28 said so. The probability level was 0.034, significant at 5%, indicating that the differences in the two groups' responses were not due to chance, but due to the factor of proficiency.

Table 2: Agreement with statement 16, according to English Language proficiency
(Item 16: I learn better when I have to use non-textbook materials.)

	Group 1 (n=22)	Group 2 (n=28)
Agree	10	4
Neutral	9	21
Disagree	3	3

Item 13 is the statement 'Textbooks enable me to learn independently.' Here also proficiency was a variable which affected students' responses. Table 3 shows that of 22 students from the high proficiency group, only 10 agreed with the statement compared with 19 out of 28 students from the low proficiency group. The probability level was also significant at 5%. These findings suggest that lower proficiency students prefer textbook materials to authentic materials. The possible reason for this might be due to the cognitive functions textbooks have.

Table 3: Agreement with statement 13, according to English Language proficiency
(Item 13: Textbooks enable me to learn independently.)

	Group 1 (n=22)	Group 2 (n=28)
Agree	10	19
Neutral	12	5
Disagree	0	4

Hypothesis 2: Activity Evaluation Questionnaires

Only 49 students completed these questionnaires. Twenty-six students, comprising 10 from the high proficiency group and 16 from the low proficiency group, completed Questionnaire set A (Textbook: structural task/Authentic materials: communicative task). The remaining 12 students from the high proficiency group and the remaining 11 students from the low proficiency group completed Questionnaire set B (Textbook: communicative task/Authentic materials: structural task).

Table 4 shows the mean of the students' responses to the affective and cognitive items for both types of materials and for the different types of tasks. All the statements were positive and the responses were recorded on a 3-point scale: 1=Agree, 2=Neutral and 3=Disagree, so *the lower the mean, the more positive* the responses are.

For the affective responses to structural tasks, there was a statistically significant difference between the two types of material (t value: 2.11, significant at 5%). As the mean for authentic materials was lower than the mean for the textbook materials, the data suggests (surprisingly) that affectively, students preferred *authentic* materials more when the task was *structural*. One reason for this might be that the exercises were designed around the topic Chow Yun-fat, which was familiar to them; the other might be that they enjoyed reading the article.

Table 4: Responses to Activity Evaluation Questionnaire
(textbook and authentic materials)

Responses	Activities	TM		AM		t value	p
		Mean	SD	Mean	SD		
Affective	Structural	1.82	0.41	1.50	0.34	2.11	*
	Communicative	1.50	0.4	1.47	0.3	0.57	–
Cognitive	Structural	1.68	0.30	1.67	0.41	0.08	–
	Communicative	1.48	0.3	1.67	0.4	1.97	*

TM: Textbook materials   AM: Authentic materials

* significant at 5% confidence interval

However, for the cognitive responses to structural activities, the mean difference between textbook and authentic materials was not significant (t value: 0.08). This suggests that cognitively students did not find any differences between the two types of materials when the task was structural. In fact, this result is predictable because the nature of the activity in both cases was exactly the same and it is natural that students would not see any differences in terms of usefulness. As for affective responses to the communicative tasks, the mean difference between the two material types was also slight, indicating that students showed little preference for either type of material when the task was communicative. This result is not surprising either, as it is likely that both activities appeared to be interesting to the learners. Affectively, they saw no difference between the two types of materials. This supports my hypothesis 2 that tasks play an important role in deciding whether materials have positive effects on learning.

Surprisingly, there was a marginally significant difference (t value: 1.97, significant at 5%) between the two types of materials when it came to cognitive responses to the communicative activities, as the mean for the textbook was lower than for the authentic materials. I can say, therefore, that cognitively students preferred to use *textbook* materials when the task was *communicative*. One possible reason for this is that as both activities were interesting, some students, especially those of lower proficiency, would prefer textbook materials as they are graded and appear to be easier and more systematic for learning. This actually confirms my previous findings that students affectively preferred authentic materials while lower proficiency students cognitively found textbook materials more useful.

Retrospective interview

In the retrospective interview, students were asked to express their opinions towards the tasks they had done and these are summarized as follows:

1. Most students from Group 2 (the lower proficiency group) said that they preferred to use textbook materials for independent learning and for grammar practice. The reason for this was textbook materials were seen to be easier and more systematic for learning. This further confirms the argument that textbooks provide a systematic framework for learning, which makes learners, especially the low proficiency ones, perceive them as cognitively more useful.

2. Most students, no matter whether they were from Group 1 or Group 2, felt that communicative tasks such as discussion were not very suitable for independent learning as there was no way for them to check whether what they had done was correct or not. Rather, they believed that when doing this sort of task, the teacher's feedback, comments or evaluation was of great importance and many of them even said they did not mind if a teacher corrected them in the middle of the task, believing that this helped them to improve their language performance. This implies that a teacher's 'instructional' role should not be regarded as having no value in a self-access mode of learning.

Conclusions

Based on the findings discussed above, I can draw the following con-clusions:

1. Authentic materials perform the affective functions better as they can make students affectively more involved. On the other hand, they can appear to lack systematic organization and may even seem daunting to some students, especially those of low proficiency. If we want to make authentic materials accessible to all students, we should pay attention to this aspect.

2. Textbook materials fulfil the cognitive function better as they are graded. Learners see them as more useful as they find they provide them with a systematic route for learning.

3. Tasks play an important role in deciding whether materials can have positive effects on learning.

Recommendations

In fact both textbook and authentic materials have their own pedagogical value. However, the recommendation I make here will focus mainly on authentic materials because they are reading texts learners will always encounter in their daily life and their future professional fields. As teachers, we should make good use of them in both classroom and self-access learning contexts so that learners know how to exploit them effectively for their own future uses.

The following is a set of suggestions on firstly, how to make authentic materials appear to be more systematic and accessible to learners; and secondly, to make learners become more 'systematic' in the use of authentic materials so they can gradually develop the pedagogic reasoning skills of selection and adaptation that they need out of the classroom to make optimum use of these materials.

Making materials accessible

Using a simple cataloguing system

Dickinson (1987) suggests the use of a PC database software program for cataloguing materials. The categories suggested are: code, title, topic, source, text type, task and task level. By having such a wide range of categories, learners can have more freedom to decide on how to choose their materials.

Providing generic guidelines for the use of authentic materials

In order to help learners to gain a better understanding of the uses of authentic materials, guidelines should be provided for learners. (See Appendix 1.)

Providing task sheets with students' notes

Students' notes for the task sheets should also be provided so that learners know how to work on the task independently.

Designing effective tasks

A set of well-chosen authentic materials accompanied by task sheets could be available as this can serve as a model for learners to design their own tasks at a later stage. Nunan's (1993) suggestions on "the development of a pedagogic task" give some insights into how to design effective tasks.

Guiding learners to select materials and design own tasks

Keeping records

Students can be advised to keep a record of the materials/tasks they have used on a chart or grid. They can also be encouraged to comment on how easy, interesting or useful the materials are. By doing this, they will be able to see patterns begin to emerge regarding the material preferences, which will help them do their materials selection later.

Providing generic task sheets

A number of generic tasks sheets can be provided so that learners can adapt them for different kinds of materials. (See Appendix 2 for an example.) The ability to adapt task sheets will prepare learners for designing their own tasks at the time they feel necessary or ready.

Selecting new texts and designing own tasks

As learners gradually develop the pedagogical reasoning skills necessary for materials selection and task design, they can be encouraged to choose their own texts and design tasks for them based on the paradigm: Input — Output — Consolidation.

Asking learners to design their own tasks might sound idealistic and unattainable. However, this could still be set as one of the goals we are trying to move towards. In this way, a self-access centre is not just a static collection of materials but rather a dynamic, evolving organism which grows in direct response to the needs and different learning styles of the learners.

Note

1. I owe a debt of gratitude to Mr Rodney Jones of the City University of Hong Kong for his stimulating ideas which helped me write up this paper. I would particularly like to thank him for the information contained in the last section of 'Guiding learners to select materials and design own tasks', which was mainly provided by him. I also wish to express my thanks to the editors and to Mr Bruce Morrison and Mr Alex Stringer of the English Language Study Centre, Hong Kong Polytechnic University for their valuable comments on the paper, and to Ms Fanny Chan for helping with the graphics.

APPENDIX 1: Example generic guidelines for the use of authentic materials

General guidelines on the use of newspaper/magazine articles

Why should you use newspaper/magazine articles?

— to familiarize yourself with authentic materials
— to prepare yourself for your everyday reading needs
— to enhance your social and cultural awareness
— to increase your exposure to different styles of written English

What can you use newspaper/magazine articles for?

— to improve reading skills such as skimming and scanning
— to extend your vocabulary
— as a springboard to prepare yourself for speaking activities such as discussion
— to prepare yourself for writing activities such as essay writing and report writing

How do you choose a newspaper/magazine article?

— identify your purpose and decide the skill you would like to practise
— choose a topic you find interesting from the newspaper index/a magazine and remember that you would probably find reading an unfamiliar topic more difficult
— if you want to use the article as a springboard for writing or speaking activities, do not choose one that is too long

How do you use a newspaper/magazine article for improving your speaking/discussion skills?

1. Read the title of the article and predict what the article is about.
2. Skim through the article quickly and check whether what you are reading matches what you have predicted.
3. Read the article again and try to guess the meaning of words or phrases you do not understand from the context.
4. If there are still words or phrases you do not understand, decide whether you need to know them to understand the passage; if so, check the words in a dictionary.
5. Read the article again and highlight the points you may want to discuss.
6. Decide on a topic you are going to discuss.

How do you decide on a discussion topic for a newspaper article?

— Think about what you have just read and write down the main idea
in one sentence.
— Ask yourself the following questions:
  • Is it about a controversial issue?
  • Is it about someone's experience?
  • Is it simply giving you some factual information?
— The discussion topic could be:
  • Giving your opinions
  • Sharing your experience with your group members
  • Giving comments on how the information is related to your life
    experience.

APPENDIX 2: Example generic task sheets for use with authentic materials

Speaking: Discussion

Classification:	Speaking — Discussion
Code:	Gen-Sp/Dis
Level:	Intermediate
Aim:	To practise expressing one's ideas fluently and confidently in a discussion context
Function:	To express opinions
Materials:	Newspaper/Magazine articles
Time:	1 hour

Pre-Discussion Activity

Step 1:	— Choose a newspaper/magazine article that you find interesting.
	— Before reading the article, predict what the article is about based on the title.
Step 2:	— Skim through the article quickly and try to get the main idea about the article.
	— Read the article again and jot down any points, vocabulary, phrases or expressions which might help you do your discussion.

| *Step 3:* | — Read the following examples carefully as they might give you some ideas on the type of discussion task you would like to do. |

Examples:

a. *Giving opinions*

Read the article 'Green posters removed as commuters see red', and then hold a short discussion on the following:
— If you were the adjudicator, would you choose the same two posters as the winners of this design competition?
— Do you think these posters should be removed?

b. *Sharing experience*

Read the article 'No merit in looking for an easy scapegoat' and then hold a discussion on the following:
— Have you ever had a very bad experience in a crowded venue? Describe your experience to your group members and say whether you saw any accidents happen.

| *Step 4:* | — Think of your own discussion task. |

Discussion Activity

— Hold a discussion with your partner(s) on the task you have decided. (10 - 15 minutes)
— Tape your discussion.
— Evaluate your performance together with a teacher/counsellor.

Consolidation Activity

Choose *one* of the following:

Song Listening — Choose a song related to the topic you have discussed.
Listening Activity — Choose a topic related to the one you have discussed.

12

Lights, camera, action: exploring and exploiting films in self-access learning

Elsie Christopher and Susanna Ho

Introduction

In the language-learning spectrum of today, there are many tools available for students to use as pathways to improving both their language proficiency and their learning efficiency. The video is one of these tools as it combines natural speech patterns with the two-dimensional visual elements of film. Today, videotapes and laserdisc technology are able to provide language learners with a wealth of authentic spoken discourse. Having access to such a wide range of choices, students are able to develop their own existing language skills by becoming more autonomous in their choices of topics for consideration. Many language teachers are beginning to realize the inherent value of autonomous learning as it allows more freedom and flexibility in learning. This is also true of group discussions. By using films as the basis for stimulating active discussion, students expose themselves to a wide range of realistic situations. The unpredictable nature of group discussions is still perceived by many language teachers as a threat to disrupting classroom order. In autonomous learning, however, this unpredictability factor can be used to motivate students, especially those who do not mind taking risks in face-to-face interaction.

In terms of the utilization of films for language skills enhancement on a self-access basis, it is problematic to consider the pedagogic value of such activities without having some type of monitoring or self-checking instruments in place for students. With this in mind, Gardner (1994: 108) points out that opportunities for active viewing activities which lead to focused language learning are useful for making films more accessible to second language learners. Active viewing and focused language learning seek to make students more aware of their own speech patterns and general spoken discourse, while at the same time, they succeed in presenting the films in more manageable chunks for greater overall comprehension.

A film discussion project was offered through the Self-Access Centre at The Hong Kong University of Science and Technology (HKUST) in the Spring semester of 1994. The aims of the project included the following:

1. To improve oral proficiency.
2. To give participants the confidence to become more independent and active viewers.

The project was primarily designed with two key factors in mind: autonomy and flexibility. In relation to students, two major characteristics were considered in the design and implementation of materials for the Self-Access Film Discussion Group:

1. As viewers, they were passive and often merely searched for general surface-level meaning in films.
2. They were active language learners who had chosen to practise their discussion skills as part of their Language Enhancement Course.

As a result, we decided to design a project that incorporated films into our own self-access materials as offered within the centre, and explored the essential benefits of using films to facilitate group discussion.

There are many reasons for using video in a self-access language learning environment such as the flexibility of viewing times, the realistic two-dimensional quality of the visual medium itself and even the sheer enjoyment factors of aspects such as music, realistic settings etc. Hill (1989: 3–5) outlines several reasons why institutions are making videos available to students on a self-access basis, the key points being more flexibility with a higher degree of autonomy, and more overall enjoyment for students.

In order to further justify the value of students participating in a video film discussion project, it is extremely important that the students themselves perceive the benefits of such a commitment. To quote one student's written self-access film project report, "Learning in this way, students can experience another learning method which is different from the normal lectures and tutorials ... Your English skills are assessed by yourself and how much work you do can be controlled by yourself." In this regard, students' perceptions of autonomy are directly related to their self-assessed progress.

Methodology

The film project

Participants of the film project were required to watch five films, one film every two weeks. After watching each film, they attended a discussion the following week. Each discussion began with a five-minute Cantonese pre-discussion. This pre-discussion in the L1 helped to clarify, explain and discuss complex issues which participants did not immediately understand in English. The remaining 55 minutes of the discussion were conducted in English. The discussions were recorded on audiotape and videotape.

Participants

The participants, having made the commitment to take part in the five prescribed film discussions, were divided into two groups based upon mutual time availability. The two groups were distinctly different in that Group 1 consisted of eight males and Group 2 consisted of four males and two females.

Materials used and procedures of the study

At the outset, participants were asked to fill in a Pre-Viewing Questionnaire which mainly required them to reflect upon their film-viewing history to date. Questions such as "How has your viewing of films changed since you were a child?" and "What are the features of a film that you most often look for when choosing what to watch?" were included. Questionnaires were produced to monitor the students' progress throughout the project and to enable participants to have a sense of achievement at the end of the project through an individual as well as comparative analysis of their own contributions within their respective groups (see question 2e of Table 1 for participants' increased confidence in speaking).

Vocabulary input exercises were also used to aid participants in acquiring vocabulary useful for discussing the background of films, such as *drama, romantic comedy, cinematography, sub-titles* etc. After these two sets of exercises were completed, participants were asked to fill in a Generic Worksheet followed by a Specific Worksheet for each of the films they watched.

The Generic Worksheet focuses mainly on the more technical aspects of the films. The genre of the film as well as the setting, atmosphere, conflicts and themes are considered with a view to heightening participants' awareness of the structured 'framework' of films in a more general sense.

Upon completion of the Generic Worksheet, participants were given a worksheet which dealt specifically with a particular film. In preparation for the ensuing discussion session which lasted for approximately one hour, participants were asked to complete the worksheet which was divided into two distinct sections (see Appendix 1). Part I of the worksheet dealt with several objective questions which required both concise and accurate responses to specific aspects of the film such as familial relationships, central conflicts, plot resolution etc. The objective questions progressed from easy to difficult (or simple to complex) and required both short and long responses. Part II of the worksheet focused predominantly upon related issues and topics which had intrinsic and emotive discussion value. Topics and issues such as dishonesty versus truth, organized crime, and death and loss were provided as 'discussion catalysts' in order to generate a natural and unstructured discussion among participants.

Consultants intervened only at a point where major learning goals had to be urgently met, as Little (1989: 80) recommends. In this case, consultants only intervened when participants came to a halt in their discussion and could not proceed any further due to a lack of clarification or misinterpretation of either the content of the film itself or a previous contribution made by another participant.

The general material design rationale attempted to provide participants with a relatively clear understanding of the films, while at the same time also providing them with the self-confidence to become independent contributors to the overall discussion. In order to help them to achieve a 'collective comprehension' of the film, participants were allowed to conduct the group discussion in Cantonese during the first five minutes of each session. They were then asked to continue the discussion in their second language, English. After completing the more general and factual questions in Part I of the specific film worksheet, participants moved on to more complex social issues in Part II.

After contributing to discussions on all five of the prescribed films, participants were given a Comparative Discussion Worksheet. This worksheet was completed near the end of the project so as to elicit personal reactions and comments from participants with regard to identifying both similarities as well as differences between all of the films discussed. The worksheet considers comparisons between such aspects of films as character development, common themes and atmosphere. The Comparative Discussion Worksheet was mainly designed in order to allow participants to recognize common elements in all films, as well as elements which make a particular film more outstanding due to specific features unique to that film.

The final item in the project was a Post-Viewing Questionnaire (see Table 1) which attempted to guide participants in identifying and commenting upon their individual progress as a result of the Film Discussion Project. Part A of the questionnaire provides participants with questions on their enjoyment of viewing films, and their perceived language improvements. Part B asks participants to describe their feelings and/or opinions regarding such aspects of the discussion as the Cantonese pre-discussion period, and their role as an active member of a discussion group.

Some of the materials were purely designed to encourage oral contributions among participants, while others served a dual purpose in the sense that they were materials genuinely used during the course of the film project, and they also acted as data collection instruments. Materials that fall into the latter category are the Pre-Viewing and the Post-Viewing Questionnaires and the Comparison Discussion Worksheet. Other instruments such as the audio and video recordings of the discussion sessions, the participants' self-access film project reports and vocabulary checklists were also used to study the effectiveness of the project. Data collected by means of these instruments were recorded in detail, and are discussed in the following section.

Data analysis and discussion

Pre-Viewing Questionnaire

It was assumed that participants who joined the self-access film project had an intrinsic interest in watching films. In order to validate this assumption, participants were asked to fill in a Pre-Viewing Questionnaire which aimed to collect information about their opinions and views on films, their habits of film watching and their personal perceptions about how they had changed as viewers. Of the fourteen participants, twelve returned the questionnaires. Given a four-point scale, the participants indicated their strong preference for romantic films by giving this category an average of 3.4. The next two popular types of films were those of human interest and science fiction, both of which scored 2.8.

Overall, participants stated that their views towards films were more simplistic when they were children, that is, they only wanted a happy ending. However, as adults, their views were much more complex. They appreciated good acting, and how themes were presented in a film, etc. In other words, they not only watch a film for the sake of enjoyment, but they also watch it from an analytical point of view. Now, after having watched a film, they try to analyze both the plot and the characters.

Comparative Discussion Worksheet and Post-Viewing Questionnaire

To further explore their taste in films, as well as their reactions to the project, the participants were asked to make recommendations for future discussion groups. All fourteen participants were asked to fill in two other questionnaires after they had watched the five pre-selected films. One of the questionnaires, which is called 'Comparative Discussion Worksheet', asked participants to compare the five films they had watched with a view to collecting student input in order to modify future discussion groups. The Post-Viewing Questionnaire aimed to collect participants' feedback on the film project as a whole. Participants were asked both closed questions and open questions. Table 1 gives a summary of the participants' responses to the closed questions.

Table 1: Participants' responses to the Post-Viewing Questionnaire (n=14)

Questions	Very much	Quite a lot	Not much	Not at all
1. To what extent has the Film Project aroused your interest in watching English films?	2	7	5	0
2. How much has the Film Project helped you improve the following:				
a) vocabulary about films?	0	2	12	0
b) listening comprehension?	0	11	3	0
c) the ability to analyze issues directly and/or indirectly stated in a film?	3	9	2	0
d) the ability to express your own opinions in small group discussions?	5	8	1	0
e) your confidence in speaking in a small group?	1	13	0	0
f) knowledge of movie types?	2	7	5	0
3. How much has the Film Project helped you learn about the following:				
a) character?	1	5	8	0
b) atmosphere?	1	5	7	0
c) theme?	1	11	2	0
d) conflicts?	0	7	7	0
e) setting?	1	4	7	2

Table 1: to be continued

Table 1: continued

4. How much have you enjoyed the film discussions?	0	14	0	0
5. Have you learned a lot from your group members?	2	9	3	0
6. How useful are the film discussions in improving your proficiency in:				
a) listening?	4	8	2	0
b) speaking?	3	10	1	0
c) reading?	0	0	10	4
d) writing?	0	1	8	5

All of them felt that they enjoyed the film discussions 'quite a lot', and more than half of them thought that the film project had aroused their interest in watching English films. They thought that the film project was most successful in helping them to improve their ability to express their opinions in small group discussions. Twelve of them also reported that the film project was either 'very' or 'quite' successful in helping them to improve their ability to analyze issues as stated (explicitly or implicitly) in films. The project also boosted their self-confidence in speaking in a small group. With regard to the four language skills, the majority thought that the film discussions were useful in improving their proficiency in both their listening and speaking skills.

More detailed responses were derived from the open questions. When asked how they felt about the five-minute Cantonese pre-discussion period, all of the participants found it very useful in helping them to clarify details, thereby increasing their overall understanding of the films. Six of them recalled that the initial Cantonese discussion helped them generate ideas which were essential to the later part of the discussion when they switched to English. The Cantonese session helped them to clarify various points about the films, and as a result, they all found it easier to express themselves in the English discussion. Indeed, one of them even commented that the Cantonese session could have been longer.

The second open question asked them what they had learned from participating in the group discussions. Their responses showed that the first aim of the film project (i.e. to improve oral proficiency) was met. Three of them said that they had improved their listening ability and thirteen of them said that they had improved their speaking ability in the sense that they had become more confident in expressing their ideas in group discussions. Two participants also said that they had learned how to organize their ideas before they presented them.

Participants were also asked whether films were a good basis for discussion. Eleven responded positively, while the other replied 'yes' — as long as they had an adequate understanding of the plot first. They said that films provided entertainment and elicited commonly-shared topics such as love and marriage and familial relationships for discussion. They also commented that as films were reflections of life, they would be useful tools for generating discussion topics. Although the majority responded favourably towards the film project, two of them were not totally convinced that using films as a basis for discussion was useful. They said that only those films which were easy to understand were a good basis for discussion. This seems to suggest that allowing time to clarify misunderstanding of a film is essential for some participants before they could move on to more in-depth discussions.

Audio and video recordings

From the audio and video recordings, it was revealed that participants did come up with their own communication strategies in order to enhance a smooth flow of discussion. Distinctly prevalent in their discussions were three types of strategies: namely, self-correction, comprehension checking and vocabulary contextualization (see Appendix 2). The first strategy, self-correction, is self-explanatory. In order to make themselves clearly understood, participants would correct themselves, even when it was not required by others in the discussion. This self-initiated correction which demonstrated an activation of passive L2 knowledge, definitely quickened the pace of discussion. The second type of strategy, comprehension checking, involved more than one participant. When ambiguities arose, they would halt their discussion and seek clarification from other group members. This strategy was often carried out by participants by repeating a word or phrase used by another participant and checking his/her own understanding of the word in question.

A third type of strategy that participants used in their discussions was vocabulary contextualization. This occurred in two ways. Sometimes, the participants used the introduced vocabulary items in their discussions, as with the word *disability* in the extract transcribed in Appendix 2. At other times, they used their own words. When used appropriately, these self-introduced vocabulary items were picked up by other participants, and became internalized by them. Since the context of the discussions was commonly shared, the 'recycled' or recurrent use of the vocabulary item(s) was found to assist greatly in participants' verbal exchanges. The contextualization and later, internalization of specific vocabulary items among participants were invested with 'situational meaning'. Corder (1966: 16) describes these situational contexts as "the people, events and things present when the bit of language is uttered". Therefore, when a new vocabulary item was introduced into the discussion, participants considered its appropriate context or situation before assigning it with a relevant meaning. Although the strategy was an interesting feature, it was not pursued in depth. This, however, could provide useful information for future research and study.

Both the audio and video recordings of the discussions provided an objective source of information for retrospective evaluation. Through the video recordings, the consultants could identify special features that took place in the participants' discussions for detailed analysis. We will focus on three interesting features, namely participants' interaction during the Cantonese session, group dynamics and improvements in the flow of communication over the course of the project.

Participants were not specifically told what they should discuss in the five-minute Cantonese discussion. Both groups automatically saw it as a chance to clarify various points in the film that they had not quite comprehended while viewing. Some of the participants tended to ask questions, while others were very good at explaining details and narrating scenes contained within the film. When speaking in their mother tongue, almost all participants spoke enthusiastically. This could be seen from their body language, which was markedly more animated in the Cantonese than in the English discussions. A comparison of L1 and L2 discussions, particularly students' use of paralinguistic features, is an interesting area for further exploration.

From the video recordings, it was observed that more interaction took place in Group 2, that is, there were more exchanges between participants and their utterances were sustained for a longer period of time. These differences could be attributed to the group combination and size. From the observations of this study, it seems that a group size of more than six does not facilitate active participation — in the larger group, participants appeared to feel less confident to speak. Another factor which could have contributed to the increased interaction in Group 2 was the fact that the two females displayed talk-support strategies (cf. Holmes 1994: 160-161), which suggests that they often played supportive roles in the discussions. For example, the females disagreed more politely and they asked questions to encourage the males to speak during the discussions. As a result of their encouragement, the males appeared to find it much easier to express themselves.

Despite the fact that there was more interaction in Group 2, both groups did conduct very successful discussions. Participants spoke most of the time, and all of them contributed to a smooth and ongoing flow of communication. Improvements in the flow of communication were particularly noticeable with Group 2, as can be seen from Table 2.

Table 2: A comparison of one-minute extracts from Discussions 2 and 5 (Group 2)

	Number of participants	Number of speaking participants	Number of turns	Number of pauses (longer than 3 secs.)
Discussion 2	5	3	9	2
Discussion 5	6	6	16	0

From the table, we can see that there is a marked improvement between the second and the last discussion. The most significant features are the number of turns as well as the frequency of pauses in the discussion. In the last discussion, all the participants contributed, and there were 16 turns in total; this was almost twice as many turns as in Discussion 2. As for the frequency of pauses, there were two of more than 3 seconds in Discussion 2 and none in the last one. (For a detailed transcription, see Appendix 3.) As a result, we may conclude that participants became more fluent in small group discussions at the end of this project.

Conclusion

The film project was successfully incorporated into one of the courses offered by the Language Centre. The project met its first goal of improving oral proficiency, as evidenced by student responses to the Post-Viewing Questionnaire and increases in the number of oral contributions made over the course of the project.

In terms of meeting its second goal of giving participants the confidence to become more independent and active viewers, the findings are more tentative. According to the Post-Viewing Questionnaire, most participants developed more self-confidence in speaking and contributing personal opinions even without any specific agenda. The participants offered their own questions and often acted as supportive group members. However, it seems that some of them were still not ready to conduct their own discussions by themselves. Three of them wanted the consultants to join the discussions and one of them would have liked more feedback from the consultants. It might be concluded that the participants had become more confident in their speaking and listening ability (see question 2 of Table 1), but they had not come to a point where they could have a discussion without the consultants present.

Although participants were directly motivated to complete the project in order to fulfil one of their course requirements, they also commented that it was genuinely interesting for them as learners. Using their mother tongue to begin the discussion promoted their self-confidence and further cultivated their interest in the project. The choice and number of films included in the project were also motivating factors. The variety of films used included romantic comedy, science fiction and human interest, and generally speaking, the participants felt that the time and effort required to complete the project were reasonable.

We can conclude that, in a general sense, the success of the project was determined by such factors as commitment on the part of the participants, the adjustment of self-access materials to suit their specific language learning needs, and the development of relevant and meaningful topics for discussion. Acknowledging that materials produced for such a project need to be continually and systematically updated and rewritten according to the perceived needs of the participants, several new films have already been added to the list, and short reading and writing tasks will also be incorporated into the overall design.

As a self-access project, students were, and will continue to be, encouraged to comment on, contribute to and ideally run their own discussion groups as a means of becoming more confident and autonomous in their own language learning.[1] Heightening awareness and providing a supportive and non-threatening atmosphere are both essential if students are to become active participants on both an individual and group basis. As one enthusiastic participant commented, "I tried to watch the movies with a group of people. This was useful for me as I could interpret the events of the movie because I could discuss them with others if I had a problem. For these reasons, my confidence was gradually enhanced and I always tried to express my ideas during the film discussion sessions."

Note

1. The project has now been running for two years. In its present form, participants are encouraged to select the films they wish to watch, which entails discussion and negotiation from the outset. They are also asked to devise their own discussion questions; using e-mail, students negotiate with each other to improve the grammar and logic of the questions, a process that appears to increase both their sense of belonging to the group and their confidence in their ability to take more control of their learning.

APPENDIX 1: Sample of Individual Film Worksheet

Self-Access Centre

Discussion Worksheet (1)

Movie: Green Card

Main Characters: Bronte, George

Part I: Discussion Questions

1. Why do Bronte and George get married?

   Bronte—
   George—

2. Bronte is a "horticulturalist", what does this mean?

3. What is George's nationality?

4. Describe Bronte and George's reaction when they see each other in the restaurant just after they get married.

5. Why do the immigration officers visit Bronte and George at home? Why do they ask Bronte and George for a second interview?

6. Who are the "Green Gorillas"? What does the group do to help the poor?

7. When do you know that Bronte and George really love each other?

8. Why must George leave at the end of the film?

Part II: Issues/Topics related to the movie which can be further discussed

1. Marriages of convenience

2. Does Marriage always = Love?

3. Dishonesty versus Truth

APPENDIX 2: Film Discussion Transcription: discussion strategies

Self-correction

F: We we can take a guess just like er er maybe the the alien in the spaceship er use the aircraft use the spaceship and so took the took the ships so that they finally drop and somewhere in the earth just like the missing airplanes they can they can because they catch the they caught the things and then they can drop it anyway [anywhere?] in the earth

Comprehension checks

M: Because song is er something like to present your friendship every people even you don't know the language of the the other country you also like a song

T: You mean just how communicate between animals and and humans?

Ta: The pilot went missing is disappear

E: What? Pardon?

Ta: The pilot went missing aeroplane went missing is disappear

Vocabulary contextualization

T: How does Christie's disability affect his life?

W: His disability er make his father dislike him.

T: It is er only a bad effect but there is also some good effect to him beco er because of his disability er he can cons he can be concentrate in er to paint and building his confident to do something something like that

APPENDIX 3: Film Discussion Transcription: a comparison of random extracts from Discussion 2 and Discussion 5

Discussion 2 (5 participants)

T: But I don't think so er because er I think Charlie found that er Irene is er er is er doing some illegal things er or just er want also want to killed him so he's disappointed and then er kill h kill her first maybe

M: But he did he know that Irene want to kill want to kill him?

T: Er maybe he guessed [pause] from the telephone conversation

M: Yeah

H: So you er you er your meaning is that Charlie er is this because Charlie realize that Irene may maybe kill her may kill him so that's why he choose family over his true love?

T: Er but also he

H: But

T: he's disappointed because er he know Irene is er employed by er er by a bad man or something like that er she she do's some illegal things or something like that so he is disappointed

H: So if if if's he he is not disappointed because er say er assume that Irene er is not er did not er will not will not kill him er is not intended to kill him er do you still think that Cha Charlie will choose family over his true love?

T: Er [pause] if Charlie believes Irene then there is no problem no sad ending I think

Discussion 5 (6 participants)

M: Why they so interest

F: You mean hu human being

M: Yeah I mean

F: If something like a UFO er happen in Hong Kong or something like that do you do you feel interest in to that to to that kind of thing?

M: I think you

F: But

M: You must

C: Excuse me very interesting to know the UFO but for example you not to go to the UFO

M: Because you know at the end of the movie er people when the door of the UFO open people was very scared

S: But how can the er alien be so brave?

C: I think they were scared

H: Do you think the creature in the film was scare scared of the people in earth?

C: Yeah

H: Why?

C: Why? Because you you you don't know each other

H: But I don't think so I think er the creature in the UFO may be much clever than us and they think that they will control us

C: But not when you in the earth you something you ever seen in the earth you will think human being is the most powerful and you see something strange then I think you will scare of it

H: Yes but I think the creatures are confident enough that they can control the earth they are more powerful than us

M: But the er the alien don't know whether we are clever than them

T: But they have come they have come to er the earth several times I think

M: But before but before they come to the earth Deniece said er when the first time the first time

T: The first visit

M: Yeah the first visit

H: But er you can see when when they come and they can destroy all the things in the earth then I think they they are sure that they are power more powerful

T: They don't know to care anything because they have much knowledge about it much power

IV

Technology

This section examines the use of technology to promote learner autonomy. As Esch points out in her chapter, technology is often seen as automatically aiding learner autonomy. In fact, technology, like materials, can hinder learner autonomy just as easily as promote it — what counts is the way in which it can be used, and the extent to which the technology controls the learner.

In Chapter 13, David Little explores the processes involved in learner autonomy and considers how these processes can be fostered by computer-based technologies. In the first part of the chapter, Little points out that autonomy (as freedom to learn) is a characteristic of humans which is, paradoxically, constrained by the equally human need to interact (i.e. dependence). He sees this "compulsion to interact" as fundamental to learning. Little draws implications from the unconscious autonomy of L1 acquisition for the conscious autonomy required for successful L2 learning in formal education, involving a combination of learning by doing and learning by reflection.

In the second part of the chapter, Little discusses ways in which information systems can facilitate the development of learner autonomy. He considers three types of interaction: interaction *with* information systems (e.g. using tutorial and pedagogic CALL programs), interaction *around* information systems (e.g. group word processing or group interaction around an interactive video program) and interaction *via* information systems (e.g. using e-mail and the World Wide Web). Little argues that an information system will develop learner autonomy to the extent that it is able to facilitate collaborative interaction and (through interaction) reflection on language and language learning. He thus sees 'inhuman' information systems as having the potential to nurture a very human characteristic — autonomy.

One of the types of system described by Little in his discussion of interaction that can take place *around* information systems is his *Autotutor* interactive video program. David Gardner and Rocío Blasco García describe another interactive video program in Chapter 14. A key feature of their program is the bilingual support provided to viewers as they watch parts of a full-length movie, and the authors consider to what extent this support could help beginning learners of Spanish develop enough confidence to watch full-length movies independently. Their findings reinforce Lee's conclusion (Chapter 11) about the need of low proficiency students for support when dealing with authentic texts. Gardner and Blasco García's data also illustrate the use made of support — an aspect of learner use of technology which is examined in more detail in Chapter 18.

Another program that provides access to authentic texts is described in Chapter 15. In this chapter, John Milton, Ian Smallwood and James Purchase describe a prototype computer program designed to aid language use. In the program, the user will have access to a variety of linguistic data, all from within his/her normal word-processing environment. The program allows for learning by doing and learning by modelling, and largely provides the opportunity for, in Little's terms, interaction *with* an information system. At the present stage, peer collaboration (interaction *around* an information system) is an optional feature of the system and it is not clear to what extent the program might develop language-learning awareness or lead to learner autonomy. But it will be interesting to see to what extent users of such a powerful tool (like certain users of word processors) are enabled to reflect on their writing and to take more control over it as a result.

13

Freedom to learn and compulsion to interact: promoting learner autonomy through the use of information systems and information technologies

David Little

Introduction

This chapter is divided into two parts. In the first part I explore the nature and processes of learner autonomy, and in the second I consider how information systems and information technologies can contribute to the development of autonomy in second and foreign language learning. Essentially, I shall argue

1. that learner autonomy is a special instance of a socio-psychological phenomenon that is central to human experience in some domains and to human potential in all domains;
2. that autonomy (as freedom to learn) combines with dependence (as biological imperative to interact) to generate communicative processes that are fundamental to a definition of what it is to be human; and
3. that information systems and information technologies can promote the development of learner autonomy to the extent that they can stimulate, mediate and extend the range and scope of the social and psychological interaction on which all learning depends.

Perspectives on learner autonomy

A working definition

The essence of learner autonomy is acceptance of responsibility for one's own learning (see, e.g., Holec 1981, Little 1991). This entails establishing a personal agenda for learning, taking at least some of the initiatives that shape the learning process, and developing a capacity to evaluate the extent and success of one's learning. According to this definition, learner autonomy has both affective/motivational and metacognitive dimensions. It presupposes a positive attitude to the purpose, content and process of learning on the one hand and well-developed metacognitive skills on the other.

Understood in this sense, autonomy is a defining characteristic of all sustained learning that attains long-term success. It is the means by which the learner transcends the limitations of the learning situation and applies what he or she has learned to the day-to-day business of living. Clearly, this is a consideration that has particular urgency in the case of second or foreign language learning: to the extent that the purpose of language learning is to develop communicative proficiency in the target language, autonomy is the learner characteristic that facilitates target language use in the larger world that lies beyond the immediate learning environment. It is also the characteristic that allows the learner to take maximum advantage of the language-learning opportunities that continually arise in language use. According to this definition, learner autonomy is not the product of one particular pedagogical style, neither is it tied to one particular organizational model. It is to be found in classrooms as well as in self-access learning schemes, among children of primary school age and adolescents as well as among university students and adults.

Terms like 'personal agenda', 'initiative', and 'self-evaluation' inevitably emphasize the individuality of each learner as regards needs, purposes, capacities, and ultimate achievement. Yet in formal educational contexts as elsewhere learning can proceed only via interaction, so that the freedoms by which we recognize learner autonomy are always constrained by the learner's dependence on the support and cooperation of others. This paradox is fundamental to human nature and human experience. Reviewing the design constraints on a unified theory of cognition, Newell (1990: 20) makes the point thus:

> Humans must live autonomously within a social community. [...] One aspect of autonomy is greater capability to be free of dependencies on the environment. [...] But, conversely, much that we have learned from ethology and social theory speaks to the dependence of individuals upon the communities in which they are raised and reside. [...] If you take us out of our communities, we become inept and dysfunctional in many ways.

The paradox of autonomy lies at the heart of first language acquisition and developmental learning.

Autonomy in first language acquisition and developmental learning

It is clear to any observant parent or caregiver that small children exercise a high degree of psychological and social autonomy in the acquisition of their first language. Their linguistic knowledge develops in a broadly predictable way that is nevertheless largely impervious to external intervention; and it does so as a result of processes of social interaction that children themselves manipulate and control. Even at the pre-linguistic stage it seems that infants are under a biological compulsion to create opportunities for learning; yet at the same time, language acquisition, socialization and acculturation depend crucially on the interactive support of others. Wells (1985: 24) summarizes the situation as follows:

> From the work of Trevarthen (1979) and Stern (1977), who observed and recorded infants interacting with their mothers, it appears that, long before they are able to interact with the physical world, infants are already behaving in ways that elicit responses from their parents and are thereby gaining feedback concerning the effects of their own behaviour. What both researchers noticed was that it is the infant who typically initiates the interaction and decides when it should end. However, it is the mother who, by the timing and aptness of her responses, gives continuity to the interaction in such a way that it looks as if the pair are engaging in something very like a conversation without words.

The fact that infants are able to interact with parents and caregivers on the basis of shared attention implies the early development of what we might call 'intersubjective awareness', that is, the development of a sense both of their separateness from their communication partners and of their essential similarity to them (Wells 1987: 35). We must suppose that, at least in the earliest stages of development, this awareness is implicit and unconscious. It is one of those metaprocesses which are "an essential component of acquisition, which continuously function at all levels of development" (Karmiloff-Smith 1983: 35f.). Another such process is 'metalinguistic' and has to do with the gradual growth of a capacity to analyze and manipulate elements of the linguistic system. In the later stages of first language acquisition, socialization and acculturation, especially under the influence of schooling, these metaprocesses have the capacity to become explicit and conscious. In other words, they become available as tools of intentional reflection, analysis and synthesis.

At this point it is necessary to confront an obvious objection to the line of argument that I am developing. It is a well-known fact that first language acquisition research has mostly been undertaken within the framework of western child-rearing practices. The child-centredness on which these practices tend to be based is by no means universal. Thus the question arises whether the 'input and interaction' model of first language development that lies behind what I have been saying is itself universally valid. Much more research must be done before we can attempt a definitive answer to this question. But since all human beings belong to the same biological species, it would be astonishing if the modes of first language development turned out to be infinitely variable. In a recent review of the available literature, Lieven (1994: 68) confirms this, finding no support for

> the idea that children can learn language in an infinite range of environments, including one in which they simply input a sufficient variety of sentences which are relatively meaningless to them into their 'Language Acquisition Device' and grammar effortlessly emerges. *The environment is made meaningful both by the child itself and by others.* (italics added)

It does, then, seem that — even allowing for large variation in cultural beliefs and social practices — first language acquisition and developmental learning are the product equally of the child's psychological and social autonomy and of the interactive support that is given by parents, siblings and caregivers. This leads us to a consideration of the relation between developmental learning and early schooling, especially from the perspective of language and discourse structure.

Learning in formal educational contexts

Educational psychologists, educational theorists and curriculum reformers have often contrasted the routine efficiency and effectiveness of developmental and experiential learning with the relative inefficiency and ineffectiveness of much schooling (see, e.g., Bruner 1966; Barnes 1976; Illich 1979). Here a word of caution is in order: our concern to define the human organism in terms of universal mechanisms undergoing universal processes must not mislead us into supposing that we can somehow bring all children, adolescents and adults to the same level of educational achievement. At the same time, however, a disjunction between developmental and experiential learning on the one hand and schooling on the other has been widely documented; and it seems reasonable enough to suppose that this disjunction causes many learners to achieve less than their capacities might otherwise allow.

Research undertaken in this area has found that the structure of classroom discourse tends to work against what I have defined as the child's natural autonomy. Tizard and Hughes (1984), for example, found that while children made 47% of the sustaining contributions to conversation at home, they made only 19% at school. Similarly, Wells (1987: 86) found that children's experience of language in use in the classroom differed significantly in emphasis from their experience of language in use at home; in particular, in the classroom they tended to be confined to a narrow range of discourse roles. What is more, Wells (ibid.: 87) found that classroom discourse differed significantly from conversation at home as regards the semantic structuring of interaction:

> Compared with parents, it is only half as often that [teachers] incorporate the meanings offered in the children's utterances, either by extending those meanings or by inviting the children to extend them themselves. By contrast, teachers are twice as likely as parents to develop the meanings that they themselves have introduced into the conversation.

Now, it is fundamental to the view I have summarized of first language acquisition and developmental learning that new knowledge can be assimilated only in terms of and in relation to what is already known. Wells (ibid.: 118) expresses the matter thus:

> [...] learning involves an *active* reconstruction of the knowledge or skill that is presented, on the basis of the learner's existing internal model of the world. The process is therefore essentially *interactional* in nature, both within the learner and between the learner and the teacher, and calls for the negotiation of meaning, not its unidirectional transmission.

If children are to integrate what they learn at school with the rest of what they know — if, to use Barnes's (1976) terms, "school knowledge" is to become part of their "action knowledge" — it is essential that classroom discourse gives full value to *their* meanings, which necessarily reflect the current state of *their* knowledge.

This consideration is implicit in Tharp and Gallimore's (1988) notion of the "instructional conversation". They follow Vygotsky (1978) in conceptualizing teaching as "assisted performance", in which teacher and learners "weave together spoken and written language with previous understanding" (Tharp and Gallimore 1988: 111). One crucial finding of the large-scale and long-term research project on which Tharp and Gallimore report was that in order to succeed, instructional conversations must establish their relevance and accessibility by adhering to the interactional and discourse norms of the community in which the learners have grown up. Bruner implies a similar point when he argues (1986: 127) that "discovery learning" is really "learning by inventing":

> It is not just that the child must make his knowledge his own, but that he must make it his own in a community of those who share his sense of belonging to a culture. It is this that leads me to emphasize not only discovery and invention but the importance of negotiating and sharing — in a word, of joint culture creating as an object of schooling and as an appropriate step en route to becoming a member of the adult society in which one lives out one's life.

What I have said about schooling so far has been concerned with the early years. But there is no reason to suppose that the nature and underlying processes of learning are somehow transformed in the more advanced stages of schooling and beyond.

According to Bruner (ibid.), "Much of the process of education consists of being able to distance oneself in some way from what one knows by being able to reflect on one's knowledge". This ability depends on the making explicit of those metaprocesses which, following Karmiloff-Smith and others, I have argued are a prerequisite both of first language acquisition and of early socialization and acculturation. In order to achieve this, it is essential that the discourse of schooling should as far as possible be characterized by the same processes of supportive negotiation as the discourse of the home. But this on its own is not enough: the autonomy that is evidently a biological imperative must be gradually supplemented by an autonomy that is the product of deliberate reflection and analysis. In relation to naturalistic processes like first language acquisition and developmental learning, autonomy is involuntary; in relation to the culturally determined processes of schooling it is conscious and intentional. I would argue that autonomy in this latter sense transcends whatever differences separate one culture from another precisely because it is an extension of autonomy in the former sense, which appears to be universal. I would also argue, however, that the modalities of learner autonomy are capable of almost infinite variation, depending on the particular cultural circumstances in which it is developed.

In general, the development of learner autonomy as a conscious and intentional phenomenon is likely to depend to a high degree on the development of literacy skills, since they greatly enhance the individual's capacity to distance him- or herself from the content and process of learning — as Goody (1977: 13) has observed, "it was the setting down of speech that enabled man clearly to separate words, to manipulate their order and to develop syllogistic forms of reasoning". The ways in which literacy skills are developed in a particular culture and the uses to which they are commonly put are likely to play a major role in determining the forms that learner autonomy will most easily take in that culture.

Implications for second language learning in formal contexts

In naturalistic contexts, language learning is inseparable from language use. Children do not first acquire their mother tongue in order then to communicate with their parents: on the contrary, acquisition is a direct product of their attempt to communicate with whatever linguistic and other resources are available to them. By contrast, one of the most persistent problems of language teaching in formal contexts, especially when it happens at a distance from the target language community, is the disjunction that can easily arise between language learning and communicative language use. Against this disjunction, Legenhausen and Wolff (see Eck et al. 1994) have proposed a model of language learning as language use. In this model, language proficiency combines communicative skills with language awareness and is underpinned by language-learning awareness, so that the learner is at once:

1. communicator — continually using and gradually developing communicative skills;
2. experimenter/researcher — gradually developing an explicit analytical knowledge of the target language system and some of the socio-cultural constraints that shape its use; and
3. intentional learner — developing an explicit awareness of both affective and metacognitive aspects of learning.

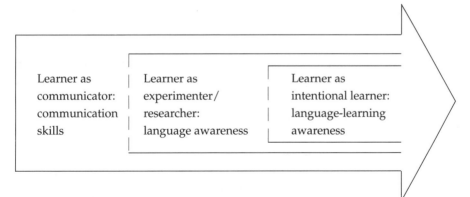

Figure 1: Dynamic model of second language proficiency: language learning as language use

It seems to me that this model can be expressed dynamically as in Figure 1 above, which makes three claims:

1. that the lowest level of proficiency in any language is a matter of developing basic communication skills;
2. that progress beyond a certain rather primitive point is possible only if learning is accompanied by metalinguistic and metacognitive processes of analysis and reflection (in first language development this is the point at which proficiency begins to depend on literacy); and

3. that in order to make the most progress possible, it is necessary to develop language-learning awareness, since only thus can we guarantee that learners will be able to draw maximum learning advantage from occasions of target language use that arise outside the classroom.

The dotted vertical lines indicate that the divisions between the components of the model are not absolute. (This way of expressing the model should not be taken to imply a pedagogical ordering. On the contrary, the development of language awareness and of language-learning awareness should be central pedagogical concerns from the beginning of the teaching/ learning process.)

The Legenhausen and Wolff model implies a pedagogy that gives equal attention to the internalization of target language forms through communicative practice and the development of analytical skills through language awareness; a pedagogy, in other words, in which learning by doing interacts thoroughly with learning by reflection. The appropriate vehicle for such a pedagogy is a version of Tharp and Gallimore's (1988) "instructional conversation" which would seek to develop the learner's communicative proficiency and language awareness by means which are both 'natural' (conversation is the engine of naturalistic language learning) and 'analytic' (instruction implies deliberation and clarity of focus). If it is to achieve our pedagogical aims, the instructional conversation must be conducted, from the earliest stages and as far as possible, in the target language.

Bruner (1986: 132f.) writes as follows on the role of the learner's first language in education:

> Language not only transmits, it creates or constitutes knowledge or "reality". Part of that reality is the stance that the language implies toward knowledge and reflection, and the generalized set of stances one negotiates creates in time a sense of one's self. Reflection and "distancing" are crucial aspects of achieving a sense of the range of possible stances — a metacognitive step of huge import. The language of education is the language of culture creating, not of knowledge consuming or knowledge acquisition alone.

These words remind us that the reflective distancing processes that are central to the success of schooling and (as I have argued) to the development of learner autonomy, also play a crucial role in the development of a sense of self. Relative to schooling in general, the autonomous learner is the one whose learning gradually enlarges his or her sense of identity; relative to second language learning in particular, the autonomous learner is the one for whom the target language gradually becomes an integral part of what he or she is.

Information systems and information technologies as tools for the development of learner autonomy

Some preliminary considerations

The purpose of the second part of my chapter is not to offer an exhaustive array of recipes but to outline a general approach to information systems as tools for the development of autonomy in second language learning. I use the term 'information system' rather than 'computer' to signal the fact that we are rapidly moving towards fully integrated multimedia. In what follows I shall take account of the use that can be made of the computer as a stand-alone device, but I also want to engage with the fact that information systems are being developed and networked worldwide as repositories of information and channels of communication. In the very near future we shall need to ask ourselves to what extent we can still talk of second language learning taking place at a distance from the target language community; and we shall also need to consider whether the capacity to interact with and via information systems should be included as a routine part of the behavioural repertoire towards which many, perhaps most, second language learners should aspire.

The perspective from which I want to consider the capacity of information systems to stimulate and support the development of autonomy in second language learning is, of course, the one that I have sketched in the first part of this chapter. I have followed Legenhausen and Wolff in proposing a model of language learning as language use in which learning by doing interacts thoroughly with learning by reflection. The pedagogy by which I believe this model should be fulfilled is founded on interaction in which meanings are negotiated on the basis of what the learners know already. I make the Vygotskian assumption that the development of a capacity for reflection and analysis, central to the development of learner autonomy, depends on the development and internalization of a capacity to participate fully and critically in social interactions. I also assume that in the great majority of cases, learner achievement will fall a long way short of the balanced bilingualism which — against centuries of counter-evidence — seems to remain the unexamined goal of so much institutional language teaching.

This latter assumption helps to explain why I think learner autonomy is so important. Most language learners are acutely conscious of the deficiencies in linguistic knowledge and communicative skill that define them as non-native speakers of their target language. In relation to the target language, their metacognitive and metalinguistic processes are inevitably less well developed than in relation to their mother tongue — but under the pressure generated by the need to communicate with partial linguistic resources, they are likely to be proportionately more explicit. Mental processes that are explicit are in principle amenable to intentional control, and it is through such control that learners can make the most of the resources available to them.

According to my model, the essential task of second language pedagogy is to engage learners in activities that will enable them to internalize those skills on which face-to-face interaction depends, develop those insights into linguistic form that will enable them to extend their linguistic skills to the performance of new tasks, and develop those insights into the learning process that will enable them to organize their learning to best effect and to derive maximum learning advantage from occasions of second language use.

The rest of my argument is organized according to three kinds of relation between language learners and information systems: interactions *with*, interactions *around*, and interactions *via* information systems.

Interacting with information systems

To date the most widespread application of computers in language learning has involved interaction *with* information systems. Two kinds of program have been used, embodying two kinds of role for the computer — defined by Higgins (1988) as "magister" and "pedagogue". In the *magister* role the computer is a substitute teacher. Programs of this kind, so-called tutorial CALL, lend themselves to delivery by self-access because the learner has only to respond to the computer's 'initiatives': there is little chance that he or she will get lost. Early in this chapter I insisted that learner autonomy is not confined to any particular organizational mode; equally, no organizational mode can in itself guarantee the development of learner autonomy. The use of tutorial CALL programs in self-access is a case in point. Let me illustrate what I mean by reference to one of the most widely used of all tutorial CALL programs, *Storyboard*.

Storyboard is an authoring program that allows the teacher rapidly to create a corpus of learning materials by assembling a directory of texts which the program then turns into so many exercises. It does this by displaying strings of asterisks instead of words. The learner's task is to reconstitute the text. There are options that allow the learner to read the text for varying amounts of time before attempting the exercise; and other options that allow the teacher/author to provide various hints and clues. If texts are used that derive from or are thematically related to other materials the learner is using, *Storyboard* can perform a stimulating and highly effective reinforcement function. The interaction that it generates is psychological and calls into play especially the learner's lexical and morpho-syntactic knowledge of the target language. When two or more learners work together on a *Storyboard* exercise, this psychological interaction is externalized and enriched, and may assume the characteristics of an 'instructional conversation' of the kind I have been advocating, which combines the performance of a language-learning task with critical reflection on the language system and (perhaps) conscious manipulation of metacognitive processes. However, there is no guarantee that this will happen spontaneously. If programs like *Storyboard* are to contribute to the development of learner autonomy, they will do so as a result of factors that lie elsewhere in the learning environment. In other words, any 'instructional conversations' that they engender will be extensions of learning discourse that has begun as interaction between teacher and learners. (I should note in passing that I do not believe this situation would be significantly changed by the introduction of intelligent programs. Suppose, for example, a version of *Storyboard* that was able to prompt the learner on the basis of incorrect input. In itself, such a program would no more develop the autonomy of the learner than a teacher standing at the front of a class and prompting responses to her questions.)

What I have said about the capacity of tutorial CALL to foster the development of learner autonomy applies also to programs in which the computer plays the role of *pedagogue*, the learner's willing helper, as the example of concordancing software shows. The possibility of exploring lexico-grammatical usage by making a keyword-in-context concordance is a powerful addition to the language learner's toolkit (see Johns 1986, 1994). But the fact that learners can use concordancing programs on their own in self-access is no guarantee that such programs will aid the development of learner autonomy. If they do, it will again be because they are being used to extend an 'instructional conversation' that has its origin in interaction between teacher and learners.

Interacting around information systems

I noted above that when tutorial CALL programs are used by two or more learners working together, they may engender an interaction that externalizes and enriches processes of psychological interaction. Such interactions *around* information systems are potentially so powerful in their effect that they require discussion in their own right. I shall consider two examples, the use of word-processing software as the basis for group writing projects, and the use of an interactive videocassette system by small groups of learners working together in self-access.

The chief argument in favour of group work as a means of developing learner autonomy is Vygotskian in origin: collaboration between two or more learners on a constructive task can only be achieved by externalizing, and thus making explicit, processes of analysis, planning and synthesis that remain largely internal, and perhaps also largely implicit, when the task is performed by an individual learner working alone. When a word-processing program is used as the tool by which learners undertake a group writing project, these effects may be achieved with particular intensity. Legenhausen and Wolff (1991), for example, found that it was much easier for learners to be explicit about, and thus explicitly develop, planning and revising strategies when they used a word processor than when they wrote with pen and paper. Their investigation suggested that using a word processor can change learners' attitudes to the writing task and also the strategies they employ in performing it. Written language is typically less tolerant of errors than spoken language, though within written language there are degrees of formality and corresponding degrees of error-tolerance. Legenhausen and Wolff propose that texts written on a computer screen combine informal and formal properties in a particularly stimulating way. The ephemeral character of the text before it is saved and the ease with which it can be revised recall the informality of spontaneous speech and encourage learners to take risks. On the other hand, the fact that word processors allow infinite revision encourages learners to refine their work and make it increasingly formal. To this it is worth adding that at every stage the cut-and-paste facility emphasizes the constructive nature of the writing task: as they are inserted, deleted, moved about the screen, words, phrases and paragraphs become the building blocks of text in a powerfully literal sense.

When used as the basis for group writing projects, then, word-processing programs have the capacity to stimulate learning conversations that include the processes of analysis and reflective negotiation essential to the development of learner autonomy. I believe that word processors are more apt to promote learner autonomy without the intervention of the teacher than group work focused on tutorial CALL programs. But again the drive to autonomy derives from the essential nature of collaboration between human beings rather than from particular characteristics of the information system that is being exploited. The same is true of my second example of interaction *around* information systems, the implementation of the *Autotutor* interactive videocassette system as a tool for group work in self-access.

The *Autotutor* was originally developed by the Centre for Language and Communication Studies, Trinity College, Dublin, as a means of delivering authentic video materials to individual language learners working in self-access mode (see Little and Davis 1986). The idea was that the computer program in which the video material was embedded should take the place of a printed worksheet, automating access to the video and providing learners with simple feedback on the pre- and post-viewing tasks they were invited to perform. The first version of the *Autotutor* used the Acorn BBC family of computers; the more recent version, *Autotutor* II, is based on the PC (for a fuller description, see Little 1994a). Throughout the successive phases of the *Autotutor* project we have been concerned with the nature and quality of the interaction between language learner and *Autotutor* program (see, e.g., Little 1987, 1988b). One of the great virtues of the *Autotutor* is the ease with which programs can be developed; the corresponding vice is that programs offer only limited interactivity. This quickly brought us to the same conclusion as many other practitioners of computer-assisted language learning (see, e.g., Stevens 1992): that the effectiveness of our programs would be greatly enhanced if we designed them to be used by small groups of learners working collaboratively in self-access (for a fuller account of the rationale behind this decision, again see Little 1994a).

This was the direction that we gave our research when we came to implement *Autotutor* II. As in our previous work, we continued to embed authentic video material in simple computer programs that provided learners with a viewing focus and post-viewing comprehension exercises. But we now inserted into our programs screens that encouraged learners to engage in discussion of various kinds — for example, pooling their linguistic resources and world knowledge to arrive at the meaning of a particular word or phrase, or sharing their often very disparate experience in order to negotiate a common focus on the video they were about to view or a common understanding of what they had just seen.

We have now conducted six experiments following this approach. Each experiment has used a different *Autotutor* program. In every case, the *Autotutor* program has stimulated a lively conversation among the learners, who have drawn on both video material and computer interaction for linguistic support. It has been noticeable that during their *Autotutor* session learners have engaged with one another as much as with the interactive video program, getting to know one another better through the processes of negotiation by which they have run the program.

We are sometimes asked whether *Autotutor* programs do anything that could not be done by a combination of videocassette, worksheets, a dictionary and a reference grammar. The answer to this question is that an *Autotutor* program provides learners with thematic content, linguistic resources, and an interactive structure that combine to make it much easier for them to conduct a learning conversation without the supporting presence of a teacher. The authentic video on which the program is based offers verbal meanings elaborated with various kinds of visual support. The computer program in which the video is embedded typically repeats and reinforces those meanings in written form. The interactive structure of the program provides the learners with a discourse framework which appears greatly to facilitate their interaction with one another.

At any particular stage in any collaborative task it is likely that one member of the group will play the role of leader or coordinator. Our experience with the *Autotutor* is no exception to this general norm. In the learning conversations that our programs have stimulated, it has evidently seemed quite natural to the learners in each group that they should take turns in assuming the role of teacher. Analysis of video recordings of these conversations suggests that this role is passed around the group according to a handful of principles — one of the most obvious has to do with successful performance. Again we are reminded of the Vygotskian principle that the psychological capacity for reflection and analysis is an internalization of social processes of negotiation. Learners who are able to assume the role of teacher in the performance of group work around an interactive videocassette program should be able gradually to internalize that role as a more refined capacity for intentional control of (aspects of) the learning process.

Interacting via information systems

My discussion of interaction *with* and interaction *around* information systems has been concerned with developments that are subordinate to the fact of language learning. In other words, without language learning there would be no *Storyboard*, no concordancing software of the kind developed by Johns (1986), no projects to exploit word processors as the basis for group writing activity, and no *Autotutor*. By contrast, the development and worldwide networking of information systems as repositories of information and channels of communication is a phenomenon larger than and wholly independent of language learning. It is part of 'real life' (for an accessible overview of the present situation, see Rheingold 1994). Over the next few years, however, these new and rapidly expanding information systems are likely to have a profound effect on the ways in which we communicate within and between societies and, by extension, on the range of skills foreign language learners need to develop. I conclude the second part of my paper by considering briefly the implications of these systems for the development of autonomy in language learning.

In the majority of learning environments, the most accessible means of exploiting international networking is electronic mail. Already there have been a number of projects designed to bring learners into contact with their peers in the target language community (see, e.g., Eck et al. 1994). Assuming the kind of group project orientation I have discussed in relation to word processing, electronic mail transcends the learning situation by carrying messages developed in the classroom to target language users at remote sites. In this way, the interactive processes involving reflection and analysis by which the message is elaborated are integrated with 'real life' interaction. In other words, processes apt to promote learner autonomy become part of a larger process whose purpose is intercultural communication. This can only strengthen the bi-directional relation between language learning and language use.

I argued earlier that word processing makes manifest the constructive nature of writing. The constructive nature of learning in general and of language learning in particular is likewise made explicit when remote information sources and communication networks are drawn into the learning environment. Research reported by Scardamalia et al. (1992) suggests that we have much to expect from growth in this area.

At present, communication via information networks proceeds mostly by writing. However, communication by voice and image is already a technical possibility and is destined to become increasingly central. As I implied earlier, within a few years learning environments that are linked to information networks will effectively be linked to the target language community. I take it that this phenomenon will encourage the development of learner autonomy in two ways. First, it will greatly extend the range and amount of information ('texts') that can provide a focus for the ex-ternalization of interactive processes that might otherwise remain internal and implicit. Secondly, it will reinforce the association between language learning and language use, adding new and powerful dimensions of social interaction. Incidentally, it will also allow learners to interact with one another at a distance: when communication is freely available via voice and image, it will be possible for 'classrooms' to be made up of network terminals separated from one another by large distances.

Conclusion

In the first part of this chapter I argued that autonomy in language learning is a special instance of a socio-psychological phenomenon that is central to human experience in some domains and to human potential in all domains. I proposed that autonomy (as freedom to learn) combines with dependence (as biological imperative to interact) to generate communicative processes that are fundamental to a definition of what it is to be human. In first language acquisition and developmental and experiential learning, these processes arise spontaneously; in formal learning environments they must be deliberately nurtured via modes of interaction that encourage the externalization and making explicit of metalinguistic and metacognitive processes. It is on this externalization and making explicit that learner autonomy crucially depends.

In the second part of the chapter I considered the role that information systems can play in the development of learner autonomy. Reviewing three modes of interaction, *with*, *around* and *via* information systems, I came to the conclusion that the decisive factor is the capacity of information systems to facilitate precisely the externalization and making explicit of meta-processes and thus to strengthen the bi-directional relation between language learning and language use.

When computers were first introduced into classrooms, there was a tendency in some quarters to talk of the dehumanization of learning. I hope I have shown that, potentially at least, the reverse is the case; that information systems have the capacity to foster the development of learner autonomy because they help us gain access to processes that otherwise can easily remain internal, implicit and relatively undeveloped. In language learning we want to develop autonomy in our learners because autonomous learners are by definition autonomous users of a language. As I have elaborated it, the ideal of learner autonomy implies that proficiency in a second language should be fully integrated with the learner's view of self. But note that the model of second language proficiency I have taken over from Legenhausen and Wolff casts the learner in three interdependent roles — communicator, experimenter/researcher and intentional learner. I conclude by pointing out that the self-determination associated with the last of these roles has implications that reach far beyond the sphere of second language learning and second language use. Learners who achieve autonomy have secured the means to become — in Michael Ignatieff's (1990) arresting phrase — "the artists of their own lives".

14

Interactive video as self-access support for language-learning beginners

David Gardner and Rocío Blasco García

Introduction

This chapter discusses an experiment with an interactive video program which was written to support beginner learners in using a target language movie as a source of authentic linguistic input. A key element of this approach is the provision of bilingual support screens at strategic points in the program which users can choose to access. The purpose of the experiment was to assess whether this kind of interactive video support program is an effective contribution towards moving learners in the direction of greater autonomy in their learning. Although this is a preliminary study with a relatively small number of users, it provides enough data to make judgements about the utility of the program and to decide whether further experimentation is justified.

Video is widely perceived as a useful language-learning medium both in the classroom (e.g. Geddes and Sturtridge 1982b; Lonergan 1984; Tomalin 1986; Cooper et al. 1991) and in self-access learning environments (e.g. Dickinson 1987; Sheerin 1989; McCall 1992; Moore 1992; Carvalho 1993; Gardner 1994). In this experiment, an interactive program was used to enhance the use of video. The immediate goal of the interactive program is to increase the learners' confidence in their ability to make use of authentic video as a language-learning tool. The ultimate goal of the program is to encourage learners to experiment with using authentic video without the support of an interactive video program. If such a goal is achieved, any target language video would become a potential source of language-learning material. The range of such material is vast, easily accessible and cheap.

The interactive program discussed here was written specifically for individual learners to use in a self-access centre. It supports the use of a Spanish language movie. However, the findings of this experiment would be equally applicable to programs written to support movies in other languages.

Background to program production

The final product (described below) is the result of careful decision making in the selection of the video material to be used and in the writing of the interactive support program. This section looks at the reasons for the choices which were made.

Self-access vs. classroom materials

All the students on the language courses from which the subjects were taken were observed to be too dependent on the teacher and the course book as the only sources of learning materials. The main aim of the program was to reduce this dependence by showing students they are able to use authentic language materials independently of the classroom environment and by encouraging them to explore the possibilities of autonomous learning.

Interactive video vs. linear video

Authentic language video without any support is too linguistically challenging for the beginners participating in this experiment. This is clear from the fact that throughout their course the learners had access to 20 target language videos in a self-access centre. Very few learners looked at them and those who did gave up very quickly and reported dissatisfaction with the experience.

To make this material accessible, careful selection of segments from within the video material is necessary and learning support materials need to be provided. This could be done by providing a paper-based worksheet with the video; however, this does not overcome what is "probably the single greatest difficulty in using video" (Gardner 1994: 108) which is simply that of the autonomous learner being able to find the correct place on the tape.

Interactive video programming is a more effective method of helping learners focus on relevant materials. It is also better than paper-based solutions at providing immediate feedback to the learner, at keeping a score for the learner's reference and at recording (for the researcher) what the learner has done while using the program. It also allows greater flexibility in the design of the non-video support materials and the provision of bilingual options is more easily handled by a computer than it can be in paper-based materials. It might also be argued that interactive video has a greater motivational effect on the learner than paper-based plus video-cassette materials. There is no conclusive evidence for such an argument and although it is important to note the argument it will not be pursued in this chapter.

Authentic video vs. language-teaching video

Little (1994b: 1) has defined authentic video materials as those which are "not specially made for language learners and serving some socio-cultural communicative purpose in the target language community". Lonergan (1984: 4) recognizes that "the outstanding feature of video films is the ability to present complete communicative situations". Such materials can overcome the disadvantages of those which are specifically written for language learning. In most language-teaching video materials the segments are rather short and concentrated on particular teaching points. Consequently, they are unlikely to sustain the learner's interest in their story lines. While this may not be a problem for learners whose interest is solely in assimilating the new language points focused on in the video, it may discourage learners whose interest is in immersing themselves in their target language community.

Language-teaching videos do not always contain natural speech, especially at beginners' level. Even at an early stage, learners should experience 'real' language (in such a way that they can cope with it). Admittedly, the language in some parts of some movies is not always the 'real' speech that would be heard in the streets — for example, it is unlikely that many Americans really speak in the cliché-ridden language of John Wayne or Sylvester Stallone. Nevertheless, movies are, in general, portraying real life — if a somewhat idealized form of it — in which real language is being used. In addition, movies generally provide a greater variety of accents, including regional, socio-economic group and gender variations. They also include a wide range of functional situations which demonstrate different uses of the language.

Moreover, an important feature of successful communication that can be better demonstrated through movies than through language-teaching videos is that it is not necessary to understand absolutely everything in order to understand the overall story.

Finally, the most obvious practical reason for choosing authentic target language video rather than language-teaching video is that there is so much of it. If the aim of encouraging learners to become autonomous in using this materials is successful, then a lot of material will be required.

Full-length movies vs. short programs or single movie segments

There are a number of reasons for choosing full-length (albeit carefully segmented) movies rather than other kinds of authentic target language video materials. The most important reason is that of building the confidence of the learners in their ability to work through an entire movie without getting lost. Using an entire movie also gives the program writer greater flexibility in choosing areas of focus which are of relevance to a particular group of learners. Other reasons for using movies revolve around the kind of language potential they offer which is not offered by other kinds of video.

Documentary programs, for example, tend to use a great deal of descriptive language but little or no interpersonal communication. They rarely use language in the kind of functional setting that the learners would have found useful. Had the aim of the learners been to use Spanish for giving a lecture, a documentary film might have been a good choice.

Single movie segments, perhaps dealing with one complete interaction within a movie, would be useful for intensive language work. However, the aim of the program was ultimately to encourage learners to make use of movies without any support. In this context, it was not useful to pursue intensive language study but rather to concentrate on building the learners' confidence by showing them that they were able to follow the gist of the story.

Bilingual support vs. target language immersion

In a previous study (Gardner 1993), the video footage and the computer screens were all entirely in the target language. This appeared to cause the learners no difficulties and avoided encouraging them to indulge in translation. Bush and Crotty (1991) also feel that the information provided by context within the video and the learners' control over the program "allow students to process meaning without translation" (p. 87). The current study, however, deals with beginners who may have felt unable to function adequately only in the target language. For this reason, bilingual support screens were provided for the advance organizer screens but not for the post-viewing question and answer screens. The use of bilingual support within the program is optional.

The program

The interactive video program is designed to support learners as they move through a movie in the target language. The program runs on an aXcess interactive video system which is an integrated videotape player with a controlling IBM PC-compatible computer. There are a number of reasons for selecting an interactive videotape system over a videodisc system (Laurillard 1984; Lambert and Hart 1991; Gardner 1993; Gardner 1994). The most important of these reasons, in the context of this study, is the enhanced choice of source material. The selection of a hardware system which uses videotape offered the flexibility to select anything available on VHS tape. By contrast, a more sophisticated interactive videodisc system would have allowed a more glossy production but would have restricted the choice of materials dramatically. While the production of an interactive program around videotape is less common than one that exploits videodisc, it is a method which has been used successfully on other occasions (Laurillard 1984; Bush and Crotty 1991; Armitage 1992; Gardner 1993).

Program structure

The program begins with an introductory sequence explaining its purpose and setting the scene for the video story. The program then shows ten segments from the video in sequential order. The segments are a variable number of minutes each and the total video viewing time by the end of the program is fourteen and a half minutes. Each segment is preceded by an advance organizer which explains to the learner what is going to happen and gives the learner a task to focus on while viewing. The advance organizers display initially in the target language but at the press of a key the learner can switch back and forth between the target language (Figure 1) and the language of instruction (Figure 2). This bilingual support is only available at this stage. After each segment, the learner answers one or two multiple-choice questions which are closely linked to the task set in the advance organizer. All questions are in the target language (with no bilingual support) and each has four possible answers. If an answer is incorrect, further tries may be made. The order in which the answer and the distractors are displayed is randomly varied for each new user. The program closes with a feedback session where suggestions for follow-up action are based on the individual's score. No time limits are set for any part of the program.

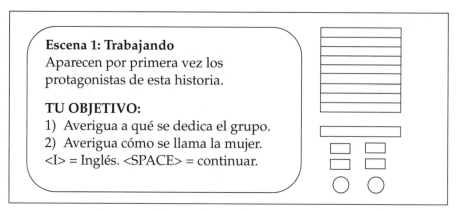

Figure 1: Advance organizer in the target language

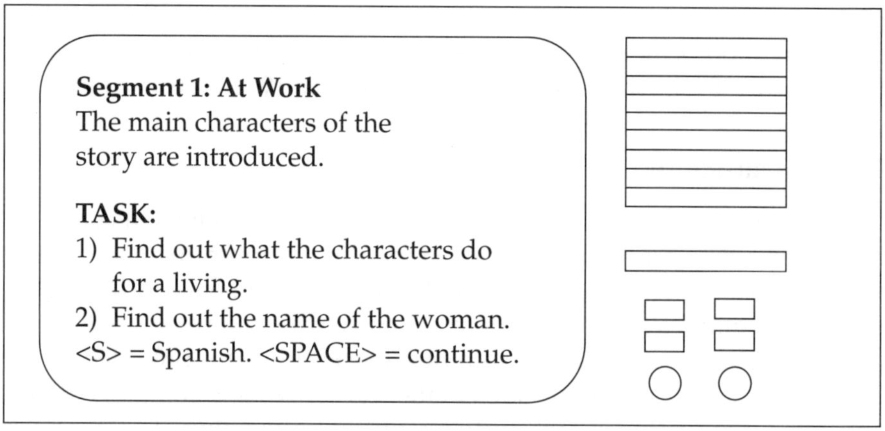

Figure 2: Advance organizer in the language of instruction

The learners

The subjects in this study were taken from students attending courses in Spanish which were open to university undergraduates from any year and any subject area (across all faculties). The group of subjects, therefore, represents a cross-section of university undergraduates. Their common points were that they were all native speakers of Cantonese, were all studying their university curriculum in English and were all beginners in Spanish. A total of 23 learners used the program within a period of two weeks (at times convenient to them). At the time of using the program all subjects had attended 55 to 60 hours of their Spanish course. Interviews with the teachers of these students suggest that the subjects were homogeneous in their level of ability in Spanish. No test of ability was given. It is the records of use by these learners and feedback from them which provide the data for this study.

Data collection methods

To assess the utility of our method as a support for autonomous learning we collected data about the use of the program in two ways:

1. The computer was programmed to record the choices that users made and how long they spent on each section of the program. This allowed data to be gathered about:
   (a) frequency of use of bilingual support;
   (b) time spent on advance organizer (in either language);
   (c) time spent on answering questions;
   (d) number of attempts at each question; and
   (e) final score.

2. All users completed a questionnaire after using the program. This allowed the collection of information about users' attitudes towards:
   (a) the hardware and software;
   (b) bilingual support;
   (c) the story line of the video;
   (d) the utility of the approach;
   (e) the level of difficulty of the program; and
   (f) the unsupported use of target language videos (pre- and post-use of the program).

The questionnaire also invited users to comment on ways of improving the program and to state preferences for story lines in future programs.

Data analysis

An analysis of the data recorded by the computer while subjects were using the program provides interesting information about a number of features of the program and the subjects' use of it.

Score

The program kept a running score by allocating one point for each answer which was correct first time. This was calculated as a percentage and fed back to the learner at the end of the program with comments about follow-up action depending on the final score achieved.

There were 19 questions and the number of correct answers per user ranged from 6 to 18 (see Figure 3). The final scores, therefore, ranged from 32% to 95%, with a median of 63% and an average of 65%. No pass mark is fixed for this program as its intention is to raise learners' confidence in their ability to comprehend rather than to test them. However, if the normal pass mark for assignments on the Spanish courses had been applied, 78% of the subjects would have passed.

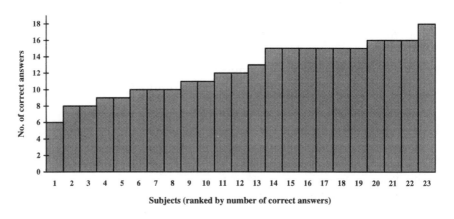

Figure 3: The number of correct answers per subject

In looking at the number of users who successfully answered questions correctly at the first attempt, it is noteworthy that none of the questions were correctly answered by all of the learners. It is also true that none of the questions were failed by all the subjects.

Two questions appeared from users' scores to be less easy to answer than other questions. The most difficult (91% of students failed to answer it successfully at their first attempt) is not recognized by the writer of the questions as being significantly more difficult than other questions. The second most difficult (78% failure) was the first question of the program. This is also not recognized as a difficult question, but it is conjectured that as it is the first question, users may not have paid sufficient attention to the advance organizer and/or the video segment.

The spread of correct answers through the users' records and the distribution of final scores indicates that the advance organizer screens and questions are pitched at the right level for the subject group. The scores also indicate that the program is successful in achieving its goal of helping users to comprehend authentic video. This may contribute to raising users' confidence.

Bilingual support

At the beginning of each of the ten sections of the program, users were presented with an advance organizer in Spanish. For each of these screens they had free access to an English translation. They were also free to switch back and forth between English and Spanish as often as they wished. There was a very clear division among the users in the use of this facility. Three of the subjects never used it at all and one used it for only 20% of the times it was available. By contrast, 19 of the subjects used the facility between 80% and 100% of the times it was available (see Figure 4). While there is no direct correlation between 100% use of bilingual support and the highest scores, it is significant that the three lowest scores in the group were among those who made little or no use of the bilingual support. There is one interesting case of a user who made no use of the bilingual support but achieved an above average score. This is, however, not the norm. In most cases there is some correlation between the use of bilingual support and a successful score.

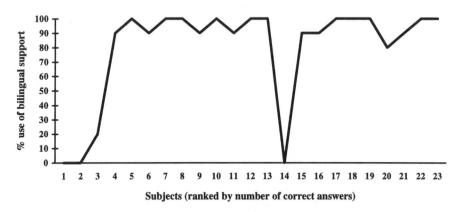

Figure 4: Use of the bilingual support

Of the 19 subjects who made extensive use of the bilingual support, it is noteworthy that a high proportion of the times when they did not use it (78%) falls within the first four sections (see Figure 5). It is difficult to know the reason for this.

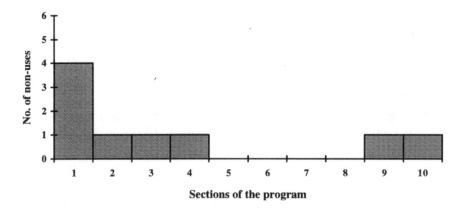

Figure 5: Non-use of bilingual support by normally high-frequency users

It is significant to note that in most cases where normally extensive users of bilingual support chose not to use it, their performance in related questions suffered. (It should be remembered that bilingual support is offered for each section, not for individual questions.) On these occasions, the number of attempts made to find the correct answers for each section was between 5% and 112% greater than in the sections where they did use bilingual support (see Figure 6). However, there is one exceptional case (subject 15) where the reverse is true. In this case, the number of attempts decreased by 22% when not using the bilingual support. The average increase in the number of attempts made to find correct answers among those subjects whose performance suffered was 55%.

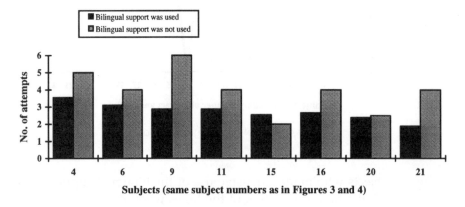

Figure 6: Average number of attempts needed to achieve a correct answer per section by the 8 subjects who used bilingual support extensively but not totally

This data clearly shows that the subjects usually made extensive use of the bilingual support in this program. It also shows that this use of the bilingual support resulted, in most cases, in an improvement in the users' ability to find the right answers.

Time

As this program is designed to allow learners to work at their own pace, there are no time limits. Nevertheless, it is important to look at the time learners might spend on the program. If they are not convinced that their time is being used efficiently, they will choose not to complete the program. In addition, if the total time needed to complete the program exceeds one hour, it is unlikely that the learners will find enough time within their busy schedules.

The computer records of use of the program show that the total time subjects spent on the program varies quite widely between 26 minutes and 50 minutes. The average time is 34 minutes. If a few minutes are added to allow time for users to organize themselves, start the hardware and load the software, the maximum time required would still fall within one hour for all users and the average time would be around 40 minutes.

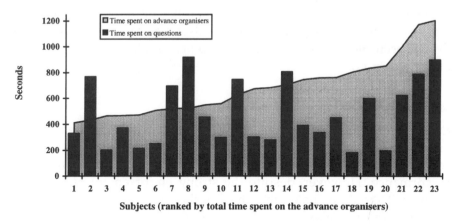

Figure 7: Time spent working on advance organizers and post-viewing questions

An interesting feature of the way subjects used the program is highlighted when comparing the time spent on pre-viewing activities (reading the advance organizers and thinking about the comprehension tasks) with the time spent on post-viewing activities (reading and answering the questions). The ratio between these two uses of their time ranges from 1:0.2 to 1:1.8

(see Figure 7). Although this is a wide range, 80% of the subjects fall into a narrower range between 1:0.4 and 1:0.8. This means that the learners are predominantly spending between 20% and 60% less time on post-viewing answering of questions than they are on pre-viewing comprehension of context and task.

User attitudes

Feedback from users was collected through a questionnaire which each subject completed immediately after using the program. This feedback supplies interesting information in a number of different areas.

Equipment and software

All the subjects found that the equipment was easy to use and that the instructions were easy to follow. This is important because unfriendly technology can prevent programs from being used effectively. A large majority of the subjects also found that the equipment did not cause unacceptable delays. This is gratifying as a concern in using videotape technology (as opposed to laserdisc technology) is that it will prove unacceptably slow when winding between segments. In the program discussed here, periods of tape winding are cached by the on-screen advance organizers and question sequences. In the case of most learners, this appears to have been successful at providing ongoing stimuli while the videotape player was busy.

Language support

Every subject agreed that the bilingual support during the advance organizer screens was helpful. This supports the evidence from the computer records that using the bilingual support may have improved performance. However, despite the strong endorsement of bilingual support, it should be noted that three of the subjects never looked at it. Two of them state this clearly while one obviously forgot and claimed to have looked at the support screens "most times".

On the question of whether post-viewing question screens should also have bilingual support, the subjects were quite evenly divided, twelve saying that they would have preferred it and ten saying that they would not. However, most of the subjects would not have liked the entire program to have been in Spanish, i.e. without bilingual support screens. These results also correlate with the computer record of the subjects' pattern of use and show a clear appreciation of the utility of the bilingual support screens.

Confidence

Subjects were asked whether they felt confident enough to watch the movie (without support) *before* using the program and *after* using it. Before using the program, 29% were confident (and none were "very confident"), but after using the program 67% felt confident (and one subject had increased to "very confident"). None of the original 29% reduced their level of confidence. Thus, an additional 38% of subjects increased their perceptions of their confidence from "not confident" to "confident". This does not, of course, mean that the subjects had improved their performance by 38%. It is, nevertheless, important to note the increased confidence which is a key feature in language learning and is particularly important in autonomous learning.

Utility

When asked whether they found the program a useful way of learning, the subjects responded very positively (with one exception). When asked whether they had enjoyed using the program, there was the same positive response and the same single dissenter. When asked whether they would use other similar programs if they were available, the response was again very positive and even the dissenter agreed. It seems clear from this evidence that the subjects value this kind of activity and would willingly commit their time to it if more programs were available.

Conclusion

It would seem that providing bilingual support during the advance organizers has helped to improve the performance of the learners who made use of it. Those who exercised their autonomy by choosing to ignore the bilingual support in certain sections performed worse, on average, in those sections than they did in the sections where they used the support. Those who chose not to use the bilingual support at all generally performed more poorly than those who used it extensively.

It is also clear that the subjects enjoyed using this program and benefited from it. There is a clear increase in their confidence in their ability to use this target language movie after using the interactive video support program. Whether this confidence will be carried over to using movies without interactive video support is uncertain.

In assessing whether the interactive video support program discussed here is an effective contribution towards moving learners in the direction of greater autonomy in their learning, we should consider two things. Firstly, we should consider whether this program has been successful in helping learners to achieve something, in the target language, outside the classroom environment. Secondly, we have to consider whether the subjects are likely to go on using target language videos but without the support provided by this program. An affirmative answer to the first issue would indicate that we have been successful in making learners aware of the potential for language learning outside the classroom, in raising their awareness of their own potential and in boosting their confidence in their own abilities to use the target language. An affirmative answer to the second issue would indicate a definite increase in the autonomy of this group of learners.

The method has only been used with one movie and has only been tried with 23 learners. It is, therefore, too soon to make conclusive statements about the value of the approach. However, the general tone of user feedback indicates that while the program is successful at providing material which supports learners' attempts at working through a video entirely in the target language, it may not be as successful in convincing learners to take the plunge and try a whole movie without support. This is further supported by the data showing that learners relied heavily on the bilingual support screens while using the program. It may be that confidence will only arrive after a learner has worked through a number of movies with interactive video support. This could only be ascertained by a longitudinal study of which the current study would form the first stage.

It is, therefore, true to say that this project has achieved its immediate goal of increasing the learners' confidence in their ability to make use of authentic video as a language-learning tool. Success in achieving the ultimate goal of encouraging learners to experiment with using authentic video without the support of an interactive video program is difficult to judge but probably has not been reached at this stage. Nevertheless, the data is encouraging and there is a clear message that more of these interactive video support programs should be produced.

15

From word processing to text processing

John Milton, Ian Smallwood and James Purchase

Introduction

This chapter describes a prototype computer-writing environment under development at the Language Centre, The Hong Kong University of Science and Technology (HKUST). It is intended to provide some of the cognitive and linguistic support which our EFL learners require as they write. We expect this self-access resource to aid both collaborative and individual composition within an academic environment by assisting in the planning, generation, formulation and organization of ideas, as well as the development of language fluency and accuracy. Assistance is keyed to the particular text-types undergraduate university students are required to produce.

A question raised repeatedly in this particular volume is the degree to which various techniques and methods encourage learner autonomy. This question certainly needs to be asked when the tutor is not always available or when the learning method might inhibit the process being learned, but is less meaningful when what is proposed is a tool that the learner will always have available, which we hope will enhance production and which learners can access at their discretion. A related concern that might be raised, and which has been the subject of considerable research, is whether the use of word processors makes people better writers. While this may have been a relevant issue as long as the future of the technology was in doubt, it has become a non-issue now that so much writing is, by necessity, done on a word processor. As teachers interested in improving the resources learners have available for the acquisition and production of language, we need to look at ways in which the features of electronic editors can be enhanced for particular users. In this chapter we propose several ways of improving and enhancing these features for learners of English. These techniques can be adapted for any writers having to produce text in a foreign language.

Hong Kong tertiary students, in common with many other students worldwide, regularly use computers to transcribe and print their coursework, but rarely compose on screen. Currently available software does little to help inexperienced writers compose in English. This situation is particularly acute when the student is an EFL learner whose proficiency in both the target language skills and basic composing strategies is limited. Most electronic programs go no further than providing English learners with testing practice of grammatical structures or lexical items. Since the technology first appeared critics have complained about the inadequacy of CALL (computer-assisted language learning) software in helping speakers of other languages to acquire the complex skills of writing in English at levels above that of the clause (cf. Last 1992).

The growing body of theory concerning both the analysis of text and the modelling of composition can facilitate the development of better computational aids for writers. This includes the relatively recent development and refinement of techniques for the analysis of text through, for example, thematic structure analysis (Berry 1989), genre analysis (Swales 1990), information structure analysis (Hoey 1983) and rhetorical structure theory (Mann and Thompson 1987). This work, combined with earlier research on the writing process (e.g. Hayes and Flower 1980), recent efforts to test theory by implementing prototype applications (e.g. Glynn et al. 1989; Sharples 1992) and research on the effects of data-driven learning (e.g. Johns 1994) have made feasible the design of electronic writing environments for EFL learners.

Theoretical background

The computer program we describe in this chapter attempts to apply some of the findings of text linguists to the development of writing skills in EFL learners. These investigators have helped bring about a shift of emphasis away from previous research into mainly syntactic and stylistic elements of composition theory, and towards the more semantic components of communication: for example, the cognitive mapping processes of learner writers and the specific functions of language in communicating meaning (see Bhatia 1993). Authors such as Halliday and Hasan (1976) combine elements of coherence and cohesion to define what is often called the 'texture' of a piece of writing. The dilemma of EFL pedagogy is how to provide guidance to learners in producing the elements that these authors identify as communicatively effective in a context where the use of English is limited.

One type of tool that can meet some of the needs of these learners is a self-access electronic environment designed to assist in the production of texts by applying some of the analytic techniques of text linguistics, viz:

1. discourse coherence, such as the observance of topic knowledge, text-form constraints and topic coherence;
2. cohesive devices, e.g. lexical patterning, clausal relationships, syntax, specialized vocabulary and punctuation;
3. thematization patterns, such as the development and interrelationships of propositions throughout the text; and
4. the matching of text to the relevant genre.

Courses are now regularly based around some form of genre-specific approach in which Science students study the language of scientific articles, laboratory reports, abstracts etc.; students in Business schools study the English of proposals, letters, reports etc., in an attempt to prepare them adequately for the specific tasks they will need to complete. However, while the findings of text linguistics have become dominant in the teaching of English for Specific and Academic Purposes (ESP/EAP), the analytical principles which have been developed have not yet been implemented in a format that is readily available to the autonomous learner. By reconstructing such techniques for the analysis of text as guides to the *production* of text, and incorporating these into a computer writing environment, the program described in this chapter attempts to apply these analytic approaches to the development of self-access writing tools.

In conjunction with research on the importance of text analysis has been work on modelling the writing process, most notably that of Hayes and Flower (op. cit.). They divide the writing process into two major components: the writer's "long term memory" and the "task environment". The former refers to the writer's awareness of topic and audience (i.e. the writer's plans to execute the task). The task environment refers to the rhetorical structure of the text. These authors identify three stages in this process which are relevant to the implementation of a computer writing environment: planning (generating ideas, organizing information and goal setting); translating (from concept to language) or composing; and reviewing (reading and editing).

Their oft-quoted model emphasizes the recursive nature of effective writing. Student writers are, however, often non-recursive, tending not to revise their written work. Although learners have at least some interactive and recursive facilities within their word processors that encourage rewriting, inexperienced writers for whom English is a foreign language are often unable to use these tools because of their unfamiliarity with the writing process, the language itself and the electronic environment. The techniques of text analysis and this kind of writing model can be more fully realized than they currently are: we return to these themes several times in this chapter. We admit of course to being very far from a complete understanding of what writing tools are most needed or will be most readily accepted by particular learners. In spite of recent research, data on cognitive processes, learning strategies and the role of social and environmental variables in second language acquisition are still scarce. Tarone et al. (1976) complained about this dearth twenty years ago. Although we now have better theoretical models, there is still much that we need to know before we can build such ideal writing environments.

The learners

Few would argue that students need assistance in finding and using appropriate vocabulary and rhetorical structures. The question of what form this assistance should take, and whether or not electronic assistance is beneficial, or even possible, is more controversial. The needs of our learners for a richer writing environment are suggested by the Hayes and Flower model: intermediate-level EFL students lack crucial knowledge in their long-term memory, which is necessary for the planning of effective writing. The translation process to which Hayes and Flower refer often includes, for our students, the literal translation of Chinese idioms into English. Because their sources of knowledge about the language are limited, their expression frequently takes the form of inappropriate application of memorized language formulas. Their unfamiliarity with both the language and the writing process inhibits the quality of their editing.

Much has been written about the particular difficulties Hong Kong students have with lexico-grammatical patterns such as cohesion (e.g. Milton and Tsang 1993), as well as more general problems of composition that are resistant to correction (Gerrard 1989). A particular problem that has frequently been associated with Hong Kong learners (and of course many other learners) is the difficulty they have in effectively incorporating source texts into their writing. The plagiarism that often results from the learners' exposure to sources is likely due to the students' lack of the lexical and rhetorical resources which are needed to present source material adequately.

Current text-analysis programs

The evidence against the success, at least for EFL learners, of the grammar-checking programs that are most often associated with text analysis is overwhelming (see, for example, Pennington 1991 and Bolt 1991). The incorrect or trivial advice that these programs generate is misleading and confusing to English learners. The techniques they employ — mostly word classification, simple parsing and narrowly defined usage rules — are neither reliable nor adequate in flagging the types of errors made by language learners, nor do they provide a basis for appropriate advice. The programs give no assistance with using or acquiring rhetorical structure, nor do they make information about language use available to the writer. Inexperienced writers have no choice but to accept the usually incorrect or inappropriate advice provided, or to skip this feature of their word processor entirely.

One concern about electronic grammar checkers, presumably based on the assumption that writers actually use them, is that inexperienced writers may become overly dependent on their assistance (e.g. Gerrard op. cit.). There is certainly not much scope for any cognitive exploration of language use in the design of these programs and it is hard to imagine how the current software, even if it does become much more accurate, can help learners to develop individual writing strategies. In criticizing these programs, Pennington (1991) proposed a set of eight "desirable attributes" which text-editing software should meet in order to be pedagogically viable. Below we outline both our own and her specifications for a better writing environment and describe how features of our program meet these specifications.

Specifications for an idea and text processor

Our specifications for the features of a writing environment are that it should help inexperienced writers exploit current composing and proofreading features of their word processor (e.g. outlining tools and spellcheckers), but go much further than available word processors by providing tools that learners can use to help them:

1. plan their writing;
2. generate and organize their ideas and language appropriately;
3. revise their written work effectively;
4. choose words and expressions that are felicitous for particular discoursal functions and relevant to particular text-types and genres;

5. avoid plagiarism in their use of source material; and
6. manage routine formatting difficulties which are associated with academic writing, such as bibliography composition.

It should also follow a pedagogical strategy that promotes autonomous learning by:

1. providing options to students as they compose;
2. allowing them to take either a structured and linear, or unstructured and nonlinear, approach to their writing, rather than forcing them through only one particular method of composition; and
3. encouraging them to explore their own composing strategies and develop their own 'voice'.

The first-time user should be encouraged to follow a highly structured route to the creation of a document, but tools should be available that can be invoked by a writer intent on making his or her own way through the writing process (users should be reminded if they fail to follow the plan they set for themselves).

Pennington's eight requirements of a computer-aided writing program are that it should:

1. be solidly grounded on a theoretical and practical base of process writing;
2. have as its primary purpose the development of editing skills, rather than the identification and/or correction of errors;
3. move users towards 'expert' performance in editing by increasing the speed, accuracy and thoroughness of editing over time;
4. instruct students in the process of finding error, making decisions about their correction and correcting error in their own work, rather than relying on the program to do so;
5. treat the editing process as an interplay of form and meaning: offer instruction in how matters of editing for style and language inform matters of content, and vice versa;
6. make available on-line help and modelling of the editing process;
7. incorporate collaborative work to develop a sense of audience in the editing process; and
8. raise the level of interactivity and user control to the point where the user drives the program and not the other way round. (ibid.: 105)

Features of an idea and text processor

In the remainder of the chapter we elaborate the features of a program which meet most of these specifications. The sections are organized around Pennington's requirements, although there is considerable overlap.

Theoretical and practical grounding

For some time there has been interest among language teachers in adapting word processors to deliver tools needed by novice writers (e.g. Nydahl 1990), but this interest has yet to result in a CALL program that is widely recognized as helping learners develop productive language skills or navigate the currents of the composing process. Some word processors do attempt to assist writers at a rhetorical level, but only by giving them choices of oversimplified 'boiler plate' (inactive) text-templates. Our experience has convinced us that learners want a more responsive writing environment that will allow them to choose particular language features to construct their own text. At the same time, they want this flexible writing environment to work invisibly with (i.e. have the same metaphors — toolbars, menus, help files etc. — as) their own word processor.

The design of the prototype program described here attempts to implement current theories of cognitive processes (e.g. drafting, brain-storming, developing a thread etc. — see Sharples and Pemberton 1990) by offering users the option of being guided through the entire writing process of idea generation, organization, referencing and proofreading, or choosing to compose according to their own habits, with independent access to writing tools. The methodology of the program is closer to what Higgins (1988) calls the "pedagogue", rather than the "magister" model (see also Little, p. 212), as its design incorporates a conscious effort to provide assistance while avoiding prescription. We concur with Little's warning that the availability of utilities of this type does not guarantee that students will develop greater autonomy; it does, however, seem a valid hypothesis that giving students greater access to information about the language and the conventions of academic writing is likely to make them more confident and less dependent on formal learning. We will test these hypotheses when the program is fully implemented.

In keeping with current text linguistics concerns (as described earlier in this chapter) to anchor the teaching of rhetorical structure to specific characteristics of the text which the student is expected to produce, the program prompts the user to identify the text-type (report, academic essay etc.) being attempted. It responds by making available corpora of authentic materials relevant to that type of text. These corpora, along with appropriate databases of set phrases, can then be directly accessed by the learner. There is a great deal of interest in using corpora in EFL teaching and in making authentic text available to language learners (e.g. Sinclair 1991), although few practical ways of providing the information contained in authentic text to the learner engaged in the writing process have yet been suggested. By implementing an efficient text-retrieval system, this program encourages users to navigate relevant text for expressions more felicitous than the student might otherwise produce. By encouraging learners to focus on specific rhetorical patterns, it makes it possible for them to explore how authentic language forges relationships between ideas and between the writer and reader.

Users are guided in the specific rhetorical elements of various text-types and the lexis of different genres. The electronic implementation of invention techniques for the development of ideas for academic essays (brainstorming, mindmapping etc.) has been previously attempted, but these have not found wide acceptance among students, probably due to their being unavailable from within the students' word-processing environment. This program integrates the idea-generation stage into the production of the complete text by offering a four-step process which mirrors the analytical methods of text linguistics:

1. the student is provided with a framework for generating and noting major topics and associated subtopics to be covered (help is provided through lists of commonly found topics and subtopics for a range of subjects);
2. graphically represented rhetorical structures for either the text as a whole or specific sections of the text are presented — the student can choose among them, combine or modify them into what seems to the writer to be a coherent structure appropriate to the task;
3. the framework of ideas is then matched to the rhetorical framework and the text as whole is constructed in note form; and
4. each section is then presented for development and completion.

At any stage of the process, writers can refer to help files for information and they can test their recognition of 'correct' grammatical, discoursal, stylistic or lexical features.

The development of editing skills

Users of this program have several options for working through the editing process. For example, one version of the program assists in the production of laboratory reports, presenting a task-specific editing screen for each of the major sections of such a report. Figure 1 shows the screen from which users can choose titles indexed by keywords. By clicking on the tabs in the display, the writer can switch between a view of authentic titles of lab reports — indexed by the main verb — to an editing screen where the titles can be modified for the specific task.

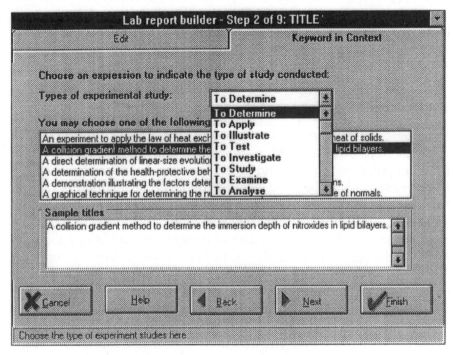

Figure 1: A dialogue box displaying lab report titles indexed by key lexical items

This screen graphic does not make clear the contrast between the function and content words of the original dialogue box: the learner is presented with only the key verbs of each sentence (e.g. *An experiment* **to** **apply** *the laws of heat exchange and* **to** **determine** *the specific heat of solids*). Only certain words are highlighted and copied because, first of all, there is very little likelihood that most of the content words will be relevant to the specific report which the learner has to write; secondly, allowing users to copy only relatively fixed expressions may help them to internalize the difference between modelling language and the plagiarism associated with the copying of entire sentences and ideas. Making relevant language available to learners at this micro-level may make it possible for them to imitate language patterns without copying larger chunks of language.

The program guides the inexperienced writer to analyze audience and clarify purpose by querying the writer on the audience and purpose of the paper. The writer is asked to identify his or her purpose and audience, and the program consults lists of lexis to prompt the user at a revision stage if apparently inappropriate language has been used (e.g., 'Are you sure a nonspecialist reader will understand this word?'). The program also uses the word processor's native outlining feature to create and make available a number of templates from which the writer can choose in order to organize ideas. It identifies possible shifts in topic and section headings by, for example, abstracting topic sentences into a skeleton outline so that students can check their implicit organization.

Towards 'expert' performance in editing

The program is designed so as to appear to supplement the features of the students' word processor and to emphasize the native editing features of the word processor (e.g. cut-and-paste, outlining, spellchecking etc.). The displays are consistent with established Windows metaphors; for example, the user can access both the wordprocessor's own tools and enhanced editing tools from a 'toolbar' located at the top of the screen by 'pointing' to an icon to see a description of the tool it represents and 'clicking' on it to invoke a 'dialogue box' (as in Figure 1). These dialogue boxes prompt the student for input; the program then processes the query or formats portions of the document according to the option selected.

Writing and word processing are becoming inextricably linked, although for many inexperienced writers a word processor is initially nothing more than a font-rich typewriter. This program provides EFL learners with task-specific knowledge in the form of access to authentic and text-relevant language. The learner also can call help files by clicking on 'buttons' available at every stage of the process. Among other notes, the help files contain information about common errors Hong Kong learners make in lexis, syntax and rhetoric. Because this information is immediately available, we expect it to be of more assistance to the learners in their editing than anything they currently have, and we expect to find users of this program more engaged in the process of editing than they otherwise would or could be. The program aids planning in various other mechanical ways, such as by reminding the user how much time has been spent on task, what percentage of the paper has been completed etc.

A research effort is currently underway at the HKUST Language Centre to identify empirically the lexis and syntax with which our students have the greatest difficulty (cf. Milton and Chowdury 1994). As we detail later in this chapter, we are also developing methods to use large corpora of NS writing as a source of linguistic information for students as they write and eventually as a data-driven component of a non-native grammar checker. When this project is complete we hope to provide a program which will give EFL learners the on-line linguistic information about English that current grammar checkers are unable to provide.

Finding errors and making decisions

The program does not attempt at this point to analyze the writer's language; however, it does provide guidance about how to detect and correct error. In addition to allowing access to relevant text, it provides students with prompts and help screens, as we've mentioned, to sensitize them to the most common grammatical and discoursal errors made by Chinese learners of English. EFL writers can practise their ability to recognize common language problems from the help screens, the main editing screen or the dialogue boxes, which represent each stage of the editing process or section of the paper. In addition to this help, users can invoke at any stage of the writing process a pop-up test which can be used to practise recognition of the common errors of syntax and lexis associated with the particular genres the students produce. The program encourages writers to improve their ability to recognize errors by giving them immediate feedback on their performance on these tests in the form of hints and statistical results.

Students are prompted to use the spellchecker and the 'errors' picked up by the spellchecker are logged. The students are later able to test themselves on these items. The program can consult vocabulary lists drawn up for specific assignments and will extract lists from corpora of authentic texts. Students can consult these lists or be tested on them, which we expect will help them to be more sensitive to the specific lexis of different text-types and to use a broader range of vocabulary in their papers.

The interplay of form and meaning

Natural language-processing research is very far from providing electronic programs with the means to interact intelligently with a writer. However, 'expert knowledge' can be made available to the writer in the form of relevant language and the formal structure of particular genres. This program does this by allowing learners to navigate within text-relevant language by focusing on both rhetorical structure and the morphology of single lexical items and expressions. They can move from one section of a report to another and search for particular morphemes, words and expressions in the text.

There is of course more to good writing than just observance of grammar rules. EFL students often lack exposure to authentic language from which they can learn the natural patterns of the language. We believe this need can be at least partly addressed within an electronic environment. One way this program encourages local connectedness is through context-sensitive help files which offer general assistance with grammatical and discoursal features. Also, and perhaps more effectively, the program enables the writer to refer at any time to examples of language serving the particular rhetorical functions within texts of a similar genre.

At each stage writers are prompted to consider the relationship between adjoining sections of text and the appropriateness of any cohesive devices used. We expect that access to appropriate rhetorical structures and examples of language commonly used at the specific stages within the text-type will help students to produce writing appropriate to the genre they are trying to replicate. The aspect of form students seem to spend the most time on is layout. Perhaps because the technology makes it possible to experiment with format, learners often make the layout of documents unnecessarily elaborate. This program generates prompts that guide users to produce appropriate layouts. These interactive templates are more detailed and relevant than those normally available with commercial word processors.

On-line help

The program's help screens provide learners with tutorials in the use of the program's electronic resources, language advice and practice, and strategies for writing. These help screens are being written according to principles of hypertext design that make it relatively easy for users to find the information they need. They are also being made interactive so that, for example, users can read about a grammatical point, click to see examples and click again to practise the recognition of correct forms in a multiple-choice or cloze test, before returning to their writing task. Along with qualitative advice, learners are also given specific information about the quantitative differences between the writing of Hong Kong English learners and the writing of native speakers (e.g. *Moreover* is used about 100 times more frequently by these learners than by NSs).

Users of this program will have access to tools that provide them with appropriate expressions for quoting source materials, dealing with other writers' ideas and formatting and compiling bibliographies. Much of the inadvertent plagiarism of student writing appears due to their inability to handle quoted material appropriately and to their difficulty in paraphrasing.

Some of these difficulties are in turn no doubt a result of their restricted vocabulary, their ignorance of the means or importance of citation and the expression of purpose in quotation. This program at least partly addresses these inadequacies: users can click on a 'Cite' tool, whereupon they are asked to select a purpose in quoting the material and are given a list of words and expressions relevant to this purpose. The program prompts the student to enter the quoted material and to specify what portions are directly quoted. It inserts this material into the student's document and applies appropriate formatting to all quoted materials and reminds the writer of how much of the paper has been copied from other sources. At a later stage students are prompted to paraphrase copied material. They have access to a simple database where they are prompted to enter reference information. The program generates a bibliography according to a specified style (MLA, APA etc.) and compiles an alphabetically indexed bibliography. It also inserts in-text references (i.e. author and year) at the appropriate place in the document.

EFL students lack information about word choice, but there are few interactive resources which provide this, other than the thesauri attached to word processors. Language learners have to approach these devices very cautiously since they often cannot distinguish between the different meanings and collocational properties of synonymous words and do not understand the complex relationship of antonymous words. Nor do electronic dictionaries yet have the features EFL learners require in order to explore semantics and usage of language adequately. One way in which this program makes word choice information available to students is by organizing words and expressions into notional/functional categories that students can use as keys to access the lists of relevant lexis and databases mentioned earlier in this chapter. For example, users can choose from a dozen generalized semantic areas (summary, argument etc.) and have access to a number of expressions relevant to the text-type they are constructing.

The implicit, and perhaps most effective, type of help the program provides is the encouragement it offers to proceed through the writing process by planning, composing and reviewing and to provide authentic models of the particular language functions in the type of text the writer is expected to produce.

Collaboration and a sense of audience

Although another reader may be simulated, the primary readers of the students' assignments are usually their tutors. The program has several features which makes it possible to clarify the expectations of these particular readers. Because the program can be networked, it gives instructors assistance in communicating the requirements of the assignments to their students and, ideally, in allowing students to share the difficulties they experience with the instructor and with other students on the course. This latter technique is the current object of much technical research and development: diverse 'groupware' products are now coming onto the market which will make it feasible for writers to edit documents cooperatively. The innovations we describe will make it possible for learners to access common databases of 'expert' knowledge to assist in peer evaluation and collaborative writing that these networking technologies make possible.

The program also helps formalize assignments and make the requirements consistent and clear. Instructors can use an electronic form to specify various expectations of particular assignments; this information is then stored in a database and can be accessed by the students at any time. Their instructors can thus provide on-line guidance which is reported to the students at the point they most need it. We expect that this facility will motivate instructors to make explicit their language expectations, as students will inevitably come to expect information from all their instructors.

Writers are informed of quantitative aspects of their writing that might be of relevance to the reader (i.e. grading). The program tracks mechanical and quantitative aspects of the students' writing and generates a report to the user based on this information; students are reminded to spellcheck, use the organizational tools etc.

Interactivity and user control

Two versions of the program are under development: one that is independent of a particular course or instructor, and another that is designed for an academic context where students are expected to meet particular assignment requirements. The latter version can be networked and records each student by name and student number and can log the student's progress. This makes it possible to report idiosyncratic habits to the student-user (e.g. 'Venus, you did not use the spellchecker; would you like to spellcheck your document?') and to track students' use of the program so that it can be evaluated and modified.

In the networked version the student is prompted for a specific course, assignment and text-type. In this way the program can call up predefined interactive templates specific to the language and formatting requirements of that assignment or type of text. Course lecturers can provide relevant guidelines, indicate marking criteria etc. We hope to include materials from course manuals in the interactive help files and so provide students with relevant information at the point they most need it.

We believe this program meets the implicit requirements of a methodology suitable for autonomous learning: users can choose to use the entire panoply of tools and features, and either be guided through the writing process or access particular features. Learners are more likely to pick and choose as they become familiar with the program, and the program will in turn undergo modification to suit the ways learners use it.

Conclusion

The general principle of the program described here is to provide guidance to the learner writer at the various stages of text planning, development and editing. We expect this support to result in a more sophisticated use of language devices appropriate to particular genres. For example, the program encourages discourse coherence and logical thematization structures by enabling writers to match their propositions to appropriate rhetorical frameworks; prompts are provided which encourage them to consider the relationship of one section of the text to another; lists of topics and subtopics also suggest appropriate organizational plans. Through such guided planning, the writer may be able to detect more clearly any illogicalities or interruptions to the text's thematic progression.

The program can supply some of the basic repetitive advice that teachers often find themselves engaged in. It also provides students with access to language that they could otherwise only acquire by intensive reading. It addresses many of the needs of EFL learner writers specified by such authors as Pennington (op. cit.) by providing an environment in which students can develop as independent learners. We believe that autonomous learning habits are more likely to be formed during the completion of authentic tasks in this type of computer writing environment, than as a result of the simulated activities of much traditional CALL software. Whether students will really write better and become more effective or independent writers as a result of interaction with this program has yet to be determined. The use of the program's features will be logged, both electronically and by observation, and modified accordingly. We will then be in a position to document the degree to which this tool is useful as an aid to the production of effective writing by EFL learners. As to the program's effectiveness in encouraging autonomous learning, we hope that this approach will help language learners develop both language awareness and a willingness to discover more about the target language: whether it will or not has of course yet to be established. However, we expect EFL writers to become skilful users of the tools for language discovery that such a program offers.

$\mathcal{V}$

The evaluation of learner autonomy

Whereas several chapters in previous sections have evaluated projects designed to help learners move towards autonomy in language learning, the final chapters of the book are concerned with the evaluation of the learning that takes place in autonomous or self-access environments. In Chapter 16, a number of fundamental questions relating to research and research methodologies are discussed; and in Chapters 17 and 18, quantitative methods are used to evaluate autonomous and self-access language learning.

In Chapter 16, Philip Riley explores methodologies and concepts appropriate for research into autonomous and self-access learning. He discusses the opposition between qualitative and quantitative approaches to research, arguing for 'alternative' or 'mixed' approaches. He then elaborates on standards for educational research that any research project should try to meet, and finally mentions a variety of research approaches that bridge or stand outside the qualitative/quantitative divide, and are appropriate for the study of self-access language learning.

The two chapters which follow exemplify two of the research approaches that Riley introduces at the end of his chapter: empirical and action research. Both chapters happen to involve quantitative data analysis.

Chapter 17 represents one of the few attempts to compare autonomous language learning with learning that takes place in a traditional classroom in terms of the language that is learned. In the chapter, Leni Dam and Lienhard Legenhausen report on a project which compares the initial vocabulary aquisition of a secondary school class learning 'autonomously' (e.g. the learners ask for/select/produce/share words of interest to them) with classes following textbook-based syllabuses. As Dam and Legenhausen make clear, theirs is a comparison rather than a controlled experimental study, but their results do suggest that the autonomous approach may be at least on a par with traditional approaches in terms of facilitating language acquisition (leaving aside other benefits); and that autonomous learning can occur with an age group often thought to have been socialized into teacher-dependence.

In Chapter 18, Vance Stevens reports on the quantitative analysis stage of an action research project investigating the use and abuse of help features in a CALL cloze program. His data show that students working on CALL programs in self-access mode may abuse help features to a greater extent than CALL developers realize. Readers may like to consider whether the depth of individual data that Stevens was able to obtain would be extended or compromised by more qualitative (and 'obtrusive') research methods.

16

'The blind man and the bubble': researching self-access

Philip Riley

Introduction

A blind man has friends who talk to him about the world which they can see but which he cannot. Amongst the things that interest him most are what his friends call 'bubbles'. He has a certain amount of factual but second-hand knowledge about 'bubbles': they can be made from soap-and-water or washing-up liquid, for example, forming extremely thin spherical membranes which are very nearly as light as air, so they float. They are beautiful, multi-coloured, fun to make and play with.

Intrigued, the blind man asks his friends to make him some bubbles, which they do, but since he cannot see them he is obliged to try to touch them. But not only are they difficult to locate, when he **does** succeed in finding one, his touch destroys it. For him, 'bubbles' will remain a matter of hearsay and a slight sensation of dampness on his fingertips. He simply does not have the appropriate tools for observing or experiencing the objects in question.

Do we? That is, if we extrapolate from my analogy to our present area of interest, do we possess the methodological and conceptual tools which are appropriate to the study of autonomy, self-directed learning and self-access? Or are we teachers and researchers in this field condemned to stumble around like the blind, gesticulating wildly and then destroying the very thing we want to understand? Is there any principled way round what Labov has called the "observer's paradox", where the simple presence of the observer suffices to destroy or distort what is observed? Can school inspectors ever 'inspect' normal classroom behaviour when their entering into a classroom changes the situation and the behaviour of the participants?

Epistemological problems of this kind, that is, problems about the *status* and *quality* of our knowledge, about *access* to knowledge and about the *representation* of knowledge are, of course, by no means limited to our little corner of the academic woods. They are the founding questions of all the world's intellectual, scientific and philosophical traditions, since, however different the answers they propose, there can by definition be no such thing as an 'intellectual tradition' until coherent decisions about such matters, about what counts as knowledge, have been reached. That is what an 'intellectual tradition' **is.**

In what follows, however, I will not be trying to give some kind of potted course in epistemology, partly because I am not particularly competent to do so, partly because I believe that the nature and development of self-access can be better understood within the framework of the sociology of knowledge as formulated by Mannheim (1936) and Schütz (1962), but mainly because I feel it would be more realistic and more useful to look at some specific topics, requirements and procedures for research in our field. The question I will be addressing is a very general one, but very important, too: what points do we need to keep in mind, what precautions do we need to take, when we design research projects and, above all, how can we ensure that the methodology we choose is appropriate, that we are not just bursting bubbles?

So here is my agenda: first, I am going to take the term 'methodology' itself for brief examination. I shall be asking what the term means and how we can tell the difference between a methodology and, say, a rule of thumb, speculation, or the mechanical application of a procedure.

Secondly, I would like to make a few points about oppositions such as 'Positivist/Non-positivist' and 'Quantitative/Qualitative' approaches to research, not because I want to rekindle the debate as to which is the 'best' or the most 'scientific', but because I believe that only by thinking carefully about the differences between them can we choose appropriately according to the nature of our object of investigation and of our particular research project.

Thirdly, I will be looking at a limited set of 'Standards for educational research' in general, as proposed by Kenneth Howe and Margaret Eisenhart (1990).

Fourthly, I will take a selection of methodologies currently in use in educational research — some 'quantitative', some 'qualitative', some mixed — and ask how they might relate to the field of autonomy and self-access.

Methodology

First, then, the term 'methodology'. The point I want to emphasize here is simple but important. It is this: there is a difference between 'a method' and 'a methodology'. A *method* is a systematic way of doing something, a knowledge community's convention for arriving at and legitimating what counts as knowledge. A *methodology*, on the other hand, is not a procedure. It is not even a set of procedures. It is a set of principles for choosing between procedures, for deciding to do something this way and not that way.

These principles cover four areas of action:

1. the identification of *appropriate procedures*;
2. forms of *argumentation*;
3. knowledge *claims*; and
4. forms of *representation* and *publication*.

The identification of appropriate procedures

Methodology sets out to identify those issues and factors which must be taken into consideration if we are to make informed decisions as to which procedures are appropriate, given the nature of the questions we are asking and of the objects we are studying.

For example, in the field of self-access language learning, the conceptual models and tools we use to investigate the four constitutive elements of that expression ('self', 'access', 'language', 'learning') must be ones which, at the very least, recognize the existence of those elements.

'Self'

There is little use in trying to investigate 'self' with a psychological model which denies the existence of or completely ignores such an entity, or which regards 'self' as universal, the unvarying expression of 'human nature'. Such approaches, in their different ways, make 'self' a no-go area and in particular prevent investigation of cultural variation in the ways in which 'self' is constructed in and through discourse (Foucault 1966; Levin 1992; Scollon and Scollon 1992).

There are cultures where "It does you good to talk about your problems", where the manifestation in discourse of certain aspects of 'self' is easily accepted, where the Donahue Show or Dr Ruth, the psychiatrist's couch, the confessional and counselling are familiar forms of interaction. On the other hand, there are cultures where this is not the case and as the last category cited (counselling) shows, this could have major repercussions for work in self-access. (This point is developed in greater detail in Riley, in press.)

'Language learning'

Similarly, there is little point in trying to investigate language learning with a psychological model which is either not linguistically sensitive or informed, or which is not interested in the learning process as such, i.e. as individual cognition, rather than as the effects of another person's behaviour, teaching.

If we bring these three requirements together (recognition of 'self', linguistic sensitivity, cognitive focus), they set up amongst themselves further constraints which enable us to specify more precisely still just what sort of model we need. It will have to be *psycholinguistic*, for example — but only in the sense that a 'psycholinguistic' approach is relevant to 'self'. In other words, the learning process will be viewed as an extension of the meanings (representations, beliefs, attitudes, values) of which the individual is capable.

Clearly, such requirements will eliminate from the range of options behaviouristic psychological models (indeed, any kind of determinism) as well as those psycholinguistic models which are accounts of data-processing, which have no 'individual' dimension. This will orient our choice towards models such as Kelly's Personal Construct Theory (see Maher 1969), Gardner (1983) on multiple intelligences, Kolb (1984) on learning styles and Bruner (1986) on cognition.

'Access'

If we confront the exigencies mentioned above with those contained in the word 'access', with its triple connotations of power, social relationships and competence, we will be obliged to temper whatever psychological model we do choose with a further set of sociological or socio-epistemic requirements. These would aim to set our investigation within the wider framework of the sociology of knowledge, where society is described as a set of structures and functions for the management (creation, organization, distribution, legitimation and utilization) of knowledge. In such a framework, the introduction of such informational economies as 'Self-access language learning' can be described and analyzed as attempts to intervene in the social knowledge system. However, this final requirement is still very much a challenge: there is no corresponding list of names and theories to refer to.

Rather than seeing the work of identification and selection as adding to our difficulties, we should consider it as a process of progressive refinement, of elimination and focusing, which enables us to choose the appropriate tools for the job. However, even this observation needs to be qualified, since it gives the impression that the researcher who has identified a question and 'has a project' has to make a choice between different ways of answering the same question. This is rarely, if ever, the case: the choice of method largely determines the question. In the words of Kenneth Burke (1955: 70), "Ways of seeing are also ways of not seeing".

Forms of argument employed

Probably the most important of the argumentative principles is that the argument must be identifiable so that it can be agreed or disagreed with. This involves matters of logic and rhetoric, of definition, of intellectual probity and probing. I believe that in the field of autonomy and self-access we have been extremely lucky to have had people of the calibre of Henri Holec, Edith Esch, Les Dickinson and David Little to argue our case, not just because it is our case, but because they have raised the quality of educational debate in general through the intellectual rigour and the 'identifiability' of their arguments.

Knowledge claims

The most important of the principles which apply to knowledge claims is that the degree of generalizability which is being claimed for results must be stated: to what other populations (etc.) can conclusions be extrapolated? It is essential that this should be done explicitly, even where it seems obvious, since principles 1 and 2 are also logically dependent on it. To take an extreme, but in my experience common, example: I have lost count of the number of times I have been told that I believe that self-direction and self-access systems are "the best way" of learning a language (for everyone, everywhere, etc.). I honestly do not think I have ever said or written such a stupid thing, but obviously I have failed to make the extent of my knowledge claim clear!

Publication

The term 'publication' is being used here in the sense of 'placing in the public domain', that is, it includes, but is not limited to, print. This principle calls for the full disclosure of results and data and of the conditions of observation and experimentation, in order to ensure replicability and critical appraisal.

Unfortunately, publication does not mean that articles and books will actually be *read*. Researchers and teachers in the field of self-access and autonomy are used to being told that their field of interest is "the latest fad", that "it will never work in practice" or that "it has never been properly researched", when in fact various forms of self-directed learning schemes and self-access centres have been operating for over 25 years and bibliographical entries run into thousands (e.g. Riley 1985; Dickinson 1987; Brookes and Grundy 1988).

It also has to be admitted that one of the main reasons why certain publications in the field are not read is that they are published in the 'wrong' language — i.e. a language other than English. The tendency to equate foreign language learning and teaching with English means that important work published in French, German, Italian, Catalan and no doubt other languages is ignored by a large section of the profession. To take a specific example: in a book published recently in the United States on independent language learning, there was not one reference to a work published in a foreign language and only two of the 40 entries had been published outside the USA.

I hope that it will be clear, in the context of the argument I have been developing, that this is not just European touchiness on my part. Neither is it principally an objection to historical revisionism, or to seeing people reinvent conceptual wheels. My main objection is that by uprooting the topic from its intellectual and scientific context, it is being deprived of its nourishment and justification, becoming just a *method*, not a methodology: *losing its principles*.

Methodology, then, is principled inquiry, but the principles are not limited to a choice of procedures: they also concern wider issues of social epistemology. What is the position, in both epistemic terms of the knowledge in question within the social knowledge system? What reality tests are being employed, what principles of relevance? Reality tests for a methodology can be of many kinds, but what they cannot be is the fruit of revelation, magic or authoritarian dicta. Only if we address such questions can we distinguish research from speculation, and this requirement applies as much to 'qualitative' as to 'quantitative' approaches.

'Qualitative' and 'quantitative' approaches

The debate between those who believe that the only valid kind of knowledge is that which is based on measurement and those who believe that there are important, valid forms of knowledge which simply cannot be measured has a long and often acrimonious history. It can be seen as the fundamental problem for the emerging social sciences in the nineteenth century, from history and anthropology to sociology and psychology. Is it possible to be 'scientific' about non-physical objects such as institutions, norms, values and behaviour? Can we be objective about subjectivity? Can social reality be investigated at all, let alone quantified?

No one won this debate because — as most physical and social scientists would now agree — it is based on an opposition ('Qualitative vs. Quantitative') that is itself flawed (with a contingent opposition 'Positivist/ Anti-positivist' which is at least as mischievous) but which at the same time prevents other considerations and approaches from being taken into account — "Ways of seeing are also ways of not seeing". In particular, to anticipate the conclusion of the argument which follows, it discounts any possibility of a 'third way', where non-physical objects can be appropriately and systematically investigated with instruments that are at least partly quantitative in nature.

Objects of study, it is now fairly uncontroversial to say, can be seen as falling into two major classes: physical objects and social objects. Physical objects — stones, trees, clouds, chemical substances — exist independently of mankind or society, though, of course, the way in which our minds actually apprehend or 'know' and 'name' such objects forms the central question of classical and Cartesian philosophy and is highly problematic. Social objects — marriage, the Conservative Party, an appointment, an uncle, Christmas Day, a good turn, shame — only exist reflexively in and through praxis. If people stop voting Conservative, getting married or celebrating Christmas, such social objects cease to exist because they are constituted intersubjectively through our social behaviour. We construct social reality using them as building blocks. They are part of that reality for as long, but only as long, as we continue to use them. In other words, they are real, because we behave as if they existed.

The development of a methodological paradigm appropriate to the study of physical objects — the empirical method — has been one of humankind's proudest intellectual and practical achievements. No one, for example, who has undergone an eye operation using laser technology can accept post-modernist arguments that modern science is just another discourse, just another ideology. However, this does not mean that the paradigm of the physical sciences can be transferred lock, stock and barrel to the social sciences, since the very different natures of their objects of study would make that inappropriate and unscientific.

This has not always been obvious or accepted. The undoubted successes of the physical sciences led to the belief that the only possible way of being scientific, the only valid methodology, was heuristic, positivist and objective. There is a single reality — 'truth' — out there, a right answer which can be known through measurement. Anything that was not amenable to this kind of investigation was dismissed as 'metaphysics', unscientific.

In the nineteenth century, the 'scientists' mounted a fierce onslaught on the metaphysicians. Any scholar interested in politics, history, anthropology or psychology was, therefore, faced with one of the two following options (a state of affairs which remained largely unchanged until about a quarter of a century ago, and of which vestiges can still be found in some departments of linguistics, education or sociology and in the editorial policies of certain academic journals):

1. to accept that their field of study was indeed not capable of being treated 'scientifically', that it was descriptive at best, subjective at worst; or
2. to attempt to apply an empirical methodology in their field, by concentrating on those aspects which were measurable.

In extreme cases — extreme but numerous and influential — the mechanical application of physical science methodology to social objects had disastrous consequences. A case in point would be 'intelligence testing', where intelligence was reduced to an IQ, those limited aspects of human cognitive functioning which could be measured with the instruments available at the time. So out went music, metaphor and creativity, eidetic thought, social skills and intersubjectivity and indexical reasoning. Interestingly enough, this left an account of intelligence, IQ, which was reduced to something strangely resembling a model for scientific logic and methodology in dealing with problems. Galton and Binet and their followers created man in their own image.[1]

As for the learning process, there was behaviouristic psychology, which, because it eschewed any consideration of mental operations as unscientific ('subjective', 'metaphysical' etc.), tried to extrapolate from rabbits and rats to human beings. This resulted in the absurd situation where conclusions about those rats and rabbits and pigeons pecking at popcorn — speechless species — were projected onto the human race, whose main distinguishing and unique characteristic is language.

It is not surprising, then, that workers on both sides of this methodological divide should see the quantitative, empirical approach and any form of social study as inimical. The 'scientists' were looking for **the** truth, the 'metaphysicians' (i.e. the social scientists) were looking for **their** truth, the world-view of the participants in the institutions and interactions they were studying. The 'scientists' were dismissive of 'speculation', their opponents were dismissive of trivial statistics, counting what could be counted instead of what counts.

Slowly, however, a third option has emerged, one that rejects the either/ or terms of the qualitative vs. quantitative debate and the absolute distinction between objectivity and subjectivity. (Ironically, this is at least partly due to developments in the physical sciences, where notions of relativity and point of view have asserted themselves with great tenacity, even in fields from which it was believed they had been forever banished.) An attempt has been made, then, to develop a methodology and techniques for the investigation of social objects which are appropriate to their nature as part of intersubjective reality, but which at the same time respect the principles for a scientific methodology which were enumerated earlier.

It is to this topic which we will now turn.

Standards for educational research

In the May 1990 issue of *Educational Researcher*, Kenneth Howe and Margaret Eisenhart published an important and influential paper entitled 'Standards for qualitative (and quantitative) research: a prolegomenon.' They argue that the polarization of the debate on educational research methodology into qualitative and quantitative methods, and positivist and anti-positivist methods, with the equations

Quantitative = Positivist

Qualitative   = Anti-positivist

(a position they regard as unchallenged "until 20 years ago") has been shown to be inaccurate and unhelpful by the development of 'qualitative' projects using quantitative instruments, and of alternative methodologies drawn from the fields of anthropology and ethnography in particular. They also argue that framing the debate in terms of a dialectical opposition between the 'positivist' and 'anti-positivist' is equally unhelpful, because it excludes all methodologies which are neither, or a mixture of both.

We will be looking at some of these 'alternative' and 'mixed' approaches in the next section. First, though, I would like to discuss the final, and most important, section of their article, where they try to get above the fray, as it were, to ask the fundamental question 'What would we require of *any* research project in education whatever, if we are to ensure that it is of adequate scientific quality?'

Their answer comes in the form of what they call "five general standards". These are necessarily high-level generalizations, and there is an inevitable (indeed encouraging) overlap between these standards and some of the points made earlier concerning methodological principles. The five standards are:

1. There should be a fit between research questions and data collection and analysis techniques.
2. Specific data collection and analysis techniques should be competently applied.
3. Researchers should be alert to their background assumptions, which should guide the research questions and methods in a coherent and consistent fashion.
4. There should be overall warrant for the project, its methodology and its conclusions.
5. External and internal value constraints should be respected.

Space permits only the briefest of comments on each of these points :

There should be a fit between research questions and data collection and analysis techniques.

I take this as meaning primarily that the principles ensuring the choice of a methodology which is appropriate to the specific research objectives (see above) must be respected. In particular, the investigation of social objects (in the widest possible sense, including representations, beliefs, attitudes, values etc.) can only be effected using instruments which are sensitive to their existence, identification, nature, variability and distribution in relation to other, social factors. However, this does not preclude the use of, for example, sophisticated statistical manipulation and analysis of data so obtained.

If, for example, you are interested in learners' representations of language and language learning (their beliefs about what language is, how you learn it, their attitudes to native speakers and the foreign culture and so on) then there really is little point in computing on the basis of outward physical behaviour of some kind, such as the number of times per lesson they use the 'Rewind' button on a tape recorder. Instead, recourse will be had to some kind of socio-psychological technique such as questionnaires or directed interviews which will produce sufficient quantities of relevant discourse for the investigators to go about identifying the interpretative repertoire of the group in question.[2]

Specific data collection and analysis techniques should be competently applied.

Presumably this is not a controversial requirement. Yet it is not unusual to come across flawed or incompetent instrument design or use. Examples include leading questions in questionnaires, or the failure to allow for the language in which a questionnaire was administered or for the ethnicity of the administrator; mathematical errors; misleading diagrams, pie-charts, tables.

Researchers should be alert to their background assumptions, which should guide the research questions and methods in a coherent and consistent fashion.

Any research project is necessarily based on what is already known about the field or object in question. The bibliographical search and the review of the literature are certainly not merely academic ritual; indeed, the whole apparatus of academic discourse from index to footnotes is a strategy for positioning this knowledge within the overarching social knowledge system. However, as recent work in the sociology of science has shown (cf. Woolgar 1988) there is no absolute defence against ideological and ethnocentric assumptions influencing research questions and methodology. This is largely because, as we saw earlier, methodology itself can be seen as a set of conventions a group employs for the validation and legitimation of knowledge.

In our own field, researchers need to be particularly vigilant then about their assumptions concerning cultural variables such as the teacher's role, educative practices, the status of discourse, their students' preferred learning styles etc., not because their opinions may be 'wrong', but because they might seriously influence the significance and generalizability of results.

There should be overall warrant for the project, its methodology and conclusions.

By this Howe and Eisenhart mean, firstly, that standards 1-3 should be respected; secondly, that the principles of argumentation mentioned above should be satisfied; and thirdly, that knowledge from outside, the particular perspective (discipline, tradition) being employed should be taken into account. When there are found to be contradictions between outside sources and the internal 'evidence', tough, critical theoretical explanations should be sought for and applied to the data. This, in turn, means that rejected or disconfirmed theories, explanations and data will receive attention and explicit discussion, not only those which are considered to be proved and accepted.[3]

External and internal value constraints should be recognized and respected.

Despite the difficulties involved, research in education has to face the problem of *external* values. 'Is it (i.e. the project) worth it?' must mean in this context 'Will it improve our understanding and practice of education?' as well as weighing the degree of priority it merits, given limited resources. This in turn implies that the research findings in question should be *accessible*, in the fullest sense, to other actors in the educational field, teachers, administrators and learners (cf. the section on 'Publication', above).

Internal value constraints are ethical and tend, in our field, to be mainly a matter of treatment of and respect for learners. To take just one problem in what is obviously a vast area: is it ethical to record counselling sessions secretly, or even openly? This clearly is directly related to a major locus of debate in anthropology and ethnography concerning the ownership of texts and the intellectual property they contain.

Some approaches to research in education

In this final section, I will be mentioning briefly some approaches to research in education which, used in appropriate circumstances, have been found to satisfy the various kinds of requirement we have been looking at.[4] Obviously there can be no question of being exhaustive, nor of entering into detail; my aim is simply to give an indication of the range of approaches available at present which are 'mixed' in the sense that they combine, or simply stand outside, 'qualitative/quantitative' and 'positivist/non-positivist' perspectives.

Ethnographic approaches

Ethnographic approaches in general aim at studying some aspect of group culture; typically, investigation involves making explicit the rules and beliefs of a competent member of the group. Such an approach is highly compatible with the learner-centred approach, since both focus on the individual's world-view, rather than imposing some external theory or taxonomy.

Techniques include participant observation, case-studies, interviews, discourse analysis, cross-cultural studies, contrastive studies, and contextual and historical studies.

Psychological approaches

Clearly, there is a need for both process-psychological and socio-psychological approaches to language learning. These include a variety of approaches, each with its own battery of methods and instruments, such as: acquisition studies (Ellis 1990); second language learning (Gaonac'h 1987); social psychology of language, and the theory of ethnolinguistic vitality (Giles and St. Clair 1979); Personal Construct Theory (Kelly 1969; Bannister and Fransella 1971); study of collective representations (Jodelet 1989); learning styles (Bickley 1989; Duda and Riley 1991); and motivation and affective factors (Laine 1987).

Ethnomethodogical approaches

Such approaches aim to investigate the ways in which the social reality of a group is acquired, constructed and maintained by its members through interaction and conversation. Examples include: identification of the interpretative repertoire (Potter and Wetherell 1988; Riley 1989, 1994; Schmitt-Gevers 1992); metaphor (Lowe 1988); cognitive and cultural models analysis (Holland and Quinn 1989); and conceptual and philosophical analysis (Trim 1976; Holec 1981).

Empirical approaches

Empirical approaches become 'hybrid' or 'quasi-experimental' as soon as social constraints are accepted. For example, if the researcher cannot choose the experimental population randomly because of institutional constraints he or she will have to work with 'classes' as established by the administration. Nonetheless, it would still be possible to test the effect, say of a learner-training programme by providing it for one part of the population but not for another.

Action research

It has to be admitted that action research is not so much a research methodology as a way of identifying research projects and priorities. Instead of starting with a 'research question' based on previous research and theory, the action researcher starts with a problem with which he or she is faced.

As such, it is well suited to educational research, especially if it is in any degree learner-centred. Once the problem has been identified, the researcher is, of course, at liberty to call on any appropriate theory, methodology or instrument. For the reasons which have been discussed above, in the social sciences this will often result in a principled methodological eclecticism.

Conclusion

Self-access centres, like all human institutions, have both material and social forms. The symbolic relations between the two, for which we use labels like 'autonomy', 'self-directed learning' or 'self-access', and their instantiation in social interaction, roles and individuals, language and language-learning activities, make it pointless to adopt an approach to research which is exclusively 'qualitative' or 'quantitative', 'positivist' or 'non-positivist'. This will imply methodologically hybrid solutions, which are not easy to find or implement. But as Piet Hein (1966) has said:

> Problems worthy of attack,
> Prove their worth by hitting back.

Notes

1. A similar, alarming piece of reductionism is to be found nowadays in the field of CALL, where learning **with** computers is increasingly confused with learning **like** computers.

2. Various examples are to be found in Holland and Quinn 1989; Riley 1989; Coupland et al. 1992; Schmitt-Gevers 1992; Riley 1994.

3. Reading the academic journals of any discipline, one has the impression that all experiments are successful, largely due to a failure to observe this 'standard'. There should be a 'Journal of Experimental Failure', not just to provide researchers with warnings and object lessons, but as a source of genuinely interdisciplinary insight and criticism.

4. There are a number of manuals for researchers in the social sciences, including Pelto (1970) and Jaeger (1988). Gardner and Miller (1994) is a collection of articles concentrating on self-access, many of them research-based. Riley (1991) examines both self-access and research amongst the various functions of university language centres.

17

The acquisition of vocabulary in an autonomous learning environment — the first months of beginning English[1]

Leni Dam and Lienhard Legenhausen

Introduction

This chapter reports on our research project LAALE (Language Acquisition in an Autonomous Learning Environment) in which the language development of a class of 21 students who learn English 'the autonomous way' is compared and contrasted with proficiency levels of classes which follow a more traditional, textbook-based syllabus. The project started in 1992, and has so far seen four different data elicitation phases. Table 1 below gives an overview of the various test formats and different language aspects focused on so far.

This chapter is only concerned with the acquisition of vocabulary in the first few months.[2] The vocabulary selected and publicly shared by the students in the first four weeks was systematically recorded and its retention tested after 7.5 and after 15 weeks, i.e. after 30 and 60 lessons respectively.

The project's aim is not to prove the superiority/inferiority of one approach over another, but mainly to illustrate that the autonomous principle does work. The test results of the more traditional classes are adduced only to facilitate the interpretation of the language development of the autonomous learners, i.e. to provide some kind of yardstick for the interpretation of test results. Learners from the traditional classes cannot serve as control groups in the strict sense of the word since independent external measures of comparability are lacking.

Table 1: Experimental design of the research project

Elicitation phase	Length of tuition/learning	Form of elicitation	Language items/abilities
1	7.5 weeks (30 lessons)	Open questions/ spontaneous recall	Productive vocabulary
2	15 weeks (60 lessons)	Vocabulary test	Receptive abilities (auditory/visual recognition); Spelling
3	30 weeks	Structure test (open and closed questions)	Structures (Pronouns, negatives, interrogatives, progressive form etc.); Written production
4	1 year, 5 months	Peer-to-peer talk/ structured interview	Oral proficiency

The learner groups

The 12-year-old autonomous learners are a mixed ability group from a Danish comprehensive school. There are altogether 10 girls and 11 boys in the class, eight of whom received remedial teaching in L1 Reading/Writing and Maths. English is taught in two double periods on Mondays and Wednesdays — each of the four lessons lasts 45 minutes. Principles of autonomous learning are only adhered to in their English classes, all other school subjects being taught the traditional way.

The first group of traditional learners, whose English course is based on *Project English* (Hutchinson 1985), comes from the same school. This is also a mixed ability class of 17 students. It can be assumed that their learning/teaching and demographic background is very similar to the class of autonomous learners. However, these learners were only able to take part in the first spontaneous production test (Elicitation phase 1).

The second group of learners whose course of English is also textbook-based — and who act as a reference group — attend a German grammar school ('Gymnasium'). The German school system is a selective three-tier system which differentiates between abilities/aptitude at a fairly early stage. This means that only 40 to 50 percent of the students of each year attend a 'Gymnasium'. These students intend eventually to take A level examinations. In other words, when it comes to comparing test results, it should be kept in mind that this group has a different learning/teaching background, and lower-ability students do not go to this school in the first place. Another difference is that the German group has five 45-minute lessons of English every week — equally spread from Mondays to Fridays.

Vocabulary acquisition in the autonomous classroom in the first few weeks

Learner autonomy and language learning

> School knowledge is the knowledge which someone else presents to us. We partly grasp it, enough to answer the teacher's question, to do exercises, or to answer examination questions, but it remains someone else's knowledge, not ours. If we never use this knowledge we probably forget it. In so far as we use knowledge for our own purposes, however, we begin to incorporate it into our view of the world, and to use parts of it to cope with the exigencies of living. (Barnes 1976: 81)

One of the basic principles and starting points for language learning in the autonomous classroom is that the learners bring to the classroom a knowledge of language and language use, e.g. communicative abilities in their mother tongue, a knowledge of interpersonal behaviour, and in many cases a knowledge of the foreign language to be learned.

This knowledge is unfortunately disregarded in many traditional language-learning classrooms. Many beginners' course books regard the students as empty bottles to be filled and from the very beginning the learners are taught that when entering the foreign language classroom 'normal' life stops — for example, they spend a long time asking people whom they have known for many years about their names.

Another important issue in the autonomous classroom is the aspect of learning versus teaching, as touched upon in the quotation above. Learning is a negotiable process between the learner's existing knowledge and the new knowledge needed by or presented to him/her — and this can only be done by the learner himself/herself (see Figure 1). It is essential that the teacher believes and accepts this.

As teachers we can support — and of course hinder — our learners' learning. It is our task partly to make the learners aware of the many possible sources of new knowledge/language (including ourselves) and partly to establish situations in which the learners can activate and develop their existing knowledge (see Figure 2).

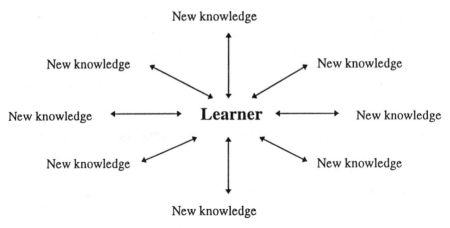

Figure 1: Learning — a negotiable process

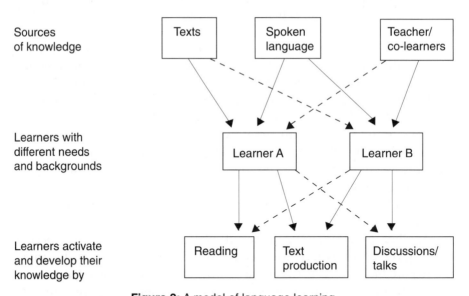

Figure 2: A model of language learning

Building up a shared language

Space does not allow us to give a detailed description of the way language learning is organized in the autonomous classroom.[3] The following sketch, therefore, focuses only on those aspects and activities which are of particular interest with regard to vocabulary acquisition.

At the beginning of term, language is introduced/developed as follows:

1. The learners are asked to bring some English language to the classroom (representing "The world outside the classroom"). The stickers, advertisements, sentences from T-shirts etc. which the children bring along are either kept in a box ("Our own materials") or written on A3 posters and put on the wall.

2. In their very first lesson, the learners are asked to present themselves in English in "My own English book". As support they are each given the *Oxford English Picture Dictionary* (Parnwell 1988) and they can ask the teacher or friends for any word or expression needed. The results are: individual, personal presentations in each diary, as well as a joint, first treasure of expressions ("New knowledge needed"), again written on posters and placed on "Our English Board". Example expressions are *My name is..., I am ... years old, I have, I like, mother/father/sister/brother, he/she is, football/swimming/dancing* etc. In the daily classroom interaction other expressions are soon needed and added such as *Sorry, I'm late* and *Sorry, I've forgotten my book.*

3. The picture dictionaries are made use of in their first lesson: the learners are asked individually to find at least five words in the dictionary that he/she would like to know/remember. They are furthermore asked to make drawings and to write the words in their diaries and then share their work with their neighbour. Again, all the learners are engaged in a 'personal', relevant language-learning task. (The same task is given as their first homework.)

4. Language input is also introduced by the teacher, in the form of nursery rhymes, songs and well-known fairy tales (e.g. *Goldilocks and the Three Bears*) which are read aloud or shown as video. In addition, words and phrases used by the teacher during the classroom discourse form a major data source. Again, expressions and structures which the teacher and/ or learners find of general interest will appear on posters, e.g. *Good morning, how are you today? I'm fine, thank you.*

5. The learners — individually, in pairs or in small groups — produce language output in the form of simple wordcards (with a drawing, photo or L1 equivalent on one side and the corresponding English expression on the other side), dominoes, picture lottos, stories, small booklets and short plays. The Picture Dictionaries, a few bilingual Danish-English dictionaries, and the posters with shared expressions and structures support these activities. Peers and, to a certain extent, the teacher

provide help as well. The produced games and texts are then made available for the other learners to play with and/or read/see.

Even though the main pedagogic value lies in the process of producing the texts — texts that can and will be used by others — it is important to stress the value of learner-produced materials as data input, if — and only if — the materials are on offer to be used when the other learners feel like it. This data is furthermore open to direct user/producer interaction: What does this mean? How is this pronounced? Used in this way, the games/texts seem to be considered as shared property and words/expressions occurring are remembered to a large extent by the users (see Figure 4 and Table 4 below).

Size and distribution of vocabulary

In order to document the process of vocabulary acquisition in the first four weeks, all the words that were made public in the classroom during this period, and written down in a form which guaranteed accessibility to all learners, were entered into a data bank. We can thus trace which words were introduced when into the classroom, by which learner(s) (or the teacher), and in what context or format.

Number of words

The data bank contains 400 different entries, which is the size of the vocabulary publicly shared by the whole learner group. Words which learners entered into their more private diaries were not included. In order to be able to interpret this figure, some kind of yardstick or reference point is called for. We will just mention two measures/figures which might prove helpful:

1. The most widely used textbook in Germany, *Green Line* (Amor et al. 1985), which implements the official language curriculum prescribed by the educational authorities in the federal states in Germany, introduces 124 different words within the same period of time, i.e. within the first four weeks.

2. The grammar school curriculum for the state North-Rhine Westfalia (where the school of our German learner group is situated) requires knowledge/mastery of 800 different words in the first year of English. This would mean that the Danish learners had already fulfilled half of the prescribed learning requirement within the first four weeks of

English — provided the words which had been made public in the classroom had actually been learned by the students. This point will be returned to below.

Semantic fields

We would first like to describe and characterize the type of words which the learners actually chose to learn. This is of great interest from a theoretical as well as from a practical point of view. The vocabulary of textbook-based courses is normally selected on the basis of criteria such as frequency, range, coverage, utility etc. All these parameters taken together aim to overcome the problem of arbitrariness regarding vocabulary selection and try to restrict the textbook author's options in a more principled way. Although textbook authors will also always make great efforts to take the learners' interests and needs into account, they can never be sure whether their predictions/anticipations and decisions turn out to be valid. To a certain extent the autonomous EFL classroom could thus be regarded as some kind of testing ground for the validity of textbook choices.

Table 2 tries to give a first answer to the question of how learners' choices compare to a textbook author's selection. The words are sorted into various semantic fields which seemed of importance to the learners. Since the number of words (n=124) introduced by the textbook *Green Line* in the first four weeks was not sufficient for a comparison of semantic fields, we almost doubled the number and used the first 233 words for comparative purposes (equivalent of 35 lessons).

Table 2: Distribution of vocabulary across semantic fields

Field	DA (totals after 16 lessons)	Textbook (totals after 35 lessons)
People	20	13
Animals	28	–
Parts of the body	8	1
Colours	13	1
Numbers	2	14
Food	12 (incl. 8 x fruit)	–
School items	3	8

DA: Danish autonomous group

Some of the differences become obvious at first glance. For example, the textbook introduces school equipment like *school-bag, rubber, biro, ruler* from the very beginning, and the numbers are systematically dealt with at an early stage. Colours are introduced much later (the colour *green* is an exception because it turns up in a song).

By contrast, the lexical fields and words of the Danish learners on the one hand seem to reflect the interests of the learner group as a whole (compare the categories 'Animals' and 'Colours'), and on the other also reflect the specific interests of individual learners. It is, for example, noteworthy that the eight different types of fruit in the category 'Food' appeared in a small booklet which the daughter of a greengrocer had made.

Comparison with a standardized frequency list

The learner vocabulary also contains hard words like *galaxy, submarine* and *parachute* which are not included in any frequency list or inventory of basic vocabulary. So in order to get a more objective picture of the semantic range and especially the frequency values of the learner vocabulary, we compared it with one of the standardized frequency lists which serve as a guideline for textbook authors and syllabus designers.

We opted for the *Leuven English Teaching Vocabulary-List* (Engels et al. 1981). The LET-List tries to combine objective frequency criteria with more subjective selection criteria. Engels and his research group have merged three well-known corpora: the Brown Corpus, the LOB Corpus and the Leuven Theatre Corpus. This procedure yielded the 2,000 most frequent words (the A-words). They formed the basis of the LET-List. Since a list of that type, however, does not contain many of the concrete everyday words (like *apple*, for example), it was checked against Richards's familiarity list (cf. Richards 1971) and supplemented by a high coverage list — the *International Reader's Dictionary* (West 1965/1977). Thus 1,493 B-words were added to the 2,000 most frequent A-words.

Figure 3 below compares the learners' first 400 words with the frequency ranges and subsections of the LET-List. It is noteworthy that:

1. after 16 lessons (4 weeks), 32% of the 500 most frequent words have emerged (or have been made public) in the classroom and
2. 10% of the vocabulary (35 words + 6 proper names) are not included in any section of the LET-List.

The right-hand column shows the distributions of the textbook vocabulary, i.e. the 233 words of the first 7 weeks. The diagram shows that:

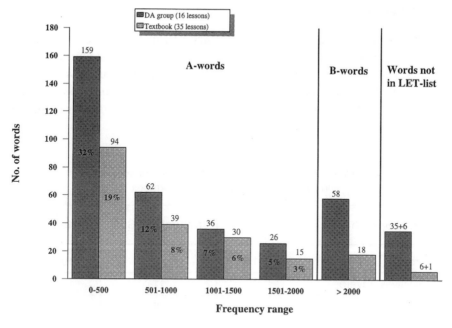

Figure 3: Comparison of learner group and textbook vocabulary with the LET-List

1. after more than twice the number of lessons, i.e. after 35 periods, only 19% of the most frequent 500 words have been introduced, and

2. only 3% (6 words + 1 proper name) are outside the LET-List. Five out of these six words have to do with the classroom discourse: *biro, vocabulary, dialogue, register* (an important concept in the German classroom) and *rhyme*. The remaining item not listed in the LET-List is the word *teddy* — the only term that can be said to reflect the specific interests of this age group, and which, incidentally, is also part of the Danish learners' first 400 words.

The 35 words of the Danish learner group which fall outside the LET-List include: vocabulary from western movies like *sheriff, revolver, duel*; special animal terms like *shark, whale* etc.; *girls' brigade/boys' brigade* (a Danish girl/ boy scout organization) and hard words like *galaxy, submarine* and *parachute* which have already been mentioned.

A comparison of the first 100 most frequent words in the LET-List with the DA group reveals that autonomous learners had learned 62% after 16 lessons, whereas the textbook — after 35 lessons — had only introduced 30% of the high frequency items.

Parts of speech

Another special feature of the vocabulary of the Danish learner group becomes apparent if we take a more detailed look at the distribution of the various parts of speech. In this case the distribution of the learner vocabulary cannot only be compared with the textbook vocabulary, but also with data from research on second language acquisition in a naturalistic environment (cf. Wode 1987).

Table 3: Percentage distribution of parts of speech
in two learner groups and the textbook

Part of Speech	DA	Naturalistic SLA	Textbook
Verbs	18	22	19
Adjectives/Adverb	12	11	16
Pronouns	5	8	5
Prepositions/Conjunctions	3	4	6
Nouns	55	31	34
Miscellaneous	6	24	20

With the exception of the noun category, the overall distribution of the various parts of speech is fairly similar across the three 'learning situations'. The overrepresentation of nouns in the Danish learner group probably results from the learners' preferred learning techniques. Since a larger percentage of vocabulary found its way into the classroom via word cards, picture lottos and dominoes, the selection of words is also determined by graphic or pictorial means of representation.

Receptive knowledge and availability of L2 vocabulary

The very fact that a large amount of vocabulary has been made public in the classroom does not yet guarantee that the learners have also acquired it. In order to follow up this question, two vocabulary tests were carried out.

Spontaneous recall test

The first test — administered after 7.5 weeks of learning (30 lessons) — was not a full-fledged traditional vocabulary test battery — but was rather an informal elicitation of all the words the learners were able to recall spontaneously. They were asked to write down as many words as they could think of. And in order to help the learners to get as many associations as possible they were given some cues. The instructions read:

---

1. Write down as many words as you can
    a. colours
    b. animals
    c. words for persons (e.g. *dreng, mor, dronning*)
    d. things you can eat
    e. things you can see in the classroom
    f. things people can do at work/in their free time (e.g. *spise, sidde, stå, ride, svømme, skrive*)

2. Write down other words or sentences in English

Figure 4 below shows the results of individual learners. The top of the column refers to the total number of words recalled. In this case every identifiable English word was recognized. The middle section of the column refers to words with one deviant grapheme. The lower black section identifies the number of orthographically correct words.

Student A was able to recall 118 English words (99 of which were correctly spelt); Student U, by contrast, recalled only nine words, none of which was error-free. It should be mentioned in this context that learner U has similar writing problems in his Danish mother tongue.

This diagram also brings out different learner approaches to the performance task. The varying ratios between total number of words recalled and error-free words will to a certain extent correlate with learner types and/or risk-taking (-avoiding) strategies. Compare, for example, the columns of safety-conscious learner F with the risk-taking student G.

The results of the Danish textbook group (DT) from the same comprehensive school and of the German textbook group from the grammar school (GT) are somewhat different (see Figures 5 and 6).

The results of individual learners from the German grammar school class are much more homogeneous, and clearly show that the students are in general better at orthography than the Danish comprehensive school

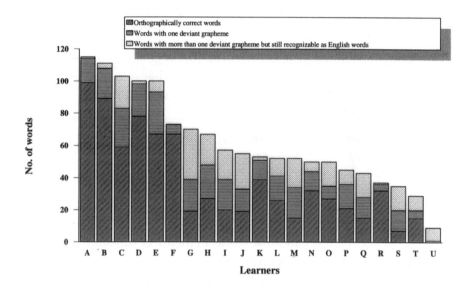

Figure 4: Number of words recalled (DA group)

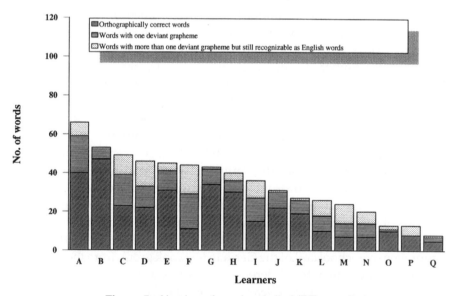

Figure 5: Number of words recalled (DT group)

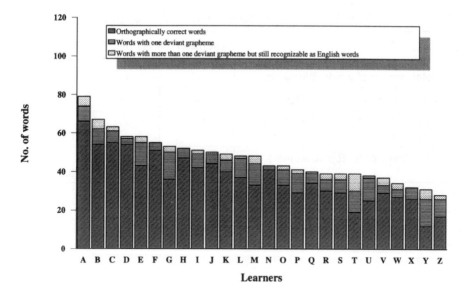

Figure 6: Number of words recalled (GT group)

students. Formal correctness (conformity) seems to be a more important teaching goal.

However, when it comes to productivity of individual learners and of the whole learner group, the overall situation is slightly different. Table 4 below shows the arithmetic means for the classes and for the 10 best and 10 least proficient students in each class. As regards most values the Danish autonomous class with mixed ability learners (DA) proves to be as good as or even better than German grammar school students (GT).

Receptive vocabulary knowledge/spelling test

The second test was administered after 15 weeks (60 lessons) and intended to assess the learners' passive vocabulary in a more systematic way. The items were all taken from the inventory of 400 words of the first four weeks, which means by then there was a time lag of 11 weeks between the vocabulary activities referred to earlier on and the test administration. In other words, the focus was on longer-term retention rates.

The test was biased towards receptive abilities (auditory and visual recognition of words) and spelling.

The test battery consisted of 5 subtests and comprised 175 items. Parameters for the selection of vocabulary items included:

Table 4: Average number of words recalled, by group

	DA (n=21)	GT (n=26)	DT (n=17)
Total number of words: Whole class	62	47	34
Error-free words: Whole class	37	37	20
Total number of words: Top 10 learners	85	59	45 (top 7: 49)
Error-free words: Top 10 learners	59	49	28 (top 7: 32)
Total number of words: Bottom 10 learners	40	36	24
Error-free words: Bottom 10 learners	16	24	11

1. How was the word introduced into the classroom? (e.g. vocabulary game/video/song/booklet/classroom discourse etc.)
2. How often was the item attested in the data bank, i.e. how many students have actively used it?
3. What difference do mono- and multisyllabic words make?

Subtests 1, 3 and 4 (55 items) tested auditory recognition and meaning recall in different formats (translational equivalents or drawings; matching). Subtests 2 (matching) and 6 (translational equivalents or drawings) covered visual recognition and meaning recall (90 items). Subtest 5 focused on spelling, i.e. 30 words were dictated. Contextual embeddings were deliberately avoided in order not to complicate things for weak readers/writers. In order to take into account the fact that some Danish learners were very weak writers, some subtests allowed the option of representing the meaning of words in the form of drawings.

The same test was also administered in the German class, although not all the words had been part of the German syllabus. Therefore the percentage figures in the last column of Table 5 refer only to that subset of vocabulary which had actually occurred in the textbook by the time of taking the test. This also explains why scores for subtest 4 could not be calculated, since only four out of 20 items were introduced by the German textbook. This subtest was intended to check to what extent words attested only once in the data bank (ten of which were multisyllabic hard words such as *corkscrew, envelope, octopus, umbrella* etc.) were recalled by the group of Danish learners. These selection criteria also explain the low success rate of 63.1% of the Danish group. The design and structure of the second vocabulary test is summarized in Table 5. The number of words that occurred in the textbook are given in brackets in the right-hand GT column.

Table 5: Structure and results of the second test

		Structure of the test			Results in %	
Sub-test	No. of Items	Source/ Selection Criteria	Abilities	Item Format	DA	GT*
1	20	Multiple attestation (1–10)/classroom discourse (11–20)	Auditory recognition/ meaning recall	Translation (drawing)	92.2	88.2 (11)
2	20	Word games (1-10)/ video films (11-20)	Visual recognition/ meaning recall	Matching	93.3	89.3 (9)
3	15	Songs/nursery rhymes	Auditory recognition/ meaning recall	Matching	98.7	90.4 (6)
4	20	Single attestation (1–20)/ multisyllabic words (11–20)	Auditory recognition/ meaning recall	Translation (drawing)	63.1	—
5	30	Random selection	Spelling	Dictation	73.1	88.7 (20)
6	70	Random selection	Visual recognition/ meaning recall	Translation (drawing)	73.3	86.1 (45)

* Numbers in brackets in the GT column refer to the number of items in each subtest which had occurred in the textbook at the time of the test.

The following tendencies can be derived from the various subtests:

1. The results of the Danish learner group are slightly better as regards auditory recognition.
2. The German learners are better when the written mode (and spelling) plays a major role.

3. Vocabulary which is presented in songs and rhymes are much better retained — especially by weaker students. This explains the score difference in subtest 3, because the items occurred in songs or rhymes only in the Danish group.
4. Multiple attestations in the data bank have an influence on retention, although frequency of occurrence can also signal increased interest on the part of the learner group.

Conclusion

The results of the two vocabulary tests convincingly demonstrate that vocabulary acquisition in the autonomous approach is very successful and compares favourably with results from more traditional textbook-based approaches. The number of words that 'emerge' in the first few months and are publicly shared by the whole learner group exceeds the requirements of official syllabus guidelines for German grammar school classes (i.e. higher ability classes). The mastery and availability of an extended vocabulary might also be due to the fact that the autonomous approach succeeds in making learners aware of the English language surrounding them in their L1 environment and in integrating this knowledge into their developing L2 competence. A subset of the words that are available to these learners would thus not be classified as 'newly acquired' but as words which they have 'become aware of'. Traditional approaches might turn out to be less successful in this regard.

Notes

1. This paper is printed here by kind permission of the editors of *Die Neuren Sprachen,* in which a different version of the article was first published (Legenhausen 1994).

2. On the development of oral proficiency cf. Legenhausen (forthcoming).

3. For further information cf. Dam (1994, 1995).

18

Use and abuse of autonomy in computer-assisted language learning: some evidence from student interaction with *SuperCloze*

Vance Stevens

Introduction

Although the situation is steadily being corrected, it has often been noted that CALL (computer-assisted language learning) has so far developed well ahead of its research base (e.g. Dunkel 1991). The result is that developers of CALL often work on intuition alone and have little real idea what students actually do with their programs (Chapelle 1990). To compound this situation, what research there is on CALL effectiveness is often done using procedures where the researcher intrudes on the learner, thus possibly contaminating the autonomous aspects of the process under study.

Feldmann and Stemmer (1987) discuss the various cognitive limits that may interfere with concentration on the task under study when students are asked to "think aloud" about what they are doing. It follows that intrusive protocols could influence results in studies such as that of Windeatt (1986), who videoed screens as his subjects thought aloud while doing computer-based cloze exercises and found that there was little use of program help features. Stevens (1991a, 1991b, 1991c), on the other hand, finds through non-intrusively tracking students working under self-access conditions that they sometimes overuse, even abuse, help features rather than rely on their competence in the language to solve problems. Thus degree of intrusion may be a factor in the outcome of such studies.

Research into what students do with CALL in self-access should ideally be carried out non-intrusively, yet due to the intrusive nature of most studies of the medium, rarely is CALL studied in its pure self-access state. One reason for this is the difficulty in controlling variables in a process which the experimenter essentially observes without interference. Also, for ethical reasons, researchers who identify individual subjects must inform them prior to including them in a study, in effect saying: "You are subjects in an experiment but please carry on as if you weren't!" As this could render it impossible to study self-access with that set of subjects, one solution, as with the present experiment, is to use subjects anonymously; that is, record their key presses on computers but take no record of who the individuals were who made them. Although many data are accordingly lost, such as relative English proficiencies of subjects exhibiting certain performance behaviours, the process under study can at least be assumed to be in a virtually uncontaminated state.

Another issue in CALL is the degree to which giving students control in self-access affects their learning. As Chapelle and Mizuno pointed out, as of 1989, the issue of optimal degree of learner control over CALL "has not yet been investigated". However, Pederson (1986) compared two groups of students, one of which was allowed to refer at any time to a reading passage during the course of answering questions on that passage, and found that the passage-unavailable treatment resulted in significantly higher levels of comprehension because those students were forced to process the text when they had their one chance to read it. One purpose of the present study is to gain further insights into how control over help features affects the degree of engagement with the target language for the students in the study.

Although CALL is typically referred to as a generic entity, in fact its manifestations are many: word processing, simulation, concordancing, database exploration, and almost anything else where computers manipulate a human language or use one as an interface. Thus, as a study of 'CALL' would rank in scope with a study of 'the world', that scope must be narrowed down.

Suggestions such as Kleinmann's (1987) that CALL should provide high levels of comprehensible input make text manipulation programs an appealing mode of CALL delivery, as they can work off virtually any ascii text. It is also argued (in Cobb and Stevens 1996) that text manipulation programs can emulate the reading process, especially in light of the "reading as a psycholinguistic guessing game" paradigm (Goodman 1967; Smith 1971; updated for ESL in Grabe 1991) — even detractors from the theory (e.g. Perfetti 1985) qualify their remarks for reading in second languages. In so far as it may promote awareness of contextual help in restoring degraded messages (Jonz 1990), cloze seems particularly suitable as a medium for text manipulation.

This chapter reports on a project in which student use of computer-based cloze is studied from data collected using non-intrusive methods. Due to the non-intrusive methods employed in data collection, the chapter presents unique insights into the use of CALL as an autonomous learning tool.

Setting and subjects

The project was carried out in the self-access Student Resource Centre (SRC) at Sultan Qaboos University in Oman, where students use computers to augment their English language skills. One major component of CALL in the SRC is a large corpus of texts taken from language courses and authentic subject course materials the students are studying. A battery of text manipulation programs provides one mode of access to these texts. Two of the text manipulation programs, *Hangman-in-Context* (Stevens and Millmore 1992–1995) and *SuperCloze* (Stevens and Millmore 1990–1995), have been configured so that when students use the programs, their key presses are recorded, making possible inferences regarding strategies used.

The students who use the SRC are Arabic-speaking male and female university students, mainly in their first year, taking English courses concurrently with subject courses at a university where English is for the most part the language of instruction. They use the computers either during scheduled class hours (when they might be directed to do certain activities by the teacher in charge) or during self-access hours in the evenings, when use would be completely unmonitored. Whether or not they themselves choose to use a certain program, once selected, students work unsupervised. Neither they nor in most cases their teachers are aware that data are being collected as they work, or that research is being carried out in the SRC. Thus we are able to collect data non-intrusively on student use of these particular programs.

Students do not log on to the stand-alone computers in the SRC, and no records were ever made of who any individual was in the study. Because of this, it is impossible to say with absolute certainty who the subjects were. It can be assumed that the interactants were all students, as the data were collected in a location used almost exclusively by students fitting the above description. In all, 54 different subjects can be distinguished as having interacted with the program at distinct dates and times, but here again, it would be impossible to say for certain that each subject was a different student, although it would be highly coincidental if any two subjects turned out to be the same student.

Although it is impossible to know from the available data the ability level of these students, assumptions can again be made based on the texts the students chose. The menus on the computers in the SRC are arranged so that students can access texts according to the courses they are taking. Accordingly, the students choosing medical texts would likely be the highest in language proficiency, followed by the English specialists (students training to be English teachers), who were the most likely users of texts from Reading for Adults and Expanding Reading Skills in addition to those from their own menu area. At the opposite end of the spectrum there are the remedial students, obviously weak in English, and students from Arts and Education, whose courses outside the Language Centre are usually conducted in Arabic. The proficiency levels of students selecting texts from the other groups such as Engineering and Science vary, but tend to fall between those of the students just mentioned. Finally, there are readings of a general nature stored on the computer (jokes and fairy tales) which could have been accessed by any of the above students.

The research perspective: findings from prior studies

Before concentrating on the present state of the research being carried out with students using *SuperCloze*, it will be useful to consider prior research done using subjects similar to those described above. Initially, a study was conducted (Stevens 1991d) in which students were asked via questionnaires to assess their attitudes towards use of the CALL facility in the SRC, of which early versions the *Hangman* and cloze programs were a prominent component. Despite the fact that most of the students were using computers for the very first time in the SRC, they reported generally favourable attitudes; e.g. that the programs were easy to use and that they perceived them as effective in improving their English.

Next, a pilot study was carried out using *Hangman*, which was chosen for this phase of the project because its code was easier to work with than that of *SuperCloze*, and data could be collected and analyzed with fewer complications than with those deriving from *SuperCloze*. Thus we could concentrate more easily on the nuts and bolts of implementation. From that standpoint, the project went well, as much was learned that could be applied to the development of the data collection component for *SuperCloze*.

But more importantly, the data revealed that, in the way it was then implemented, *Hangman* may not have been what we had assumed it was: an effective CALL program. To gather these data, each student response to the program had to be characterized as either deriving from a competency-based effort to solve the linguistic puzzle or just a random key press. A competency-based effort might be, when confronted with the letters "whi--", typing in the letter 'c' even though the word in question might be *whisk*. Another competency-based effort might be to request a hint to reveal "whis-", and then use that as a basis for solving the problem. Non-competency-based efforts include, besides random and clustered key presses, using hints for more than half the letters in a word or invoking the 'See Solution' feature, which in *Hangman* essentially solves the problem for the student.

It was found that students were engaging more than half the time in non-competency-based behaviours, with only 47% of their keystrokes suggesting use of some strategy clearly utilizing linguistic competence in arriving at a solution to any given problem. These results suggested numerous improvements to the program and led to the development of a stand-alone module which we now call *Hangman-in-Context*. As the name suggests, *HMIC* strives to emphasize the most crucial aspect of text manipulation: its relationship to the curriculum as reflected in the text base. This relationship is highlighted in *HMIC* through provision of a portion of the text surrounding the target word; that is, the surrounding context as it occurs in the text from which that word was extracted, except that this context is masked until the student unmasks it as needed and at the cost of points.

In addition, *HMIC* encourages productive strategies in solving text manipulation puzzles by:

1. imposing limits on use of hints;
2. detecting use of clustered key presses and signalling this awareness to the student; and
3. tracking correct vs. incorrect key presses both in the point system and by display of a progress-at-a-glance graphic.

As to the present project, work on *Hangman* has suggested a pattern of development that is being applied to *SuperCloze*, and whose steps are (a) implementation of a prototype CALL program, (b) data collection and analysis during trial on students, and (c) development of an improved version of the program which can be shown to be more pedagogically sound than the original. This chapter reports work with *SuperCloze* as it proceeds through these steps.

The *SuperCloze* program and its relation to the text base

As noted previously, the corpus of texts on the computers in the SRC is broken down into numerous files accessible through a menu of courses the students are in, so that students using *SuperCloze* should in theory be working on texts relevant to what they are doing in their current coursework. Accordingly, our text manipulation programs were designed to work from ascii text, and so serve as templates acting on any of the files in the corpus.

As one of these computer-based template programs, *SuperCloze* generates cloze exercises from any text file the student selects. After selecting a text, students have the option of choosing how they want the cloze passage to appear. The default is for every 5th word to be targeted for deletion, but any deletion rate ranging from every word to every 9th word may be selected, as well as deletion by word lists (e.g. lists of prepositions, helping verbs, determiners etc., or all words containing *n* number of letters, or more than *n*, or less, etc.). Students may also select texts that have been 'marked'; that is, a teacher has indicated words in the text that are those most appropriately deleted, and the program targets these.

Once students have settled on how they want the cloze passage to appear, the program generates cloze exercises from the selected text one paragraph at a time. In these exercises, the cursor appears at the first letter of the first targeted word. When students type a letter, the cursor moves to the next character blank until a word is completed, at which point students press 'Enter' for the program to compare their answer with the original text. If correct, the word remains in the text and the cursor moves to the next blank; if not, the incorrect answer is erased and the student can try again. At any point, the student can move the cursor to another blank, or request a hint (the correct letter at the cursor position), or have a look at the original paragraph and then either return to the problem or request another.

When the program is configured for research, all student moves are recorded into a data file on the hard disk, as well as particulars about the problem, such as the passage as it appeared to the student, the length of each paragraph, and how many gaps and words there were. Although the program records all key presses, students are never asked to identify themselves, and no records are made as to identity of individuals.

Data analysis

Two areas of analysis are suggested in the data collected: items that can be tallied, and moves made by students which we can attempt to understand in light of inferred linguistic competence. The present analysis focuses on the quantitative results. These include:

1. how much of the available text students appear to be working on;
2. whether they approach the text linearly or holistically;

3. how many problems they attempt, and how many are correct and incorrect;
4. how much time they spend on the text; and
5. how often and to what extent they use the help features provided in the program.

Because 100 is both a robust sample and a convenient number for calculating percentages, student interactions with 100 paragraph-length cloze exercises were used in the study. These 100 interactions were taken at random from the hundreds of interactions recorded. That is, a data file was opened at random and the interactions recorded there were analyzed, another file was opened and its contents analyzed, and so on until 100 interactions had been studied.

The data are presented in accompanying tables with column headings described in a key in the Appendix. The tables are designed so that interactions by the 54 subjects in the study can be easily traced. Towards this end, all subjects #1 to #54 who worked more than one paragraph are assigned letter designations to order the different paragraphs attempted. For example, as can be seen in Table 1, the first subject listed, #1, worked two paragraphs, a and b, spending just over a minute with each one. Apparently a medical student, this student chose his/her second text from the general reading section, and on both texts, attempted a single gap in each (that is, pressed some key besides 'F9-Quit' or 'Enter') but got no problems right. Some subjects appear on all three tables. For example, subject #4, probably a remedial English student, took eight minutes to solve the first two gaps in the first two of seven sentences in the first paragraph worked (Table 2: 4a) but used 'See Solution' and hints extensively in the process (Table 3: 4a). The student then quit that paragraph and peered into four others (Table 1: 4b, 4c, 4d and 4e), using 'See Solution' once more (Table 3: 4d), before completing all seven gaps in a sixth paragraph successfully (Table 2: 4f).

Results and discussion

Computer-surfers prone to browsing know that it is not unusual to open a software application only to exit it after a few seconds. In light of this, it was not surprising to find in the data numerous instances of 'window-shopping'; in fact, almost half the interactions recorded in this study evidenced non-fruitful use of the program. Taken optimistically, this means that over half the interactions were fruitful, while a fifth of all sessions recorded were worked by students to the very end (i.e. Number of gaps solved = Number of gaps attempted), an encouraging finding indeed in a setting of pure self-access.

In all, a total of 333 minutes of interaction time were examined, which suggests that students spent on average approximately three and a half minutes on each paragraph. Of this time, 280 minutes (84% of the total time) were spent in productive work, for an average of 5.38 minutes per paragraph dealt with interactively. Further distinctions between fruitful and non-fruitful sessions are elaborated below.

Non-fruitful sessions

As just noted, almost half of the sessions initiated by students with the *SuperCloze* program resulted in interactions for which no language-learning behaviours could be inferred. These non-fruitful sessions are indicated in the data wherever there are low time values, zero (or perhaps one) problems attempted, and of course zero numbers of gaps solved correctly. In other words, these are sessions where students looked at a passage, but made negligible effort to solve any of it. The data for such sessions are recorded in Table 1.

Table 1: Non-fruitful sessions

Subject and paragraph number	Type of text chosen	Deletion option selected	Number of gaps attempted	Number of gaps solved	Time on passage (min.)	Time per gap attempted
1a	M	determiners	1	0	1.1	1.1
1b	G	helping verbs	1	0	1.1	1.1
2	A	default: 5th	0	0	0.8	–
3a:f	A	default: 5th	0	0	5.9	–
3g	A	default: 5th	0	0	0.3	–
3h	A	default: 5th	0	0	0.1	–
3i	A	default: 5th	1	0	0.8	0.8
4b	R	default: 5th	0	0	0.2	–
4c	R	default: 5th	0	0	0.1	–
4d	R	default: 5th	1	0	1.2	1.2
4e	R	default: 5th	0	0	0.3	–

Table 1: to be continued

Table 1: continued

Subject and paragraph number	Type of text chosen	Deletion option selected	Number of gaps attempted	Number of gaps solved	Time on passage (min.)	Time per gap attempted
5	Eng	default: 5th	1	0	1.3	1.3
6	G	default: 5th	0	0	0.2	–
10	ERS	default: 5th	0	0	0.1	–
11	A	default: 5th	0	0	0.3	–
12	R	default: 5th	0	0	1.2	–
14a:h	G	default: 5th	0	0	10.2	–
15	Eng	default: 5th	0	0	0.3	–
16	E	default: 5th	0	0	0.3	–
18a	AE	default: 5th	0	0	1	–
18b	AE	default: 5th	0	0	1.3	–
19	G	default: 5th	1	0	0.7	0.7
20b	G	default: 5th	0	0	0.1	–
20c	G	default: 5th	0	0	0.1	–
21	AE	default: 5th	1	0	0.9	0.9
22	G	default: 5th	0	0	0.7	–
23	E	default: 5th	0	0	1	–
24	Eng	default: 5th	0	0	2.5	–
26a	AE	all	0	0	0.3	–
28	AE	default: 5th	0	0	0.1	–
30c	Eng	default: 5th	1	0	0.2	0.2
30d	Eng	default: 5th	0	0	0.1	–
30e	Eng	default: 5th	0	0	0.1	–
30f	Eng	default: 5th	0	0	0.1	–
33	Eng	default: 5th	0	0	0.3	–
35	M	default: 5th	0	0	0.8	–
41	E	default: 5th	0	0	1.5	–

Table 1: to be continued

Table 1: continued

Subject and paragraph number	Type of text chosen	Deletion option selected	Number of gaps attempted	Number of gaps solved	Time on passage (min.)	Time per gap attempted
43	E	default: 5th	0	0	3	–
45b	Eng	default: 5th	0	0	2	–
45c	Eng	default: 5th	1	0	1.9	1.9
45d	Eng	default: 5th	1	0	1.1	1.1
46	S/M	default: 5th	1	0	3.3	3.3
47	Eng	default: 5th	0	0	0.1	–
50	Eng	default: 5th	0	0	0.1	–
51	Eng	default: 5th	1	0	0.6	0.6
52a	Eng	default: 5th	1	0	0.5	0.5
52b	Eng	default: 5th	1	0	1	1
53b	Eng	default: 5th	1	0	1.5	1.5
Total	–	–	15	–	52.7	17.2
Average	–	–	–	–	1.1	1.15

Key to text types				
A	Reading for Adults	G	General Reading
AE	Arts and Education	M	Medicine
E	English specialists	R	Remedial
Eng	Engineering	S	Science
ERS	Expanding Reading Skills		

In the data, there are 33 instances of zero problems attempted — a third of the interactions recorded (but only 35.5 minutes, or 10.66% of the students' time spent). Some of these might indicate that a student wanted to look the text over before attempting it, a possibility in the case of subject 14a:h (Table 1), who chose, looked at, and quit from eight passages in succession over ten minutes' time with no recorded interaction (i.e. no gaps attempted, or no keys pressed other than 'Enter' or 'F9-Quit' in response to a blank). Another such interaction is 3a through h (Table 1), which in fact represents a student's looking at eight paragraphs one after another via the 'See Solution' (as indicated in Table 3: 3a:g) and 'Next passage' option for over six minutes before finally requesting a single hint (Table 3: 3i) just prior to logging off (Table 1: 3i).

Interaction 3i is representative of another example of non-fruitful interaction, where the student performed some action (an 'attempt') regarding a gapped item, but without success (i.e. attempted a problem and got it wrong or, as in the present case, requested a hint, then quit). In my sample data, there are 15 such items, which appear to be variations on window-shopping.

In summary, of the 100 cloze passages examined, about half (33 + 15 = 48) got essentially nowhere. In these cases, the students either looked at one or more paragraphs but did nothing more, or made a single move towards solving a gap and then quit without success or follow-through.

As noted, the interactions in this study in which such behaviour was exhibited constituted only 16% of the total time spent with the program by all students in the study. It is furthermore possible, since only data on student interaction with *SuperCloze* are considered in this study, that these students might have gone on to something else in the SRC that was productive and more suited to them. Unfortunately, there are no data on whether they did or not, as student movements are not tracked throughout the SRC.

However, it should be kept in mind that the existence of 'window-shopping' does not necessarily imply that students ultimately wasted their self-access time. They may have simply been captured in an act of browsing at a time when they were not in the mood for the task they had wandered into, and they may have found something else to do in the SRC that sharpened their linguistic skills a week, a day or a moment later, in the same way that window-shopping in real life leads ultimately to buying something, somewhere, from someone.

Fruitful sessions

Although it is interesting to note the large number of students who failed to take advantage of the opportunity to improve their English using *SuperCloze*, the main interest in the present study is with the students who did utilize the program. It is encouraging to find that the remaining 52% of the interactions, comprising 84% of the time spent with the program, were in some way fruitful. In these 52 interactions, the following data emerge, as shown in Table 2:

Table 2: Fruitful sessions

Subject and paragraph number	Type of text chosen	Deletion option selected	Number of sentences addressed	Linear or non-linear	Total gaps in passage	Number of gaps attempted	Number of gaps solved	Time on passage (min.)	Time per gap attempted
4a	R	default: 5th	2 out of 7	linear	7	2	2	8.0	4.0
4f	R	default: 5th	all	linear	7	7	7	4.5	0.64
7a	E	every 3rd	all	linear	14	14	14	5.9	0.42
7b	E	–	2 out of 3	linear	14	8	8	3.3	0.41
8a	E	default: 5th	all	linear	10	10	10	1.3	0.13
8b	E	–	all	linear	27	27	27	5.8	0.21
8c	E	–	all	linear	6	6	6	1.9	0.32
9	ERS	default: 5th	1st only	linear	7	2	1	1.5	0.75
13	G	default: 5th	1st only	linear	21	5	4	2.0	0.4
17a	AE	default: 5th	all	linear	16	16	16	30.4	1.9
17b	AE	default: 5th	4 out of 14	linear	23	5	4	4.2	0.84
18c	AE	default: 5th	1st only	linear	18	2	1	2.5	1.25
20a	G	default: 5th	1st only	linear	12	2	1	2.3	1.15
20d	G	default: 5th	4 out of 7	linear	15	8	7	3.9	0.49
25	ERS	default: 5th	1st only	linear	8	2	0	1.2	0.6
26b	AE	default: 5th	1st only	–	13	1	1	0.8	0.8
27	ERS	determiners	global	non-linear	25	6	5	1.7	0.28
29a	S	default: 5th	2 out of 3	linear	15	5	4	1.8	0.36
29b	S	default: 5th	1st only	linear	29	3	2	0.6	0.2

Table 2: to be continued

Table 2: continued

Subject and paragraph number	Type of text chosen	Deletion option selected	Number of sentences addressed	Linear or non-linear	Total gaps in passage	Number of gaps attempted	Number of gaps solved	Time on passage (min.)	Time per gap attempted
30a	Eng	default: 5th	4 out of 14	linear	32	6	6	13.1	2.18
30b	Eng	default: 5th	1st only	linear	11	4	4	4.2	1.05
30g	Eng	default: 5th	global	non-linear	17	2	0	1.7	0.85
31a	E	marked text	all	linear	6	6	6	5.2	0.87
31b	E	marked text	all	linear	16	16	16	6.0	0.38
31c	E	marked text	all	linear	2	2	2	0.6	0.30
32a	G	default: 5th	1st only	–	20	1	1	1.6	1.60
32b	G	default: 5th	all	linear	20	20	20	4.8	0.24
32c	G	default: 5th	all	linear	12	12	12	3.2	0.27
34	M	default: 5th	all	linear	12	12	12	2.0	0.17
36a	ERS	default: 5th	2 out of 6	linear	12	3	2	5.4	1.80
36j	ERS	default: 5th	global	non-linear	8	3	1	1.6	0.53
36u	ERS	default: 5th	2 out of 2	linear	7	4	3	2.5	0.63
36v	ERS	default: 5th	1st only	linear	11	2	1	1.5	0.75
36x	ERS	default: 5th	1st only	–	3	1	1	1.1	1.10
37b	Eng	default: 5th	1st only	linear	11	4	4	2.0	0.50
38a	Eng	default: 5th	3 out of 5	linear	26	11	11	12.5	1.14
38b	Eng	default: 5th	all	linear	7	7	7	7.9	1.13
38c	Eng	default: 5th	all	linear	12	12	12	6.8	0.57

Table 2: to be continued

Table 2: continued

Subject and paragraph number	Type of text chosen	Deletion option selected	Number of sentences addressed	Linear or non-linear	Total gaps in passage	Number of gaps attempted	Number of gaps solved	Time on passage (min.)	Time per gap attempted
39b	Eng	default: 5th	all	linear	8	8	8	6.7	0.84
40	E	default: 5th	1st only	linear	10	3	2	0.8	0.27
42	AE	default: 5th	1st only	linear	12	3	2	2.3	0.77
44	R	default: 5th	1st only	linear	9	2	1	18.1	9.05
45a	Eng	default: 5th	1st only	non-linear	21	4	0	4.8	1.2
48a	ERS	default: 5th	1st only	linear	7	2	1	9.1	4.55
48b	ERS	default: 5th	all	non-linear	15	15	15	25	1.67
49a	M	default: 5th	all	linear	12	12	12	5.2	0.43
49b	M	default: 5th	all	linear	19	19	19	14.7	0.77
49c	M	default: 5th	all	linear	16	16	16	6.3	0.39
49d	M	default: 5th	3 out of 6	linear	23	12	11	11	0.92
52c	Eng	default: 5th	all	linear	22	9	6	1.6	0.18
53a	E	marked text	1st only	–	3	1	1	0.9	0.9
54	AE	helping verbs	all	non-linear	12	12	10	6.4	0.53
Totals	–	–	–	–	721	377	345	280.2	–
Averages	**–**	**–**	**–**	**–**	**13.87**	**7.25**	**6.63**	**5.39**	**0.74***

* Calculated from total time on passage divided by total number of gaps attempted

1. In 19 of the sessions recorded, students correctly solved all of the blanks presented.
2. Thirty-four interactions with the program involved all or a substantial portion of the passage presented. Twenty-one subjects addressed blanks found in all the sentences in the passage.
3. In the remaining 18 of the 52 fruitful sessions examined, interaction was constrained to within the first sentence.
4. Of all cloze passages in the database in which more than one gap was addressed, only six were addressed in anything but a strictly linear, solve-one-gap, go-on-to-the-next manner.

Regarding the latter finding, the tendency for students to work linearly with CALL has been noted elsewhere (e.g. Edmondson et al. 1988). Windeatt (1986) also finds that his students working cloze went linearly from blank to blank instead of employing more holistic reading strategies. Considering that the range of choices possible with computers should promote more holistic approaches, the consistency of these findings suggests that student users of computers typically fail to realize this advantage. A practical purpose of studies such as this, then, is to identify such patterns of use and then reconfigure the courseware to channel students into optimally productive behaviours.

Along the same lines, another tendency of students (85% of all interactions) was to accept the default option of every 5th word deleted rather than experiment with the other settings. Again, if experimentation is to be encouraged, then it must be somehow proposed to the students rather than simply being available to them. In summary, although 18 of the students worked only within the first sentence of the cloze exercise, over a third of all interactants in the study (34) did substantial work with the program. In fact, almost a fifth (19) of all exercises attempted in this study were worked to completion.

Use, and abuse, of 'Help'

Both text manipulation programs referred to in these studies, *Hangman* and *SuperCloze*, had two help features: 'Hint' and 'See Solution'. In either program, a request for a hint reveals one letter. 'See Solution' works differently in each program. In *Hangman* it reveals the target word and then takes the student on to the next problem; whereas in *SuperCloze* it shows learners the paragraph intact, without any words blanked out, and then allows them to either return to the original gapped paragraph or skip to the next one. These help features are provided so that students can always in one way or another find a correct answer rather than become frustrated. However, the help features can be abused if students use the computer to feed themselves answers rather than think them through themselves. One purpose of this research, then, is to determine the extent of such abuse and then configure the program to counter it appropriately. In the pilot study using *Hangman*, there was found a high instance of abuse of the on-line help features, to the extent that just over half the interactions with the program favoured reliance on help over applying strategies based on an emerging competence in the target language (Stevens 1991a). In other words, a surprisingly large number of students engaged in random key presses, or had answers fed to them hint by hint until the problem was solved for them, or in some cases even saw one solution after another with no attempt at all to try on their own to discern the solution to the word puzzle.

If this behaviour were typical of students working text manipulation programs on computers during self-access sessions when they thought no one was looking over their shoulders, then it might be expected that work with *SuperCloze* would be similarly non-productive. Considering that student use of *SuperCloze* includes window-shopping activities which seemingly have no result, and that students engage in such behaviour in about half the log-ons to the program, perhaps there is a relationship here with the *Hangman* data. Perhaps the 50% of the students who would be expected to window-shop simply found it easier to wander around in *Hangman*, but had no more intention of buying than the 50% who paused at the door of *SuperCloze*, had a peek, and abruptly exited. On the other hand, such behaviour might be particular to *Hangman* or with that particular computer-based implementation of it, with *SuperCloze* being taken more seriously as a language-learning activity. In fact, the data show that abuse of help features was less predominant in *SuperCloze* than with *Hangman*, suggesting that students were by and large invoking competency-based strategies.

The hint feature in *SuperCloze* was, if anything, underutilized by most students, especially by those who had little or no interaction with the program. As can be seen from Table 3, there were only isolated incidents of heavy use of hints (see subjects #8 who used hints to solve approximately half the characters in the gaps presented in paragraphs b and c; #26b who solved a single word entirely through use of hints; and #30 who used hints to solve more than half the letters in all the words presented in paragraphs a and b).

'See Solution' appears to have been more widely abused. Twenty-five of the 34 passages in which there was significant interaction registered some use of 'See Solution', and some of this was exorbitant (e.g. #4a who used

Table 3: Use of hints and 'See Solution'

A	B	C	D	E	F	G	H
Subject and paragraph number	Number of times 'see Solution' requested	% of solutions seen per gaps solved correctly	Number of gaps for which hints requested	% of gaps for which hints requested per gaps attempted	Total number of hints requested in all gaps in the passage	Total number of characters in all words for which hints requested	% of hints in Column F per characters in Column G
3a:g	7	none solved	–	–	–	–	–
3i	–	–	1	100.0	1	7	14.3
4a	7	350.0	1	50.0	1	4	25.0
4d	1	none solved	–	–	–	–	–
7a	3	21.4	–	–	–	–	–
7b	4	50.0	–	–	–	–	–
8a	–	–	1	10.0	1	5	20.0
8b	–	–	7	25.9	16	28	57.1
8c	–	–	4	66.7	8	17	47.1
17a	5	31.3	1	6.3	1	3	33.3
17b	1	25.0	–	–	–	–	–
20a	1	100.0	–	–	–	–	–
20d	3	42.9	–	–	–	–	–
25	–	–	2	100.0	3	11	27.3
26b	–	–	1	100.0	3	3	100.0
30a	1	16.7	5	83.3	16	27	59.3
30b	3	75.0	3	75.0	13	23	56.5
30c	–	–	1	100.0	1	10	10.0
31a	1	16.7	1	16.7	1	3	33.3

Table 3: to be continued

Table 3: continued

A	B	C	D	E	F	G	H
31b	1	6.3	—	—	—	—	—
32b	3	15.0	—	—	—	—	—
32c	5	41.7	—	—	—	—	—
34	—	—	1	8.3	3	9	33.3
36a	—	—	2	66.7	3	8	37.5
36j	—	—	—	—	1	3	33.3
37b	1	25.0	1	25.0	1	2	50.0
38a	4	36.4	1	9.1	1	6	16.7
38b	4	57.1	6	85.7	6	31	19.4
38c	5	41.7	7	58.3	7	30	23.3
39b	4	50.0	3	37.5	3	15	20.0
42	1	50.0	—	—	—	—	—
45d	—	—	1	100.0	1	5	20.0
48a	1	100.0	—	—	—	—	—
48b	1	6.7	3	20.0	4	14	28.6
49a	1	8.3	—	—	—	—	—
49b	5	26.3	—	—	—	—	—
49c	2	12.5	—	—	—	—	—
49d	3	27.3	—	—	—	—	—
52a	—	—	1	100.0	1	5	20.0
52c	—	—	1	11.1	1	8	12.5
53b	—	—	1	100.0	1	9	11.1
Totals	78	33.3	56	34.8	98	286	34.27
Averages	2.89	—	2.33	—	3.92	11.4	—

'See Solution' 7 times to solve 2 gaps; and subject #30 who, in addition to abusing hints, used 'See Solution' in 3 of 4 gaps solved in paragraph b). In many cases, 'See Solution' appears to act in the manner of a drug — students try faithfully to solve gaps until they 'discover' the feature, at which point its frequency of use increases.

A signature strategy for at least two different subjects was to use a hint to expose a single letter in an unknown word, perhaps make an attempt at solving the problem, but failing that (or sometimes directly, without overt attempt at an answer) to use 'See Solution' to get the rest of the word. Still another pattern (3a:g, 4d) was to look at the solution, return to the problem, and still fail to solve the gapped item. The fact that hints were underutilized by students in window-shopping mode suggests that the existence of this and other features should be emphasized somehow to the casual user while access to these features should be limited for those engaged in the task. In the most recent version of *SuperCloze*, the number of hints available has in fact now been restricted to half the number of characters blanked in a given word, and the number of times a student can invoke 'See Solution' has been limited to two per paragraph.

Healthy use of hints and 'See Solution'

Perhaps the most encouraging finding in the study is that half the interactions with *SuperCloze* are fairly productive ones. Interaction 48b (Tables 2 and 3) is one example, in which the student solved all gaps, resorting occasionally to reasonable use of hints, and skipping but later cycling back through gaps not solved the first time around. 'See Solution' was used only at the very end of the session, to reveal the word *Mashona* (the name of an ethnic group in Southern Africa).

Numerous instances of this kind of competency-based problem solving in the data suggest that use of this and similar CALL programs can be healthy and warranted for language learning. The next stage of the analysis will be to examine more closely what is going on in these more productive interactions in the hope of isolating strategies that should be encouraged in order to revise the *SuperCloze* program accordingly.

Conclusion

This study has attempted to shed some light on how students approach CALL text manipulation in purely self-access mode. Although intrusive protocols such as introspection during problem solving or follow-on interviews can be revealing, such protocols can raise doubts about whether students are engaging in self-access when they know their behaviour is being monitored. Therefore, a non-intrusive protocol was used in the present study to increase chances of being able to observe the phenomenon under study, even though loss of individual data on the students means that explanations for some behaviour can only be inferred.

The findings of the present study and of the pilot one with *Hangman* suggest that students working in self-access mode tend to abuse help features more than CALL developers might realize, though this tendency was more marked with *Hangman* that with *SuperCloze*. With both programs, there is an element of 'window-shopping', with students dropping in on the program, just having a look, and perhaps going on to something else that will help them improve their linguistic abilities, or perhaps not. More optimistically, with both programs, half the interactions are serious ones with ample evidence that the students are using their budding linguistic competence in working towards solutions to the problems.

This paper is based on a quantitative analysis of certain elements in the data. It is hoped that more insights may be gained using a qualitative approach to the vast amounts of data being collected. This is action research, in that these insights are being directed towards improvements to the program that will make it an even more effective medium for fruitful, competency-based interaction with authentic texts in the study of second languages.

APPENDIX: Key to Tables

Table 1: Non-fruitful sessions

Subject and paragraph number	Numbers each subject in the study and assigns a letter to paragraph-long cloze exercises attempted (in the order attempted).
Type of text chosen	Gives the category of text each subject selected, from which inferences regarding student proficiency level can be made.
Deletion option selected	Records the deletion target option selected by each subject.
Number of gaps attempted	Gives the number of gaps in the passage which each subject attempted to solve.
Number of gaps solved	Records the number of gaps successfully solved by each subject (in non-fruitful sessions, this number is always zero).
Time on passage	Gives the amount of time in minutes each subject spent on each paragraph.
Time per gap	Computes the average time each subject spent on each gap attempted.

Table 2: Fruitful sessions

In addition to all of the elements in Table 1, Table 2 contains the following:

Number of sentences addressed	Records the number of sentences considered by each subject in working each cloze paragraph. The purpose of this measure is to quantify how much of the passage the student might have read as inferred from the position in the paragraph of gaps addressed. Notations are: "1st only" (the student appears to have looked only at the first sentence), "all" (students may have considered all the sentences in the paragraph), something like "2 out of 7" (the student addressed gaps found in the first two of the seven sentences in the passage), and "global" (the student attempted gaps at various places in the paragraph).
Linear or non-linear	Records whether the subject approached the gaps sequentially or not.
Total gaps in passage	Gives the number of gaps in that particular cloze exercise.

Table 3: Use of hints and 'See Solution'

A	Subject number	These are the same subjects as in Tables 1 and 2.
B	Number of times 'See Solution' requested	Gives the number of times the student saw the solution while viewing that paragraph.
C	% of solutions seen per gaps solved correctly	Relates the frequency of 'See Solution' use to the number of gaps solved; a high number here implies overuse of this feature.
D	Number of gaps for which hints requested	Gives the number of gaps in the passage which were addressed through some use of hints.
E	% of gaps for which hints requested per gaps attempted	Relates the figure in D to the number of gaps the subject attempted in the entire passage.
F	Total number of hints requested in all gaps in the passage	The total number of times the student in requested hints in a given paragraph irrespective of the number of gaps.
G	Total number of characters in all words for which hints requested	This is the sum of the number of letters in all the words where the student asked for the hints.
H	% of hints in Column F per characters in Column G	Gauges degree of reliance on hints by showing (on average) the percentage of characters revealed through use of hints in the words where hints were used.

References

Ager, D.E., E. Clavering & J. Galleymore (1980) 'Assisted self-tutoring in foreign languages at Aston.' *Recherches et Échanges* 5: 16–29.

Allwright, D. (1988) 'Autonomy and individualizaton in whole-class instruction.' In A. Brookes & P. Grundy (eds.) *Individualization and Autonomy in Language Learning*, pp. 35–44. ELT Documents 131. London: Modern English Publications/The British Council.

Allwright, R. (1981) 'What do we want teaching materials for?' *ELT Journal* 36(1): 5–17.

Altman, H.B. & C.V. James (1980) *Foreign Language Teaching: meeting individual needs*. Oxford: Pergamon.

Amor, S. et al. (1985) *Learning English — Green Line*. Stuttgart: Klett-Verlag.

Armitage, S. (1992) 'Using a videotape-based system for management learning.' *Interactive Learning Journal* 8: 37–44.

Assinder, W. (1991) 'Peer teaching, peer learning: one model.' *ELT Journal* 45(3): 218–229.

Aston, G. (1993) 'The learner's contribution to the self-access centre.' *ELT Journal* 47(3): 219-227.

Bachman, L.F. & A.S. Palmer (1982) 'The construct validation of some components of communicative proficiency.' *TESOL Quarterly* 16: 449–465.

Bacon, S.M. (1992) 'The relationship between gender, comprehension, processing strategies, and cognitive and affective response in Foreign Language listening.' *The Modern Language Journal* 76(2): 160–178.

Bacon, S.M. & M.D. Finnemann (1990) 'A study of the attitudes, motives, and strategies of university foreign language students and their disposition to authentic oral and written input.' *Modern Language Journal* 74(4): 459–473.

Bailey, K.M. (1991) 'The process of innovation in language teacher development: what, why and how teachers change.' Paper presented at the RELC Conference, Singapore, April 1991.

Baker, D.O. & D.P. Jones (1993) 'Creating gender equality: cross-national gender stratification and Mathematics performance.' *Sociology of Education* 66: 91–103.

Balla, J., L. Gow, D. Kember, J. Hunt & P. Barnes (1988) 'Using evaluation as a source for information for students.' *Education Technology Newsletter* 4(5): 14–24.

Balla, J., M. Stokes & K. Stafford (1991) 'Changes in student approaches to study at CPHK: a three year longitudinal study.' *AAIR Conference Refereed Proceedings*, pp. 7–31. Melbourne: AAIR.

Ballard, B. & J. Clanchy (1991) *Teaching Students from Overseas*. Melbourne: Longman Cheshire.

Bannister, D. & F. Fransella (1971) *Inquiring Man: the psychology of personal constructs*. Harmondsworth: Penguin.

Bare, J. (1994) 'Re: speaking partners.' E-mail report from jsbare @maroon.tc.umn.edu.

Barnes, D. (1976) *From Communication to Curriculum*. Harmondsworth: Penguin.

de Bary, W.T. (1991) *Learning for One's Self: essays on the individual in neo-Confucian thought*. New York, NY: Columbia University Press.

Beatty, C.J. (1994) 'Re: conversation partners.' E-mail report from cameronb @cc.snow.edu.

Belkin, G.S. (1984) *Introduction to Counselling*. Dubuque, IA: W.M.C. Brown.

Benesch, S. (1993) 'ESL, ideology and the politics of pragmatism.' *TESOL Quarterly* 27(4): 705–716.

Benson, P. (1995) 'Self-access and collaborative learning.' *Independence* (newsletter of the IATEFL Learner Independence SIG) 12: 6-11.

Benson, P. (in press) 'The philosophy and politics of learner autonomy.' In P. Benson & P. Voller (eds.) *Autonomy and Independence in Language Learning*. Harlow: Longman.

Berry, M. (1989) 'Thematic options and success in writing.' In C.S. Butler, R.A. Cardwell & J. Channell (eds.) *Language and Literature: theory and practice*, pp. 14–31. Nottingham: University of Nottingham.

Bhatia, V.K. (1993) *Analysing Genre: language use in professional settings*. New York, NY: Longman.

Bickley, V. (ed.) (1989) *Learning and Teaching Styles in and across Cultures*. Hong Kong: Institute for Language in Education.

Biggs, J.B. (1979) 'Individual differences in the study processes and the quality of learning outcomes.' *Higher Education* 8: 381–394.

Biggs, J.B. (1987) *Student Approaches to Learning and Studying*. Hawthorn: Australian Council for Educational Research.

Biggs, J.B (1991) 'Approaches to learning in secondary and tertiary students in Hong Kong: some comparative studies.' *Educational Research Journal* 6: 27–39.

Biggs, J.B. (1992) *Why and How Do Hong Kong Students Learn*? Education Paper 14. Hong Kong: Faculty of Education, University of Hong Kong.

Blanche, P. & B. J. Merino (1989) 'Self-assessment of foreign-language skills: implications for teachers and researchers.' *Language Learning* 39(3): 313–340.

Block, D. (1991) 'Some thoughts on DIY materials design.' *ELT Journal* 45(3): 211–217.

Blue, G.M. (1988) 'Self-assessment: the limits of learner independence.' In A. Brookes & P. Grundy (eds.) *Individualization and Autonomy in Language Learning*, pp. 100–118. ELT Documents 131. London: Modern English Publications/The British Council.

Boekaerts, M. (1991) 'Subjective competence, appraisals and self-assessment.' *Learning and Instruction* 1: 1–17.

Bolt, P. (1991) 'An evaluation of grammar-checking programs as self help learning aids for learners of English as a Foreign Language.' *Occasional Papers* 5(1–2): 49–91. Hong Kong: Hong Kong Polytechnic.

Bolton, R. (1987) *People Skills: how to assert yourself, listen to others, and resolve conflicts*. Brookvale: Simon & Schuster.

Boud, D. (1988) *Developing Student Autonomy in Learning*. London: Kogan Page.

Brindley, G. (1989) *Assessing Achievement in a Learner-Centered Curriculum*. Sydney: NCELTR.

Brindley, G.P. (1991) 'Issues in Assessment.' *Interchange* 17: 3–6.

Brockett, R.G. and R. Hiemstra (1991) *Self-Direction in Adult Learning: perspectives on theory, research, and practice.* London: Routledge.

Brookes, A. & P. Grundy (eds.) (1988) *Individualization and Autonomy in Language Learning.* ELT Documents 131. London: Modern English Publications/The British Council.

Brookfield, S. (1985) 'Self-directed learning: a critical review of research.' In S. Brookfield (ed.) *Self-Directed Learning: from theory to practice*, pp. 5-16. San Francisco, CA: Jossey-Bass.

Brookfield, S. (1993) 'Self-directed learning, political clarity, and the critical practice of adult education.' *Adult Education Quarterly* 43(4): 227–242.

Brown, A.L., J.D. Bransford, R. Ferrara & J. Campione (1983) 'Learning, remembering, and understanding.' In J.H. Flavell & E.M. Markham (eds.) *Carmichael's Manual of Child Psychology*, Vol. 1. New York, NY: Wiley.

Bruner, J. (1986) *Actual Minds, Possible Worlds.* Cambridge, MA: Harvard University Press.

Bruner, J.S. (1966) *Toward a Theory of Instruction.* Cambridge, MA: Harvard University Press.

Bruner, J.S. (1983) 'The social context of language acquisition.' In R. Harris (ed.) *Approaches to Language,* pp. 31–61. Oxford: Pergamon.

Burke, K. (1955) *Permanence and Change.* New York, NY: New Republic.

Bush, M.D. & J. Crotty (1991) 'Interactive videodisc in language teaching.' In W.F. Smith (ed.) *Modern Technology in Foreign Language Education: applications and projects*, pp. 75–95. Chicago, IL: National Textbook Company.

Candy, P.C. (1988) 'On the attainment of subject-matter autonomy.' In D. Boud (ed.) *Developing Student Autonomy in Learning*, pp. 59–76. London: Kogan Page.

Candy, P.C. (1989) 'Constructivism and the study of self-direction in adult learning.' *Studies in the Education of Adults* 21: 95–116.

Candy, P.C. (1991) *Self-Direction for Lifelong Learning.* San Francisco, CA: Jossey-Bass.

Carkhuff, R.R. (1969) *Helping and Human Relations: a primer for lay and professional helpers.* Vol. 2: Practice and Research. New York, NY: Holt, Rinehart & Winston.

Carvalho, D. (1993) *Self-Access: appropriate material.* Manchester: The British Council.

Cathcart, R. & S. Vaughn (1993) *Real Conversations: beginning listening and speaking activities.* Boston, MA: Heinle & Heinle.

Chan, V. & A. Hui (1974) *The Education of Chinese in Toronto: an initial investigation.* Toronto: Chinese Businessmen's Association.

Chapelle, C. (1990) 'The discourse of computer-assisted language learning: toward a context for descriptive research.' *TESOL Quarterly* 24(2): 199–225.

Chapelle, C. & S. Mizuno (1989) 'Student strategies with learner controlled CALL.' *CALICO Journal* 7(2): 25–47.

Chiang, M. (1963) *Chinese Culture and Education.* Taipei: The World Company.

Clarke, D. F. (1991) 'The negotiated syllabus: what is it and how is it likely to work?' *Applied Linguistics* 12(1): 13–28.

Cobb, T. & V. Stevens (1996) 'A principled consideration of computers and reading in a second language.' In M.C. Pennington (ed.) *The Power of CALL*, pp. 115-136. Houston, TX: Athelstan.

Cohen, L. & L. Manion (1989) *Research Methods in Education.* Third edition. London: Routledge.

Cooper, R., M. Lavery & M. Rinvolucri (1991) *Video.* Oxford: Oxford University Press.

Corder, S.P. (1966) *The Visual Element in Language Teaching.* London: Longman.

Coupland, N., H. Giles & J. Wiesmann (1992) "Talk is cheap'... but 'my word is my bond': beliefs about talk.' In K. Bolton & H. Kwok (eds.) *Sociolinguistics Today: international perspectives*, pp. 218–243. London: Routledge.

Dalwood, M. (1977) 'The reciprocal language course.' *Audio Visual Language Journal* 15: 73–80.

Dam, L. (1994) 'How do we recognize an autonomous language classroom?' *Die Neueren Sprachen* 93(5): 503–527.

Dam, L. (1995) *Learner Autonomy 3: from theory to classroom practice.* Dublin: Authentik.

Dam, L. & G. Gabrielsen (1988) 'Developing learner autonomy in a school context: a six-year experiment beginning in the learners' first year of English.' In H. Holec (ed) *Autonomy and Self-Directed Learning: present fields of application*, pp. 19–30. Strasbourg: Council of Europe.

Davidson, E. & G. Henning (1985) 'A self-rating scale of English difficulty: Rasch Scale analysis of items and rating categories.' *Language Testing* 2: 164–179.

Dearden, R.F. (1972) 'Autonomy and education.' In R.F. Dearden, P. Hirst & R. Peters (eds.) *Education and the Development of Reason*. London: Kogan Page.

Dickinson, L. (1987) *Self-Instruction in Language Learning*. Cambridge: Cambridge University Press.

Dickinson, L. (1988) 'Learner training.' In A. Brookes & P. Grundy (eds.) *Individualization and Autonomy in Language Learning*, pp. 45–53. ELT Documents 131. London: Modern English Publications/The British Council.

Dickinson, L. (1992) *Learner Autonomy 2: learner training for language learning*. Dublin: Authentik.

Duda, R. & P. Riley (eds.) (1991) *Learning Styles*. Nancy: Presses Universitaires de Nancy.

Duffy, G.G., R.L. Roehler, M.S. Meloth, L.G. Vavrus, C. Book, J. Putnam & R. Wesselman (1986) 'The relationship between explicit verbal explanations during reading skill instruction and student awareness and achievement: a study of reading teacher effects.' *Reading Research Quarterly* 21(3): 237–52.

Dunkel, P. (1991) The effectiveness of research on computer-assisted instruction and computer-assisted language learning.' In P. Dunkel (ed.) *Computer-Assisted Language Learning and Testing: research issues and practice*, pp. 5–36. New York, NY: Newbury House.

Eck, A., L. Legenhausen & D. Wolff (1994) 'Der Einsatz der Telekommunikation in einem lernerorientierten Fremdsprachenunterricht.' In W. Gienow & K. Hellwig (eds.) *Interkulturelle Kommunikation und prozeßorientierte Medienpraxis im Fremdsprachenunterricht: Grundlagen, Realisierung, Wirksamkeit*, pp. 43–57. Frankfurt: Lang.

Edmondson, W., S. Reck & N. Schroder (1988) 'Strategic approaches used in a text-manipulation exercise.' In U.O.H. Jung (ed.) *Computers in Applied Linguistics and Language Teaching*, pp. 193–211. Frankfurt: Verlag Peter Lang.

Egan, G. (1986) *The Skilled Helper: a systematic approach to effective helping.* Belmont, CA: Brooks/Cole Publishing.

Ellis, G. & B. Sinclair (1986) 'Learner training: a systematic approach.' *IATEFL Newsletter* 92: 13–14.

Ellis, G. & B. Sinclair (1989) *Learning to Learn English: a course in learner training.* Cambridge: Cambridge University Press.

Ellis, R. (1990) *Instructed Second Language Acquisition: learning in the classroom.* Oxford, and Cambridge, MA: Basil Blackwell.

Engels, L.K., B. Van Beckhoven, T. Leenders & I. Brasseur (1981) *L.E.T. Vocabulary-List: Leuven English Teaching Vocabulary-List based on objective frequency combined with subjective word-selection.* Dept. of Linguistics, Catholic University of Leuven. Leuven: Acco.

Entwistle, N. (1987) 'A model of the teaching-learning process.' In J.T.E. Richardson, M.W. Eysenck & D.W. Piper (eds.) *Student Learning: research in education and cognitive psychology,* pp. 13-28. Milton Keynes: Society for Research into Higher Education/Open University Press.

Entwistle, N.J. & P. Ramsden (1983) *Understanding Student Learning.* London: Croom Helm.

Esch, E. (1994) *Self-Access and the Adult Language Learner.* London: CILT.

Evans, M. (1993) 'Flexible learning and modern language teaching.' *Language Learning Journal* 8: 17-21.

Eveland, L. (1994) 'Speaking partners.' E-mail report from leveland @umdacc.bitnet.

Exum, H. & E. Lau (1988) 'Counseling style preference of Chinese college students.' *Journal of Multicultural Counselling and Development* 16(2): 84–92.

Fairclough, N. (1993) 'Discourse and cultural change in the enterprise culture.' In D. Graddol, L.Thompson & M. Byram (eds.) *Language and Culture,* pp. 44–55. Clevedon: Multilingual Matters.

Feldman, S.S. & D.A. Rosenthal (1991) 'Age expectation of behavioural autonomy in Hong Kong, Australian, and American youth: the influence of family variables and adolescents' values.' *International Journal of Psychology* 26(1): 1–23.

Feldmann, U. & B. Stemmer (1987) 'Thin____ aloud a____ retrospective da____ in C-te____ taking: diffe____ languages — diff____ learners –

sa____ approaches?' In C. Faerch & G. Kasper (eds.) *Introspection in Second Language Research,* pp. 251–266. Clevedon: Multilingual Matters.

Fok, A.C.Y.Y. (1981) *Reliability of Student Self-Assessment.* Hong Kong: Language Centre, University of Hong Kong.

Foucault, M. (1966) *Les Mots et les Choses.* Paris: Gallimard.

Frankel, F. (1982) 'Self-study materials: involving the learner.' In M. Geddes & G. Sturtridge (eds.) *Individualisation,* pp. 52–60. London: Modern English Publications.

Galloway, V. & A. Labarca (1990) 'From student to learner: style, process, and strategy.' In D.W. Birckbichler (ed.) *New Perspectives and New Directions in Foreign Language Education,* pp.111–158. Lincolnwood, IL: National Textbook Company.

Gaonac'h D. (1987) *Théories d'Apprentissage et d'Acquisition d'une Langue Étrangère.* Paris: Hatier.

Gardner, D. (1993) 'Interactive video in self-access learning: development issues.' In *Interactive Multimedia '93,* pp. 150–152. Warrenton, VA: Society for Applied Learning Technology.

Gardner, D. (1994) 'Creating simple interactive video for self-access.' In D. Gardner & L. Miller (eds.) *Directions in Self-Access Language Learning,* pp. 107–114. Hong Kong: Hong Kong University Press.

Gardner, D. & L. Miller (eds.) (1994) *Directions in Self-Access Language Learning.* Hong Kong: Hong Kong University Press.

Gardner, H. (1983) *Frames of Mind.* New York, NY: Basic Books.

Garner, R. (1990) 'When children and adults do not use learning strategies: toward a theory of setting.' *Review of Educational Research* 60: 517–529.

Garrison, D.R. (1992) 'Critical thinking and self-directed learning in adult education: an analysis of responsibility and control issues.' *Adult Education Quarterly* 42(3): 136–148.

Gathercole, I. (ed.) (1990) *Autonomy in Language Learning.* London: CILT.

Geddes, M., S. Chalker & P. Eaves (1986) *Fast Forward 3.* Oxford: Oxford University Press.

Geddes, M. & G. Sturtridge (eds.) (1982a) *Individualisation.* London: Modern English Publications.

Geddes, M. & G. Sturtridge (1982b) *Video in the Language Classroom.* London: Heinemann.

Gerrard, L. (1989) 'Computers and basic writers: a critical view.' In G.E. Hawisher & C.L. Selfe (eds.) *Perspectives on Computers and Composition Instruction*, pp. 8–18. New York, NY: Teachers' College Press.

Gibbs, B. (1979) 'Autonomy and authority in education.' *Journal of Philosophy of Education* 13: 119–132.

Giles, H. & R.N. St. Clair (1979) *Language and Social Psychology*. Oxford: Blackwell.

Glisan, E.W. & V. Drescher (1993) 'Textbook grammar: does it reflect native speaker speech?' *Modern Language Journal* 77(1): 23–33.

Glynn, S.M., D.R. Oaks, L.F. Mattocks & B. Britton (1989) 'Computer Environments for managing writers' thinking processes.' In B. Britton & S. Glynn (eds.) *Computer Writing Environments*, pp. 1–15. Hillsdale, NJ: Lawrence Erlbaum.

Goodman, K.S. (1967) 'Reading: a psycholinguistic guessing game.' *Journal of the Reading Specialist* 6: 126–135.

Goody, J. (1977) *The Domestication of the Savage Mind*. Cambridge: Cambridge University Press.

Gow, L., J. Balla, D. Kember & K.T. Hau (in press) 'Learning approaches of Chinese people: a function of the context of learning?' In M. H. Bond (ed.) *Handbook on the Psychology of the Chinese People*. Hong Kong: Oxford University Press.

Gow, L. & D. Kember (1990) 'Conceptions of teaching and their relationship to student learning.' *British Journal of Educational Psychology* 63: 20–33.

Gow, L., D. Kember & B. Cooper (1994) 'The teaching context and approaches to study of accountancy students.' *Issues in Accounting Education* 9(1): 118–130.

Grabe, W. (1991) 'Current developments in second language reading research.' *TESOL Quarterly* 25(3): 375–406.

Gremmo, M-J. & P. Riley (1995) 'Autonomy, self-direction and self access in language teaching and learning: the history of an idea.' *System* 23(2): 151-164.

Grotjahn, R. (1987) 'On the methodological basis of introspective methods.' In C. Faerch & G. Kasper (eds.) *Introspection in Second Language Research*, pp. 54–81. Clevedon: Multilingual Matters.

Hall, S. (1991) 'The effect of split information tasks on the acquisition of mathematical vocabulary.' Unpublished dissertation, Victoria University of Wellington, New Zealand.

Halliday, M.A.K. & R. Hasan (1976) *Cohesion in English.* London: Longman.

Hammond, M. & R. Collins (1991) *Self-Directed Learning: critical practice.* London: Kogan Page.

Harding, E. & A. Tealby (1981) 'Counselling for language learning at the University of Cambridge: progress report on an experiment.' *Mélanges Pédagogiques* 95–120. CRAPEL, Université de Nancy II.

Harding-Esch, E. (ed.) (1976) *Self-Directed Learning and Autonomy.* Cambridge: Dept. of Linguistics, University of Cambridge.

Harris, K. (1994) 'Conversation partners.' E-mail report from kaharris @ casbah.acns.nwu.edu.

Hatano, G. & K. Inagaki (1990) *Chiteki Koukishin [Intellectual Curiosity].* Tokyo: Chuuou Kouron.

Haughton, G. & L. Dickinson (1989) 'Collaborative assessment by masters' candidates in a tutor based system.' *Language Testing* 5(2): 233–246.

Hayes, J.R. & L.S. Flower (1980) 'Identifying the organization of writing processes.' In L.W. Gregg & E.R. Steinberg (eds.) *Cognitive Processes in Writing*, pp. 3–30. Hillsdale, NJ: Lawrence Erlbaum.

Heath, S.B. (1992) 'Literacy skills or literate skills? Considerations for ESL/ EFL learners.' In D. Nunan (ed.) *Collaborative Language Learning and Teaching*, pp. 40–55. Cambridge: Cambridge University Press.

Hein, P. (1966) *Grooks.* London: Hodder.

Helmore, H. (1987) *Self-Directed Learning: a handbook for teachers.* Sydney: Sydney CAE.

Henner-Stanchina, C. (1985) 'Two years of autonomy: practice and outlook.' In P. Riley (ed.) *Discourse and Learning*, pp. 191–205. London: Longman.

Higgins, J. (1988) *Language, Learners and Computers.* London: Longman.

Hill, B. (1982) 'Learning alone: some implications for course design.' In M. Geddes & G. Sturtridge (eds.) *Individualisation*, pp. 71–75. London: Modern English Publications.

Hill, B. (1989) *Technology in Language Learning: making the most of video.* London: Bourne Press.

Ho, J. and D. Crookall (1995) 'Breaking with Chinese cultural traditions: learner autonomy in English language teaching.' *System* 23(2): 235-243.

Hoey, M. (1983) *On the Surface of Discourse*. New York, NY: Allen & Unwin.

Holec, H. (1980) 'Learner training: meeting needs in self-directed learning.' In H.B. Altman & C.V. James (eds.) *Foreign Language Learning: meeting individual needs*, pp. 30–45. Oxford: Pergamon.

Holec, H. (1981) *Autonomy and Foreign Language Learning*. Oxford: Pergamon. (First published 1979, Strasbourg: Council of Europe.)

Holec, H. (1985) 'On autonomy: some elementary concepts.' In P. Riley (ed.) *Discourse and Learning*, pp. 173–190. London: Longman.

Holec, H. (1987) 'The learner as manager: managing learning or managing to learn?' In A. Wenden & J. Rubin (eds.) *Learner Strategies in Language Learning*, pp. 145–156. Hemel Hempstead and Englewood Cliffs, NJ: Prentice Hall.

Holec, H. (ed.) (1988) *Autonomy and Self-Directed Learning: present fields of application*. Strasbourg: Council of Europe.

Holland, N. & N. Quinn (eds.) (1989) *Cultural Models in Language and Thought*. Cambridge: Cambridge University Press.

Holmes, J. (1994) 'Improving the lot of female language learners.' In J. Sunderland (ed.) *Exploring Gender: questions and implications for English language education*, pp. 156–162. Hemel Hempstead: Prentice Hall.

Howe, K. & M. Eisenhart (1990) 'Standards for qualitative (and quantitative) research: a prolegomenon.' *Educational Researcher* 19(4): 2-9.

Hsu, E. (1992) 'Transmission of knowledge, texts and treatment in Chinese medicine.' PhD dissertation, University of Cambridge.

Hughes, G. (1982) 'Classroom techniques for one-to-one teaching.' In M. Geddes & G. Sturtridge (eds.) *Individualisation*, pp. 64–70. London: Modern English Publications.

Hutchinson, T. (1985) *Project English*. Oxford: Oxford University Press.

Hyde, J. S. & M.C. Linn (eds.) (1986) *The Psychology of Gender: advances through meta-analysis*. Baltimore, MD: Johns Hopkins University Press.

Ignatieff, M. (1990, January 7) 'We are the artists of our own lives.' *The Observer*. London.

Illich, I. (1979) *Deschooling Society*. Harmondsworth: Penguin. (First published 1971, New York: Harper & Row.)

Ingram, D.E. & E. Wiley (1984) *Australian Second Language Proficiency Ratings.* Canberra: Australian Government Publishing Service.

Jacobs, G. (1988) 'Miscorrection in peer feedback in writing class.' *RELC Journal* 20(1): 68–76.

Jaeger, R.M. (ed.) (1988) *Complementary Methods for Research in Education.* Washington, DC: American Educational Research Association.

Jin, L. & M. Cortazzi (1993) 'Cultural orientation and academic language use.' In D. Graddol, L. Thompson & M. Byram (eds.) *Language and Culture*, pp. 84–98. Clevedon: Multilingual Matters.

'Jobs or husbands?' (1994, April 19) *The New Paper*, p. 15. Singapore.

Jodelet, D. (1989) *Les Représentations Sociales.* Paris: P.U.F.

Johns, T. (1986) 'Micro-concord: a language learner's research tool.' *System* 19: 51–62.

Johns, T. (1994) 'From printout to handout: grammar and vocabulary teaching in the context of data-driven learning.' In T. Odlin (ed.) *Perspectives on Pedagogical Grammar*, pp. 293–313. Cambridge: Cambridge University Press.

Jones, J. (1994) 'Self-access and culture: retreating from autonomy.' Paper presented at the conference on 'Autonomy in Language Learning', Hong Kong University of Science and Technology, 23-25 June 1994. Also published (1995) in: *ELT Journal* 49(3): 228-234.

Jones, L. (1992) *Communicative Grammar Practice.* Cambridge: Cambridge University Press.

Jones, R.L. (1985) 'Some basic considerations in testing oral proficiency.' In Y.P. Lee, C.Y.Y. Fox, R. Lord & G. Low (eds.) *New Directions in Language Testing*, pp. 77–84. Oxford: Pergamon.

Jonz, J. (1990) 'Another turn in the conversation: what does cloze measure?' *TESOL Quarterly* 24(1): 61–83.

Karmiloff-Smith, A. (1983) 'A note on the concept of 'metaprocedural processes' in linguistic and non-linguistic development.' *Archives de Psychologie* 51: 35–40.

Kelly, G. (1969) In B.A. Maher (ed.) *Clinical Psychology and Personality: the selected papers of G. Kelly.* New York, NY: Wiley.

Kelly, J. (1991) 'A study of gender differential linguistic interaction in the adult classroom.' *Gender and Education* 3(2): 137–144.

Kember, D. & L. Gow (1991) 'A challenge to the anecdotal stereotype of the Asian student.' *Studies in Higher Education* 16(2): 117–128.

Kleinmann, H. (1987) 'The effect of computer-assisted instruction on ESL reading achievement.' *The Modern Language Journal* 71(3): 267–276.

Knowles, M. (1973) *The Adult Learner: a neglected species*. Houston, TX: Gulf Publishing Company.

Knowles, M.S. (1975) *Self-Directed Learning: a guide for learners and teachers*. New York, NY: Association Press; and Cambridge Adult Education Company.

Knowles, M.S. (1980) *The Modern Practice Of Adult Education: from pedagogy to andragogy*. Chicago, IL: Follett Publishing Company.

Kolb, D. (1984) *Experiential Learning: experience as the source of learning and development*. Englewood Cliffs, NJ: Prentice Hall.

Krippendorff, K. (1980) *Content Analysis: an introduction to its methodology*. Beverly Hills, CA: Sage.

Kumaravadivelu, B. (1990) 'Ethnic variation in classroom interaction: myth or reality.' *RELC Journal* 21(2): 45–54.

Kumaravadivelu, B. (1991) 'Language learning tasks: teacher intention and learner interpretation.' *ELT Journal* 45(2): 98–107.

Laine, E.J. (1987) *Affective Factors in Foreign Language Learning and Teaching*. Jyväskylä Cross-Language Studies No. 13. Jyväskylä: Dept. of English, University of Jyväskylä, Finland.

Lambert, B. & I. Hart (1991) 'Interactive videodisc for the rest of us.' In *Interactive Instruction Delivery*, pp.118–120. Warrenton, VA: Society for Applied Learning Technology.

Last, R. (1992) 'Computers and Language Learning.' In C.S. Butler (ed.) *Computers and Written Text*, pp. 227–245. New York, NY: E. Horwood.

Laurillard, D. (1984) 'Interactive video and the control of learning.' *Educational Technology* 24(6): 7–15.

LeBlanc, R. & G. Painchaud (1985) 'Self-assessment as a Second Language placement instrument.' *TESOL Quarterly* 19(4): 673–687.

Legenhausen, L. (1994) 'Vokabelerwerb im autonomen Lernkontext.

Ergebnisse aus dem dänisch-deutschen Forschungsprojekt LAALE.' *Die Neueren Sprachen* 93(5): 467–483.

Legenhausen, L. (forthcoming) 'The impact of classroom culture on attitudes and communicative behaviour.' In L. Dam & G. Gabrielsen (eds.) *Proceedings from the 4th Scandinavian Conference on Autonomous Language Learning.* Copenhagen.

Legenhausen, L. & D. Wolff (1991) 'Der Micro-Computer als Hilfsmittel beim Sprachenlernen: Schreiben als Gruppenaktivität.' *PRAXIS des neusprachlichen Unterrichts* 346–356.

Levin, J. (1992) *Theories of the Self.* Basingstoke: Taylor & Francis.

Lewis, R. (1995) 'Open and distance learning in Europe: add-on or mainstream?' *Open Learning* 10(3): 52-56.

Lieven, E.V.M. (1994) 'Crosslinguistic and crosscultural aspects of language addressed to children.' In C. Gallaway & B.J. Richards (eds.) *Input and Interaction in Language Acquisition,* pp. 56–73. Cambridge: Cambridge University Press.

Lim, S. (1992) 'Investigating learner participation in teacher-led classroom discussions in junior colleges in Singapore from a second language acquisition perspective.' Unpublished doctoral dissertation, National University of Singapore.

Little, D. (1987) 'Interactive video and the autonomous language learner.' *Fremdsprachen und Hochschule* 19: 15–23.

Little, D. (1988a) 'Autonomy and self-directed learning: an Irish experiment.' In H. Holec (ed.) *Autonomy and Self-Directed Learning: present fields of application,* pp. 77–84. Strasbourg: Council of Europe.

Little, D. (1988b) 'Interactive video: teaching tool or learning resource?' *Journal of Applied Linguistics* (Greek Applied Linguistics Association) 4: 61–74.

Little, D. (ed.) (1989) *Self-Access Systems for Language Learning.* Dublin: Authentik.

Little, D. (1991) *Learner Autonomy 1: definitions, issues and problems.* Dublin: Authentik.

Little, D. (1994a) 'Interactive videocassette for self-access: a preliminary report on the implementation of Autotutor II.' *Computers in Education,* 23 (1–2): 165–170.

Little, D. (1994b) 'Learning and talking.' Keynote paper delivered at EUROCALL 94, Karlsruhe, September 1994.

Little, D. (1994c) 'Learner autonomy: a theoretical construct and its practical application.' *Die Neueren Sprachen* 93(5): 430-442.

Little, D. (1996) 'The politics of learner autonomy.' *Learning Learning* (newsletter of the JALT Learner Development N-SIG) 2(4): 7-10. Paper presented at the Fifth Nordic Workshop on Developing Autonomous Learning, 24-27 August 1995, Copenhagen, Denmark.

Little, D. & E. Davis (1986) 'Interactive video for language learning: the Autotutor project.' *System* 14: 29–34.

Littlejohn, A.P. (1983) 'Increasing learner involvement in course management.' *TESOL Quarterly* 17(4): 595–607.

Lockhart, C. & P. Ng (1993) 'How useful is peer response?' *Perspectives* 5(1): 17–30.

Logan, G.E. (1980) 'Individualized foreign language instruction: American patterns for accommodating learner differences in the classroom.' In H.B. Altman & C.V. James (eds.) *Foreign Language Teaching: meeting individual needs*, pp. 94-110. Oxford: Pergamon.

Lonergan, J. (1984) *Video in Language Teaching*. Cambridge: Cambridge University Press.

Lowe, G. (1988) 'On teaching metaphor.' *Applied Linguistics* 9(2): 125–147.

Lublin, J.R. (1980) 'Student self-assessment: a case study.' *Assessment in Higher Education* 5: 263–272.

MacCargar, D.F. (1993) 'Teacher and student role expectations: cross-cultural differences and implications.' *The Modern Language Journal* 77(2): 193–207.

Maher, B.A. (ed.) (1969) *Clinical Psychology and Personality: the selected papers of G. Kelly*. New York, NY: Wiley.

Mann, W.C. & S.A. Thompson (1987) *Rhetorical Structure Theory: a theory of text organization*. Los Angeles, CA: Information Sciences Institute, University of S. California.

Mannheim, K. (1936) *Ideology and Utopia: an introduction to the sociology of knowledge*. London: Routledge Kegan Paul.

Marsh, H.W., B. Byrne & R.J. Shavelson (1988) 'A multifaceted academic self-concept: its hierarchical structure in relation to academic achievement.' *Journal of Educational Psychology* 80: 366–380.

Marton, F. & R. Säljö (1976) 'On qualitative differences in learning outcome, and process II: outcome as a function of the learner's conception of the task.' *British Journal of Educational Psychology* 46: 115–127.

Maslow, A.H. (1954) *Toward a Psychology of Being.* New York, NY: Van Nostrand Reinhold.

Mason, R.J. (ed.) (1984) *Self-Directed Learning and Self-Access in Australia: from practice to theory.* Proceedings of the AMEP conference, 21-25 June 1984, Melbourne, Australia. Melbourne: Council of Adult Education.

May, R. (1967) *Psychology and the Human Dilemma.* New York, NY: Van Nostrand Reinhold.

McCall, J. (1992) *Self-Access: setting up a centre.* Manchester: The British Council.

McMullen, C. (1993) 'Teaching overseas students.' *Occasional Papers Series* 1: 1–9. Professional Development Centre, The University of New South Wales.

Melton, C.D. (1990) 'Bridging the cultural gap: a study of Chinese students' learning style preferences.' *RELC Journal* 21(1): 29–54.

Mezirow, J. (1991) *Transformative Dimensions of Adult Learning.* San Francisco, CA: Jossey-Bass.

Miller, L. (1992) *Self Access Centres in South East Asia.* Research Report No. 11. Hong Kong: Dept. of English, City Polytechnic of Hong Kong.

Miller, L. & D. Gardner (1994) 'Directions for research into self-access language learning.' In D. Gardner & L. Miller (eds.) *Directions in Self-Access Language Learning*, pp. 167–174. Hong Kong: Hong Kong University Press.

Milton, J. & N. Chowdury (1994) 'Tagging the interlanguage of Chinese learners of English.' In L. Flowerdew & A.K.K. Tong (eds.) *Entering Text*, pp. 127–143. Hong Kong: Language Centre, Hong Kong University of Science and Technology.

Milton, J. & E.S.C. Tsang (1993) 'A corpus-based study of logical connectors in EFL students' writing.' In R. Pemberton & E.S.C. Tsang (eds.) *Studies in Lexis*, pp. 215–246. Hong Kong: Language Centre, Hong Kong University of Science and Technology.

Mittan, R. (1989) 'The peer review process: harnessing students' communicative power.' In D. Johnson and D. Roen (eds.) *Richness in Writing*, pp. 207–219. New York, NY: Longman.

Moore, C. (1992) *Self-Access: appropriate technology*. Manchester: The British Council.

Müller, M., G. Schneider & L. Wertenschlag (1988) 'Apprentissage autodirigé en tandem à l'Université.' In H. Holec (ed.) *Autonomy and Self-Directed Learning: present fields of application*, pp. 65–76. Strasbourg: Council of Europe.

Munby, J. (1978) *Communicative Syllabus Design*. Cambridge: Cambridge University Press.

Murphey, T. (1991) *Teaching One to One*. Harlow: Longman.

Murphy, D. (1987) 'Offshore education: a Hong Kong perspective.' *Australian Universities Review* 30(2): 43–44.

Murphy, R. (1987) *English Grammar in Use*. Cambridge: Cambridge University Press.

Newell, A. (1990) *Unified Theories of Cognition*. Cambridge, MA: Harvard University Press.

Nolan, R.E. (1990) 'Self-direction in adult second language learning.' In H.B. Long & Associates (eds.) *Advances in Research and Practice in Self-Directed Learning*, pp. 265-278. Oklahoma Research Center for Continuing Professional and Higher Education of the University of Oklahoma.

Nunan, D. (1987) 'Communicative language teaching: the learner's view.' In B. Das (ed.) *Communicating and Learning in the Classroom Community*, pp. 176–190. Singapore: RELC.

Nunan, D. (1988) *The Learner-Centred Curriculum: a study in second language teaching*. Cambridge: Cambridge University Press.

Nunan, D. (1993) 'Communicative tasks and the language curriculum.' In S. Silberstein & J.E. Alatis (eds.) *State of the Art TESOL Essays: celebrating 25 years of the discipline*, pp. 53–67. Alexandria, VA: TESOL.

Nunan, D. (1994) 'Self-assessment and reflection as tools for learning.' Paper presented at the Assessment Colloquium, International Language in Education Conference, University of Hong Kong, December 1994.

Nunan, D. (1995a) *ATLAS: learning-centred communication*. Book 3. Boston, MA: Heinle & Heinle.

Nunan, D. (1995b) *Learning Matters*. Hong Kong: The English Centre, University of Hong Kong.

Nydahl, J. (1990) 'Teaching word processors to be CAI programs.' *College English* 52(8): 32–48.

Nyikos, M. (1990) 'Sex-related differences in adult language learning: socialization and memory factors.' *The Modern Language Journal* 74(3): 273–287.

O'Hanlon, W.H & M. Weiner-Davis (1989) *In Search of Solutions: a new direction in psychotherapy*. New York, NY: W.W. Norton.

O'Malley, J.M. & A.U. Chamot (1990) *Learning Strategies in Second Language Acquisition*. Cambridge: Cambridge University Press.

O'Malley, J.M., A.U. Chamot, G. Stewner-Manzanares, L. Kipper & R.P. Russo (1985) 'Learning strategies used by beginning and intermediate students.' *Language Learning* 35(1): 21–46.

Oskarsson, M. (1990) 'Self-assessment of language proficiency: rationale and applications.' *Language Testing* 6(1): 1–13.

Oxford, R.L. (1990) *Language Learning Strategies: what every teacher should know*. Boston, MA: Heinle & Heinle.

Oxford R.L. (1993) 'Instructional implications of gender differences in Second/Foreign Language (L2) learning styles and strategies.' *Applied Language Learning* 4(1–2): 65–94.

Page, B. (1992) *Letting Go – Taking Hold: a guide to independent language teaching by teachers for teachers*. London: CILT.

Parnwell, E.C. (1988) *Oxford English Picture Dictionary*. Oxford: Oxford University Press.

Pask, G. (1976) 'Styles and strategies of learning.' *British Journal of Educational Psychology* 54: 228–234.

Pederson, K.M. (1986) 'An experiment in computer-assisted second language reading.' *Modern Language Journal* 70(1): 36–41.

Pelto, P.J. (1970) *Anthropological Research: the structure of inquiry*. New York, NY: Harper & Row.

Pennington, M. (1991) 'Computer-based text analysis and the non-proficient writer: can the technology deliver on its promise?' In J.C. Milton & K.S.T. Tong (eds.) *Text Analysis in CALL: applications, qualifications and developments*, pp. 89–108. Hong Kong: Language Centre, Hong Kong University of Science and Technology.

Pennycook, A. (1989) 'The concept of method, interested knowledge, and the politics of language teaching.' *TESOL Quarterly* 23(4): 589–618.

Perfetti, C.A. (1985) *Reading Ability.* New York, NY: Oxford University Press.

Pierce, B.N. (1989) 'Toward a pedagogy of possibility in the teaching of English internationally: People's English in South Africa.' *TESOL Quarterly* 23(3): 401–420.

Potter, J. & M. Wetherell (1988) 'Discourse analysis and the identification of interpretative repertoires.' In C. Antaki (ed.) *Analysing Everday Explanation.* London: Sage.

Qian, W.C. (1985) *Proceedings of the Siu Lien-ling Visiting Fellows Programme.* Hong Kong: Chung Chi College.

Rheingold, H. (1994) *The Virtual Community: finding connection in a computerized world.* London: Secker & Warburg.

Richards, J.C. (1971) 'Word familiarity as an index of vocabulary selection with indices for 4,495 words.' Doctoral dissertation, Université de Laval, Canada.

Richards, J.C. (1994) 'Beyond the text book: the role of commercial materials in language teaching.' *RELC Journal* 24(1): 1–14.

Riley, P. (ed) (1985) *Discourse and Learning.* London: Longman.

Riley, P. (1988) 'The ethnography of autonomy.' In A. Brookes & P. Grundy (eds.) *Individualization and Autonomy in Language Learning,* pp. 12-34. London: Modern English Publications/The British Council.

Riley, P. (1989) 'Learners' representations of language and language learning'. In G. Willems & P. Riley (eds.) *Foreign Language Teaching and Learning in Europe.* Amsterdam: Free University Press.

Riley, P. (1991) 'There's nothing as practical as a good theory: research, teaching and learning functions of Language Centres.' In M.T. Zagrebelsky (ed.) *The Study of English Language in Italian Universities.* Alessandria: Edizioni dell'Orso. (First published 1989: Mélanges Pédagogiques 73-87. CRAPEL, Université de Nancy II.)

Riley, P. (1994) ''Look in thy heart and write': students' representations of writing and learning to write.' Paper given at the Academic Writing Research Symposium, University of Helsinki, May 1994.

Riley, P. (in press) 'The guru and the conjurer: aspects of counselling for self-access.' In P. Benson & P. Voller (eds.) *Autonomy and Independence in Language Learning.* Harlow: Longman.

Riley, P., M-J. Gremmo & H. Moulden (1989) 'Pulling yourself together: the practicalities of setting up and running self-access systems.' In D. Little (ed.) *Self-Access Systems for Language Learning*, pp. 32–61. Dublin: Authentik.

Rubin, J. (1987) 'Learner Strategies: theoretical assumptions, research history and typology.' In A. Wenden & J. Rubin (eds.) *Learner Strategies in Language Learning*, pp. 15–29. London: Prentice Hall.

Rubin, J. & R. Henze (1981) 'The foreign language requirement: a suggestion to enhance its educational role in teacher training.' *TESOL Newsletter* 15: 17,19,24.

Sanguinetti, J. (1992–93) 'Women, 'empowerment' and ESL: an exploration of critical and feminist pedagogies.' *Prospect* 8 (1–2): 9–37.

Sato, C.J. (1981) 'Ethnic styles in classroom discourse.' In M. Hines & W. Rutherford (eds.) *On TESOL '81*, pp. 11–24. Washington, DC: TESOL.

Scarcella, R. & R. Oxford (1992) *The Tapestry of Language Learning: the individual in the communicative classroom.* Boston, MA: Heinle & Heinle.

Scardamalia, M., C. Bereiter, C. Brett, P.J. Burtis, C. Calhoun & N. Smith Lea (1992) 'Educational applications of a networked communal database.' *Interactive Learning Environments* 2(1): 45–71.

Schank R. & L. Birnbaum (1994) 'Enhancing Intelligence.' In J. Khalfa (ed.) *What is Intelligence?*, pp. 72–107. Cambridge: Cambridge University Press.

Schmitt-Gevers, H. (1992) 'La notion d'aisance dans la production et la réception en langue étrangère.' *Mélanges Pédagogiques* 21: 129–147. CRAPEL, Université de Nancy II.

Schumann, J.H. (1978) 'The Acculturation Model for second language acquisition.' In R. Gringas (ed.) *Second Language Acquisition and Foreign Language Teaching.* Arlington, VA: Centre for Applied Linguistics.

Schütz, A. (1962) *Collected Papers I: the problem of social reality.* The Hague: Nijhoft.

Schwartz, B. (1977) *Permanent education. Final Report.* CCC/EP (77) 8 revised. Strasbourg: Council of Europe.

Scollon, R. & S.W. Scollon (1992) *Individualism and Binarism: a critique of American intercultural communication analysis.* Research Report No. 22. Hong Kong: Dept. of English, City Polytechnic of Hong Kong.

Sharples, M. (1992) *Computers and Writing: issues and implementations.* Dordrecht: Kluwer Academic Publishers.

Sharples, M. & L. Pemberton (1990) 'Models of writing.' In N. Williams (ed.) *The Computer, the Writer and the Learner,* pp. 36–41. Berlin: Springer-Verlag.

Sharwood-Smith, M. (1993) 'Input enhancement in instructed SLA: theoretical bases.' *Studies in Second Language Acquisition* 15(2): 165–179.

Sheerin, S. (1989) *Self-Access.* Oxford: Oxford University Press.

Sheerin, S. (1991) 'Self-access.' State of the Art Article. *Language Teaching* 24(3): 143–157.

'She's my everything, says superstar Chow' (1993, June 27) *South China Morning Post.* Sunday Morning Post, p. 3. Hong Kong.

Sinclair, B. & G. Ellis (1992) 'Survey review: learner training in EFL course books.' *ELT Journal* 46(2): 209–225.

Sinclair, J. (1991) *Corpus, Concordance and Collocation.* Oxford: Oxford University Press.

Sinha, D. & H.S.R. Kao (1988) 'Introduction: values–development congruence.' In D. Sinha & H.S.R. Kao (eds.) *Social Values and Development — Asian Perspectives,* pp.10–27. New Delhi: Sage Publications.

Skehan, P. (1989) *Individual Differences in Second-Language Learning.* London: Edward Arnold.

Slimani, Y. (1992) 'Evaluating classroom interaction.' In J.C. Alderson & A. Beretta (eds.) *Evaluating Second Language Education,* pp. 197–221. Cambridge: Cambridge University Press.

Smith, F. (1971) *Understanding Reading: a psycholinguistic analysis of reading and learning to read.* Third edition. New York, NY: Holt, Rinehart & Winston.

Soars, J. & L. Soars (1989) *Headway Advanced.* Oxford: Oxford University Press.

Spaventa, L.J. & J.S. Williamson (1989) 'Participatory placement: a case study.' In M. Pennington (ed.) *Building Better English Language Programs*, pp. 75–93. Washington, DC: NAFSA.

The State-Administered Examinations for Self-Learners in China (1992) Beijing: Peking University Press.

Stern, D. (1977) *The First Relationship: infant and mother.* London: Open Books.

Stevens, V. (1991a) 'Computer HANGMAN: pedagogically sound or a waste of time?' Revised version of a paper presented at the 24th TESOL Convention, San Francisco, March 1990. ERIC Document No. ED 332 524.

Stevens, V. (1991b) 'Strategies in solving computer-based cloze: is it reading?' Paper presented at the 25th TESOL Convention, New York, March 1991. ERIC Document No. ED 335 952.

Stevens, V. (1991c) 'Reading and computers: Hangman and cloze'. *CAELL Journal* 2(3): 12–16.

Stevens, V. (1991d) 'A study of student attitudes toward CALL in a self-access student resource centre.' *System* 19(3): 289–299.

Stevens, V. (1992) 'Humanism and CALL: a coming of age.' In M.C. Pennington & V. Stevens (eds.) *Computers in Applied Linguistics*, pp. 11–38. Clevedon: Multilingual Matters.

Stevens, V. & S. Millmore (1990–95) *SuperCloze.* Shareware available from the authors, CELIA and through the TESOL/CALL Interest Section's MS-DOS/Windows UG.

Stevens, V. & S. Millmore (1992–95) *HangMan-in-Context.* Shareware available from the authors, CELIA and through the TESOL/CALL Interest Section's MS-DOS/Windows UG.

Sturtridge, G. (1982) 'Individualised learning: what are the options for the classroom teacher?' In M. Geddes & G. Sturtridge (eds.) *Individualisation*, pp. 8–14. London: Modern English Publications.

Swales, J.M. (1990) *Genre Analysis: English in academic and research settings.* Cambridge: Cambridge University Press.

Tarone, E., M. Swain & A. Fathman (1976) 'Some limitations to the classroom applications of current second language acquisition research.' *TESOL Quarterly* 10(1): 11–23.

Tarone, E. & G. Yule (1989) *Focus on the Language Learner.* Oxford: Oxford University Press.

Taxdal, V. (1994) 'Speaking partners.' E-mail report from taxdal @wam.umd.edu.

Tharp, R.G. & R. Gallimore (1988) *Rousing Minds to Life: teaching, learning, and schooling in social context.* Cambridge: Cambridge University Press.

Thomson, C.K. (1992) 'Learner-centered tasks in the Foreign Language classroom.' *Foreign Language Annals* 25(6): 523–531.

Tizard, B. & M. Hughes (1984) *Young Children Learning: talking and thinking at home and at school.* London: Fontana.

Tomalin, B. (1986) *Video, TV and Radio in the English Class.* London: Macmillan.

Toronto Board of Education (1969) *Main Street School and Regional Reception Centres: a comparison of "graduates".* Report No. 81. Toronto: Toronto Board of Education.

Tough, A. (1971) *The Adult's Learning Projects: a fresh approach to theory and practice in adult learning.* Ontario: The Ontario Institute for Studies in Education.

Trevarthen, C. (1979) 'Communication and co-operation in early infancy: a description of primary intersubjectivity.' In M. Bullowa (ed.) *Before Speech.* Cambridge: Cambridge University Press.

Trim, J.L.M. (1976) 'Some possibilities and limitations of learner autonomy.' In E. Harding-Esch (ed.) *Self-Directed Learning and Autonomy*, pp. 1–11. Cambridge: Dept. of Linguistics, University of Cambridge.

Tyacke, M. (1991) 'Strategies for success: bringing out the best in a learner.' *TESL Canada Journal/Revue TESL du Canada* 8(2): 45–56.

Vygotsky, L. (1978) *Mind in Society.* Cambridge, MA: Harvard University Press.

Waxer, P. (1989) 'Cantonese versus Canadian evaluation of directive and non-directive therapy.' *Canadian Journal of Counselling* 23(3): 263–272.

Wells, G. (1985) 'Language and learning: an interactional perspective.' In G. Wells & J. Nicholls (eds.) *Language and Learning: an interactional perspective*, pp. 21–39. London: Falmer Press.

Wells, G. (1987) *The Meaning Makers.* London: Hodder & Stoughton.

Wenden, A. (1987) 'Incorporating learner training in the classroom.' In A. Wenden & J. Rubin (eds.) *Learner Strategies in Language Learning*, pp. 159–167. Hemel Hempstead and Englewood Cliffs, NJ: Prentice Hall.

Wenden, A. (1991) *Learner Strategies for Learner Autonomy: planning and implementing learner training for language learners.* Hemel Hempstead and Englewood Cliffs, NJ: Prentice Hall.

Wenden A. & J. Rubin (eds.) (1987) *Learner Strategies in Language Learning.* Hemel Hempstead and Englewood Cliffs, NJ: Prentice Hall.

West, M. (1965/1977) *An International Reader's Dictionary.* London: Longman.

Widdows, S. & P. Voller (1991) 'PANSI: a survey of ELT needs of Japanese university students.' *Cross Currents* 18(2): 127–141.

Widdowson, H.G. (1979) *Explorations in Applied Linguistics.* Oxford: Oxford University Press.

Willing, K. (1988) *Learning Styles in Adult Migrant Education.* Adelaide: National Curriculum Resource Centre.

Willing, K. (1989) *Teaching How to Learn: learning strategies in ESL.* Sydney: NCELTR.

Windeatt, S. (1986) 'Observing CALL in action.' In G. Leech & C. Candlin (eds.) *Computers in English Language Teaching and Research,* pp. 79–97. London: Longman.

Wode, H. (1987) 'Einige Grundzüge des natürlichen L2-Erwerbs des Wortschatzes.' In H. Melenk, J. Firges, G. Nold, R. Strauch & D. Zeh (eds.) *11. Fremdsprachendidaktikerkongreß,* pp. 483–496. Tübingen: Narr.

Woolgar, S. (ed.) (1988) *Knowledge and Reflexivity: new frontiers in the sociology of knowledge.* London: Sage.

Yee, A. (1989) *A People Misruled.* Hong Kong: API Press.

Young, R. (1987) 'The cultural context of TESOL: a review of research into Chinese classrooms.' *RELC Journal* 18(2): 15–30.

Index